120334

THE GOSPEL OF REDEMPTION

THE GOSPEL

of

REDEMPTION

By

WALTER T. CONNER

BROADMAN PRESS
NASHVILLE, TENNESSEE

Printed in the United States of America

This Book Is Dedicated to the Memory of
ALBERT VENTING, JUNIOR

PREFACE

This book is a revision and enlargement of some things that I published on the same line some years ago. I have followed rather closely the second half of my former book, *A System of Christian Doctrine*, and have added a section on the church.

The views expressed are essentially the same. In places, however, the discussion has been enlarged somewhat and the emphasis slightly changed.

This book, with my former volume, *Revelation and God*, is intended to cover in a general way the field of Christian doctrine. I recognize that the treatment is inadequate. The nature of the subject precludes adequacy. Who could give an adequate treatment to such a theme?

There are radical and rapid changes taking place in the field of theology. One ventures the opinion that most of the changes right now are in the right direction. Men are turning their thoughts in the direction of the need and the fact of revelation, of man's sin and helplessness, of both the individual and social failure of man without God, of the adequacy of God's grace for man's need, and of the centrality of Christ and his saving work for human history. It has come to pass again that men are not ashamed to be known as theologians. They have actually ceased talking about the "science of religion" as if all that theology meant was a factual account of man's religious life without reference to any supernatural or superhuman reality. There was never a more vain idea than the one that all of reality, so far as man could know it, could be brought under the head of science, in the modern and technical sense of that noble term. It is time that theology declared its independence of science and stood on its own feet. This is not to say that science is not important, or that it is not performing a useful function in life. Any man of middle age will realize by looking backward that science has revolutionized our lives as to physical comfort and the means to sustain our natural life on this earth. But things do not constitute life. Man does not live by bread alone. It is more important that man have something to live for than that he have something to live on; and life without God is not true life. Modern man needs to face that fact and realize it.

Someone may think that more attention should have been given in a discussion of redemption to the work of the Holy Spirit. One reason for the omission is that I have discussed the principles involved in the Spirit's work in our salvation in another volume, *Revelation and God*.

The Scripture quotations used in this volume are, in most instances, according to the American Standard Version, Thomas Nelson & Sons, publishers.

I am indebted to many persons for suggestions and stimulation in my thoughts concerning the redemptive work of Christ. I am especially grateful to President E. D. Head of the Southwestern Baptist Theological Seminary for encouragement, and to Professor Stewart A. Newman for helpful suggestions in the field of the Philosophy of Religion. I am also grateful to Rev. Boyd Hunt for the preparation of the indexes.

THE AUTHOR

CONTENTS

THE GOSPEL OF REDEMPTION

SIN: MAN'S NEED OF REDEMPTION

Introduction: Man saved from something to something

I. Preliminary Considerations

1. Sin as against God
2. Temptation as related to sin

II. The Nature of Sin

1. Sin as due to bodily appetites and instincts
2. Sin as weakness and limitation
3. Sin as rebellion against God
   (1) The element of wilfulness in sin
   (2) Sin and knowledge
   (3) Sin as unbelief
   (4) Against God as a person
   (5) Sin as guilt
   (6) Sin as depravity
   (7) Sin as bondage
   (8) Sin as an evil heart

III. Original Sin

1. A preliminary survey
2. The Augustinian and Federal theories
3. Race unity
4. Individual responsibility in relation to race unity
5. The salvation of infants

IV. The Results of Sin

1. Sin alienates from God
2. Sin degrades the sinner
3. Sin disrupts the social order
4. Sin causes suffering
5. Sin brings death

CHAPTER I

SIN: MAN'S NEED OF REDEMPTION

In treating the Christian doctrine of salvation, it will be necessary to have some understanding of the nature and ruin of sin. Christ came to seek and to save those who were lost in sin. We need to appreciate the awfulness of that from which he saves us. This is not to be taken to mean that salvation is only deliverance *from* something. It is positive in its nature. We are saved *to* something as well as *from* something. Salvation includes all the riches of the blessings involved in the life of fellowship with God into which he brings us by his grace. In fact, we are not truly saved from sin except as the life of sin is displaced by a life of fellowship with God.

I. Preliminary Considerations

In this chapter we will consider mainly the nature of sin and the ruin it brings on man. Leading up to this, however, there are certain other aspects of the matter that need consideration. We can understand better the nature of sin and the ruin it brings on man if we keep these other phases of the subject in mind.

1. *Sin as against God*

Sin is a religious conception. Crime is against the state. Immorality is against society.[1] But sin is against God. In a godless world the idea of sin would have no meaning. As men lose the consciousness of God the sense of sin also goes out of their minds and hearts. On the other hand, as the vision of God is renewed in an individual or a society of people, he (or they) will be smitten with a sense of sin.

The Old Testament centers in God and his activity in the world. The writers of the Old Testament view man

---

[1]By this statement the author does not mean to concede that one can have a satisfactory ethical system apart from God or religion.

and the world in relation to God and his dealings with man. We would, therefore, expect to find much in their writings concerning sin. And that is what we do find. There are a striking number and variety of words in the Old Testament (as well as in the New) dealing with sin. It will be shown below, however, that the fullest disclosure of sin and its nature comes only in relation to the final revelation of God in Christ.

What we have just said does not mean that crime against the state, or an immoral life, is not sin. It means rather that these are sin only by virtue of the fact that the state and the human social order are phases of the divine order of the world. Both the state and human society are ordained of God. They are partial expressions of the will of God. So far as these are expressions of the will of God, then, crime against the state or a violation of the will of God as expressed in human society is sin. The idea of sin would have no meaning in a godless world.

This does not mean that a man must be directly conscious of God to commit sin. In most cases the sinner is not directly conscious of God. It is this lack of a consciousness of God (perhaps implying a rejection of God) that is the central thing in man's state of sin. The very heart of sin is the putting of God out of man's thoughts and life.

2. *Temptation as related to sin*

Sin comes as the result of temptation. Temptation is an incitement or inducement to sin. Temptation can hardly be said to be the cause of sin; it is rather the occasion. Sin perhaps would not be without temptation, but the cause of sin is the will of man. Yet to speak of a cause for sin may be too mechanical. It might be better to speak of it in terms of moral decision and moral responsibility. Causality sounds too much like one brick in a row knocking others over. Moral responsibility lies in man's will. Temptation influences the will, but it does not determine it. The will is self-determining.

Otherwise it is not will; apart from the power of self-determination it would be a mechanical force, not personal will.

All the way through the Bible temptation is an inducement to sin coming from without. It is thus possible because man is not a self-contained being. He is a finite creature. He is social in his nature and can exist only in relation to other beings and forces. Evil in the Bible is regarded as a system with the devil as its head.

Many people today deny that there is any personal devil. They hold that this idea of a personal devil is opposed to what they are pleased to call the "scientific" view of the world. But the question as to whether there is a personal devil or not is not one that properly comes within the range of scientific investigation. And as to the bearing of philosophy on the question, the only principle that would necessarily exclude a personal devil is the principle that would deny all personal agency in the world and reduce the universe altogether to a system of impersonal forces. But this would not only exclude a personal devil; it would also exclude God as a person and man as well. Such a view is intolerable in religion.

The idea is sometimes advanced that to attribute sin to the agency of the devil would be to lessen man's sense of responsibility for sin. But this is a mistaken notion. This is shown by the fact that it did not have this effect with the biblical writers. No writers have ever shown such a penetrating sense of the guilt and power of sin, yet at the same time they looked upon sin as being due to satanic temptation. The same thing is true with reference to Christians who believe in Satan. Instead of lessening their sense of the awfulness and ruin of sin, it has rather been increased. Such a man as Martin Luther is a good example. On the other hand, there is good reason to question at least if a disbelief in a personal devil does not have a decided tendency to make men view sin as a light thing. It is not against this view that the idea of a devil and evil spirits is to be found in other religions. The idea of a god is to be found in other religions. But we do not reject the idea for that reason. The agency of a powerful personal evil spirit would help to explain the power and persistence of sin in human life. It is said that the idea of a personal devil is to be attributed to the spontaneous tendency of the mind to attribute phenomena the cause of which is not understood to personal agency of some kind. This might be granted. The question is not whether the belief is to be attributed to such a psychological tendency, but whether it leads us in the direction of truth or not. On other questions, such as the existence of God and the immortality of the soul, we usually say that a natural tendency of the mind, leading to practically a universal belief, is to be trusted. At least this would not be against the belief in a personal devil.

There are at least two things that favor the view that there is a personal devil. One is the existence, power, and persistence of moral evil in the world. That sin and sinners exist, no one with the least moral perception can deny. But it is not only a question of accounting for sin and sinners, it is also a question of accounting for the power and persistence of sin, for what seems to be a kingdom of evil. In the second place, that there is such a kingdom of evil under Satan as the head is the view presented in the Bible. The thing that we insist on here is that there are certain phenomena which can best be accounted for on the hypothesis that such an evil personality exists and operates in human life to promote sin, destroy man, and thwart the purposes of God.

The origin of Satan is a question on which little or no light is thrown in the Bible. There are two things that we can affirm with a fair degree of confidence on general grounds, not by specific Scripture teaching. One is that Satan is a created being. We can affirm this for two reasons. One is that the Scriptures teach that God made all things both visible and invisible (Col. 1:16). The other reason is that in the nature of the case there can be only one eternal and uncreated being. God is the only self-existent being. The other thing we feel confident of is that God did not make Satan a sinful being. God probably made him, but did not make him a devil. Satan doubtless made himself a devil by rebellion against God and then by giving himself to the work of enticing others to sin. But as to how and when this took place we have no light. Since the days of Milton, or before, the view has been prevalent that Satan was the chief of the fallen angels. But for this view there is no specific Scripture teaching. It may be true or it may not. Scripture authority cannot be claimed for it. The Bible, then, gives us no account of the origin of sin in the universe. It gives only the origin of sin among men. It traces the origin of sin among men to satanic temptation.

It is often assumed that temptation can appeal only to that which is evil in man, to that which is degraded and corrupted. But this is untrue. The temptation of Eve, as well as the temptation of Jesus, makes this clear. Let us examine the temptation of Eve with reference to this point.

In Genesis 3:6 it is made clear that the forbidden fruit appealed to three desires on Eve's part, every one of which is a normal desire. The first was the physical appetite or the desire for food. Eve saw that the tree was good for food. It looked good to eat. And certainly it is not morally wrong to be hungry or to desire food. To eat is perhaps within itself a morally indifferent act. Ordinarily, at least, it is not wrong. It was to this perfectly natural and normal desire for food that the devil appealed in tempting Eve and also in tempting Jesus. Then it is said that Eve saw that the tree was a delight to the eyes. It appealed to the sense of the beautiful. And to desire the beautiful is certainly not wrong within itself. Then it is said that she saw that the tree was to be desired to make one wise. It appealed to the desire for knowledge. This again is a desire that is normally right.

So the devil tempted Eve by appealing to these three desires that are normal in any healthy human being. Wherein, then, consisted her sin? In trying to satisfy these normal desires of her being in the wrong way, contrary to the will of God.[2]

This helps us to understand how temptation makes its appeal to desires of our nature which, if satisfied in the right way, are entirely normal and right. It is a mistaken idea that temptation must appeal to the base and ignoble. It may appeal to that which is highest and best. Sin is the perversion of the good and the worst sin may be the perversion of the best.

Against Manichæus, who attributed an independent existence to the devil and held that the devil produced corrupt natures, Calvin said that nothing in the universe is "evil in its nature; since neither the depravity and wickedness of men and devils, nor the sins which proceed from that source are from mere nature but from a corruption of nature."[3] Not the use, but the abuse, of God's world causes trouble. This helps to correct another false impression with reference to sin. We sometimes think that the higher one goes in the moral and spiritual life the less subject to temptation he will be. This is not true, as every Christian knows who has made any progress in spiritual matters and as the example of the Saviour himself shows. It would be nearer the truth to say that the higher one goes in the spiritual life the subtler and stronger does temptation become. It also helps us to understand how the worst sins are the perversion of the highest and holiest relations in life. Sin always appears in the guise of a good. Otherwise it would be no temptation.

The epistle of James tells us that a man is tempted when he is drawn away and enticed by his own lust (1:14). The author says that lust produces sin, and sin

---

[2]For a discussion of this point as related to the Person of Christ, see my book, *Revelation and God*, pp. 198-199.
[3]*Institutes*, Vol. I, p. 153. Cf. Augustine's statement that evil is not a substance. *Confessions*, Bk. VII, (XII), 18.

death. This does not mean to deny temptation from outside of man. It is describing the psychological course of sin and death. The thing contemplated is not a temptation unless desired. Unless there is an appeal to man's desire, temptation would be lacking.

James also tells us that God cannot be tempted and that he does not tempt man (1:13). God cannot be tempted because his goodness and wisdom are absolute. He does not tempt man for the same reason. As absolutely good he is the source of all good and of nothing that is morally evil.

Yet we find in the Bible that God tries men. He tests or tries men that he may develop and confirm them in goodness. The devil tempts men that he may destroy them. The same event in a man's life may be from God's standpoint a testing to develop the man, and from the devil's point of view a temptation to destroy him.[4]

II. The Nature of Sin

We now look more carefully at the nature of sin. What is the fundamental nature of sin? There are three views which we will consider.

1. *Sin as due to bodily appetites and instincts*

The first may be summed up in the statement: Sin is due to man's possession of a body. This connects sin with man's physical organism. In its extreme form it is based on the theory that matter is essentially evil. Hence man is a sinner by virtue of his possession of a body. It gains some plausibility from the use of the term flesh in the Bible to denote man as weak and mortal, and, at least in Paul, as sinful. But while the term "flesh" does denote man as weak and mortal, and while Paul uses the term to denote the sphere of the operation of the sin principle, still the biblical writers never look upon

---

[4]There probably could be no moral goodness in a world where sin was an impossibility. Sin is the frustration of the good, the good is the overcoming of evil. It may also be worth thinking about that evil can only be overcome by grace. Punitive righteousness can suppress, but not overcome, evil.

the body as being evil within itself. This idea came into Christian theology from Greek philosophy. It was reinforced by the doctrine of original sin, especially in the extreme form in which it was held by Augustine. This led to the idea that all things natural were evil. The natural instincts and propensities of the body were evil and should be suppressed. A pious life and a vigorous body could hardly go together. Hence, the idea that to cultivate a life of piety one must withdraw from the world and subdue one's body with all its natural desires and propensities.

This view has in recent times taken on a somewhat modified form due to the theory of evolution. This theory has led to the tendency to regard sin as the remains of animal instinct in man. Sin, therefore, is not so much a thing that is culpable as it is certain animal tendencies that must be curbed and brought under the control of man's rational will. There was no fall of man according to this theory.

Neither form of this theory is a sufficient account of sin. The body is never regarded as evil in the Scriptures. Paul does not mean by the term "flesh," when used as a synonym for the sin principle, the body. He does not regard the body as sinful in itself. He speaks about the mind or thoughts of the flesh (Rom. 8:6-7). And he includes envy, strife, jealousy, etc., as works of the flesh, which shows that the flesh was a spiritual and not simply a bodily principle (Gal. 5:19-21).

Sin cannot be regarded simply as the remains of animal instinct in man. It is true that much of man's sin is connected with his bodily organism and physical desires and instincts, but the most diabolical factor in sin is not connected primarily with the animal appetites or instincts of man. Such sins as pride and ambition can hardly be regarded as the remains of animal instincts.

Jesus denounced most severely, not those who were guilty of what we call sins of the flesh, such as drunkenness and sexual immorality, but those who were guilty of self-righteous pride and hypocrisy,

2. *Sin as weakness and limitation*

Another theory as to the nature of sin can be summed up in the statement: Sin is limitation due to man's finiteness. It is not deliberate and wilful transgression; it is weakness and error. This theory goes back in different forms at least as far as Socrates. He taught that no man would deliberately do that which he knew would harm himself; that man does wrong because he does not know better. Sin, therefore, is not wilful. Theodore Parker is a good representative of this view among early New England Unitarians. He said that sin bears the same relation to man's developing spiritual life that falling does to a child's learning to walk. The child cannot learn to walk without falling. But by falling the child learns to walk. So by his moral blundering man learns the lessons necessary to the development of his moral and spiritual life.

This view takes the elements of wilfulness and guilt out of sin. But the Scriptures say that these elements are there, as conscience testifies also—particularly an enlightened Christian conscience. Socrates and Paul held opposite philosophies with reference to the matter. Socrates said in substance: "What man needs is knowledge as to what is right and what is wrong; and when he knows the right, he will do it." Paul said in effect: "When a man knows what is right, he will not do it because he cannot. He does not have the moral ability. There is in him a principle of sin that is too strong for him. What man needs is not simply a knowledge of what is right, but some motive power to enable him to do the right. Without this power he is helpless."[5] Parker's view that man learns to do right by doing wrong will not bear the test of experience. Experience shows that about all man learns by sinning is to sin.

---

[5] See especially **Romans**, chap. 7.

It is true that man could not be tempted and hence could not sin unless man were finite. God cannot be tempted because he is infinite in wisdom and power. Man's finiteness, his creatureliness, makes him subject to temptation, and hence to sin. But it is not true that his creatureliness within itself constitutes sin.

Moreover, there is a moral weakness that grows out of sin. Sinning produces a state of sin that inevitably leads to further sinning. Sin is more than a mistake or blunder. As already noted, this is the error in the view that man learns to walk morally by falling. Falling does not produce strength to walk; it only causes weakness of character that leads to further falling.

3. *Sin as rebellion against God*

Suppose we take for a tentative definition of sin the statement that sin is rebellion against the will of God. To make clear the nature of sin as rebellion against God, the following points need emphasis:

(1) *The element of wilfulness in sin*

One factor in man's personality, one thing that marks him as a being created in the divine image, is the power of will. To be capable of obedience or disobedience, man must have the power of choice. The obedience of physical elements or of animals to the law of their being deserves no praise because these have no choice. With them it is a matter of physical necessity or animal instinct. Their conformity to the law of their being is obedience only in a secondary sense. Man obeys because he wills to obey.

As free to obey or disobey, man receives commands from God. Why was man singled out at the beginning as the one being whom God had created to whom God should address a specific command, unless it be that man by virtue of his personality has the power of obedience or disobedience? This principle as a presupposition underlies all God's dealings with man as recorded in the

Bible. Man is more than a mechanism; he is a person. Even God his Creator respects his personality.

This comes out even more clearly in the fact that God not only commands man, but also entreats, persuades, exhorts him. God's respect for man's will comes out in the fact that God uses men as his messengers to persuade their fellows to obey God. One of the most impressive things about the biblical revelation of God is the infinite patience of God in dealing with erring and sinful man. God was never without his witnesses, and after he had entered into covenant relations with Israel as a nation, the record is one long story of the backsliding and unfaithfulness of Israel and of the faithfulness and longsuffering of Jehovah. This comes out through the whole of Old Testament history and is the theme of such psalms as the seventy-eighth.

This principle is impressively brought out also in the life and teachings of Jesus. Jesus weeps over Jerusalem as he sees the impending doom of the city. He gives as the reason for its coming desolation that its inhabitants would not be gathered to him (Luke 13:34). But this comes out nowhere more clearly than in Paul's great saying in 2 Corinthians 5:19-20. He says God is in Christ reconciling the world unto himself. Then he adds: "We are ambassadors therefore on behalf of Christ, as though God were entreating by us: we beseech you on behalf of Christ, be ye reconciled to God." It is not a surprising thing that God the Creator should command man his creature. But it is surprising that God should entreat man. It shows distinctly the respect that God has for man's will and the element of wilfulness in man's rebellion against God.

(2) Sin and knowledge

If man's sin is wilful, then it must be sin against light. Where there is no knowledge of moral truth, there can be no sin in the full sense of the term. Perhaps this is implied in Paul's statement that where there is no law, neither is there transgression (Rom. 4:15). He also says

that through the law is the knowledge of sin (Rom.
3:20). In Romans 7 Paul describes a state in which he
says that at one time he was alive without the law. But
when the commandment came, "sin revived, and I died."
When he came to know a certain thing as forbidden of
the law, he did not thereby refrain from doing that thing,
but rather came to do it. This shows that there was an
intimate connection between a knowledge of the will of
God and sin as an active principle in human life. (See
vv. 7-11.)

But knowledge of moral and spiritual things, particularly knowledge of God and his will, presupposes revelation on God's part. As a matter of fact, we find the
idea of sin in the Bible intimately related to two other
ideas—revelation on God's part and a knowledge of that
revelation on man's part. In general, there are four
stages in this revelation, all connected with the idea of
sin in the New Testament. The first is the revelation
of God in nature or the physical world. This, Paul discusses in Romans 1:18 ff. The invisible things of God
are clearly seen, being perceived through the things that
are made, even his everlasting power and divinity. Paul
says that this knowledge of God that comes through
nature leaves men without excuse. Although men knew
God as thus revealed, they would not honor him and
serve him. As a consequence they became blinded.
They were plunged into idolatry and all sorts of moral
and spiritual degradation. In Acts 14:17 Paul speaks
also of the works of nature as being a witness of God.
We find this thought in the Old Testament in Psalm 19
and other places.

The next stage in the revelation of God as related to
sin is his revelation in reason and conscience, or man's
rational and moral nature. Paul says that the Gentiles,
who have not the law, "are a law unto themselves;
in that they show the work of the law written in their
hearts, their conscience bearing witness therewith, and
their thoughts one with another accusing or else excus-

ing them" (Rom. 2:14-15). The heart here is probably a general term denoting about what we mean by moral nature. It seems that Paul is setting forth that the requirements of the law, at least in a general way, are revealed in man's moral consciousness, and that obedience to these requirements of the law as thus made known is virtually obedience to the law. The knowledge of the distinction between right and wrong, with the consciousness that we are bound to do the right and avoid the wrong, with some knowledge as to what is right and what is wrong—this is at least a partial revelation of the moral requirements of the law and thus of the moral nature of God. To live up to the light thus given is so far to keep the law. Not to live up to the light thus given is to violate the law and thus to sin.

A third stage in God's revelation may be denoted by the term law. This is Paul's great term when thinking of God's revelation of himself in relation to man as sinful. By this he means primarily the Old Testament or Mosaic law. Sometimes he uses the term without the article, sometimes with it. With the article it is clear that he means the Mosaic law. And without the article he also means primarily the Mosaic law, but he is thinking also of that law as embodying universal principles of righteousness or moral requirement. When he uses the article he is thinking of the Mosaic law more as a concrete system of particular requirements. Without the article the Mosaic law is still in mind but rather as made up of universal principles of general application.[6]

The law is the embodiment of the moral requirements of God in published ordinances. The center of the Old Testament law looked at as moral requirement is the Ten Commandments. The requirement of the law is perfect obedience to its mandates. The law as such allows of no exceptions and makes no provision for any

---

[6]Cf. Stevens, *Pauline Theology*, p. 160. I find myself recently, however, more inclined to the view that when Paul uses the term law without the article, he means any system of moral requirement, Mosaic or otherwise. Certainly it carries that implication.

remission of penalty. It condemns without mercy every violator of its precepts. We mean by this the law as moral requirement, which seems to be the chief, if not the exclusive, point of view of Paul when discussing the law in relation to sin. There was, it is true, provision for ceremonial cleansing and forgiveness in the Mosaic law. But Paul does not seem to include this aspect of the law in his use of the term; at least ordinarily he does not, if ever.

Sin as against the command or moral requirement of the law Paul calls a trespass or transgression. (See Romans 5:12 ff., and other places.)

The function of the law in relation to sin was not to justify or to save from sin, but rather to awaken one to a consciousness of sin, to one's helplessness in sin, to one's need of the Redeemer, and thus to serve as the pedagogue to lead the sinner to Christ. (Romans 7; Galatians 3.)

The climax of revelation in relation to sin came in the revelation of the grace of God in Christ which saves from sin. The point we are interested in here is not the light which we get in this revelation concerning grace, but the light which grace throws upon sin. We might get the impression from some statements by Paul that the full doctrine of sin came in connection with the revelation of the law as a means of developing the nature of sin and giving a knowledge of sin. But we do not get the complete doctrine of sin until we see the grace of God that saves from sin. The awful blackness of sin does not make its full impression on us until we see it in contrast to the radiant grace of God and as rejection of that grace. This may be illustrated in the case of Paul himself, who seems to have had a deepening consciousness of sin until in his old age he calls himself the chief of sinners (1 Tim. 1:15). His own conduct in persecuting the church he thought to be right until he was given the revelation of God's grace. Then he became a guilty sinner in his own eyes. This thought is also illustrated in the teaching of Jesus. Jesus says that because of his presence and teaching in their midst, the cities of his day will receive a greater condemnation than Sodom and Gomorrah (Matt. 11:20 ff.). The servant who has the knowledge of the master's will and does it not will be beaten with many stripes, while the servant who knew not his master's will will be beaten with few stripes (Luke 12:47-48). Again, Jesus says that, if he had not come, those who reject him had not had sin. Now they have no excuse for their sin (John 15:22). Men are condemned because they love darkness rather than light. The condemnation is that light is come into the world, and men love darkness rather than light, because their deeds are evil (John 3:19). The light of God's grace does two things for the sinful heart: it reveals its darkness and it increases that darkness in case of those who reject the light of grace.

The Johannine writings bring out this contrast between sin and grace most clearly. Sin is set forth as darkness and hatred and error, while grace is light and love and truth. Between the two there has been a never-ceasing conflict, and there will continue to be until grace finally conquers sin. The conflict of the future is graphically set forth in the book of Revelation, which contains the most vivid portrayal of the forces of evil in conflict with the forces of righteousness to be found anywhere in this literature. In John's Gospel and First Epistle we find the contrast between the darkness of sin and the light of righteousness strikingly presented. And sin takes its final form in unbelief or rejection of Christ as the Son of God and Saviour of the world. He that believeth not is condemned already, because he hath not believed on the name of the only begotten Son of God (John 3:18). He that disobeyeth the Son shall not see life, but the wrath of God abideth on him (John 3:36). When the Holy Spirit is come, he will convict the world in respect of sin, of righteousness and of judgment (John

16:8 ff.). This last passage is worthy of special emphasis in this connection and we will dwell on it for a time.

The Holy Spirit's work in convicting concerning righteousness is intimately related to his work in convicting concerning sin. In fact, these are not two works but simply two phases of one convicting work. This bears out our position that the final revelation as to sin does not come until we get to the grace of God in Christ. The revelation of righteousness in Christ reveals the nature of sin. The conviction both as to righteousness and to sin centers in Christ.

The conviction as to judgment consists in the fact that the prince of this world has been judged. The devil's judgment of Jesus becomes his own judgment. The world's condemnation of Jesus became the world's condemnation. The final revelation of the diabolical character of sin came in the rejection by the world of the sinless Son of God. In thus denuding it of all its embellishments and attractions and showing it up in its true character, sin was condemned in the eyes of every enlightened moral intelligence. This again shows that the final revelation of the character of sin came in connection with the revelation of the grace of God. Sin crucified the Son of God. But in so doing, sin forever undid itself in that it forever disclosed its own character as sin.

The conviction as to sin lies in the fact that men believe not on Christ. This probably means, not that unbelief in Christ is evidence of the world's sin, but that the world's sin consists in its unbelief in him. This position is justified not only by this passage, but also by the statements elsewhere in the Johannine writings as to unbelief. It is everywhere identified with moral darkness. In the First Epistle the liar is the man who denies that Jesus is the Christ (1 John 2:22). Perhaps the sin unto death is the final and obdurate rejection of Jesus as the Son of God (1 John 5:13-17).

(3) *Sin as unbelief*

What has just been said would favor the view that unbelief is the essence of sin. This does not mean, however,
unbelief in the sense of a refusal to accept a doctrine
or a dogma. It is unbelief in one's rejection of moral
and spiritual light, particularly as that light is embodied
in Jesus Christ. It is the rejection of God's final revelation of himself as made in Jesus Christ. When this rejection becomes definite and wilful, it becomes the sin
unto death.[7] It is then a wilful treading under foot of
the Son of God, counting the blood of the covenant
wherewith he was sanctified an unholy thing, and doing
despite to the Spirit of grace (Heb. 10:29). It thus becomes moral suicide. It is putting out one's own spiritual
eyes. It does not take place except in connection with a
high degree of enlightenment. It is deliberate, wilful,
malicious rejection of Christ as God's revelation, knowing that he is such a revelation. It is deliberately calling
white black.

At first sight this does not seem to agree with what
Jesus says about blasphemy against the Holy Spirit,
because he says that all sins and blasphemies shall be
forgiven, but not the blasphemy against the Holy Spirit
(Matt. 12:22 ff.). But if we remember that the sin that
men were committing which led Jesus to utter this warning was the sin of attributing his works to the power of
the devil, thus denying that they were wrought by the
power of God, then he is not thinking of sin or blasphemy
against the Spirit irrespective of the Spirit's relation to
the Father or the Son. He is thinking of the Spirit as
embodied in his own life and works and thus revealing
the presence of God, giving men light to see and recognize God in him. When men thus enlightened by the
Spirit deliberately reject his works as the works of God
and attribute them to the devil, they blaspheme the
Spirit, and there is never forgiveness for their sin. This

---

[7] As above, preceding page.

is essentially unbelief in its final form as set forth by
John and wilful sin as described in Hebrews.

Some have defined the essential principle of sin as
selfishness—not selfishness as opposed to benevolence
toward one's fellow man, but selfishness in the sense of
the assertion of one's own will as opposed to submission
to the will of God. To live in sin, then, is to live a life
centered in self, to erect one's own will as the law of
life. This, it is said, is shown to be the essential principle of sin in the fact that love to God is the essence of
virtue. Therefore, the opposite must be the essence of
sin. Again, the fact that Jesus made the first condition
of discipleship to be self-denial would indicate that selfishness is the essential principle of sin. But, as a matter
of fact, selfishness as thus defined is practically the same
thing as unbelief as set forth above. Each is the principle of self-assertion as opposed to humble submission
and trust in God. Each is rebellion against God. Each
is practically the same thing that John had in mind when
he said that sin is lawlessness. And violation of the
moral order established by God is rebellion against God.

(4) *Against God as a person*

Consider another phase of the doctrine of sin. Sometimes sin is contemplated as a violation of the moral
order or law, sometimes it is considered as a personal
offense against God. At times at least, Paul views it in
relation to law. He conceives of nature, man's heart and
conscience, and the whole Old Testament revelation as
an expression of the righteous will of God in an objective
moral order. Sin is a violation of this moral order and
brings upon man the wrath of God. It is not necessary
that there should be a written law whose commands man
shall violate in order to bring upon himself the wrath
of a righteous God. He may sin against God who reveals himself in nature and man's own moral constitution. And when he does so, he brings on himself the
condemnation of a holy God.

In other places sin is thought of as a personal offense against God. This comes out in Psalm 51:4 when the writer, looking at the enormity of his sin, says: "Against thee, thee only, have I sinned, and done that which is evil in thy sight." The writer does not mean that he has not sinned against his fellow man, but means to assert in emphatic form that his sin is first of all against God.

What has just been said, however, shows that sin in its final and most deadly form is sin against a personal God revealed in Christ as a God of mercy and love.

(5) *Sin as guilt*

Viewing sin as personal ill desert, we describe it by the term guilt.

There is probably no single term in the Old or New Testament denoting just this idea, yet the thought goes all the way through both divisions of the Bible. The sense of shame and ill desert caused Adam to clothe himself with fig leaves and hide himself from his Maker (Gen. 3:8). Adam tried to shift the blame to his wife, and Eve in turn to the serpent; but in each case there was clearly the sense of ill desert.

The guilt of sin manifests itself in consciousness. Man knows himself as blameworthy on account of his sin. This consciousness of ill desert is a general phenomenon of human life, especially of man's religious life. This is true in spite of the fact that there is a general disposition to hide one's sense of ill desert and cover up or deny one's responsibility for sin. In fact, the attempt to cover up one's guilt is itself an evidence of guilt. A clear conscience is not so quick to attempt to justify itself as a guilty one. This sense of guilt manifests itself also in the fact that men blame one another with reference to their deeds. The desire to justify oneself in one's own eyes and in the eyes of others leads to much "rationalization," or giving of false reasons for one's beliefs and conduct. One may often think that the false reasons, given to oneself and to others, are the real reasons when they are not. One may deceive himself as well as others by such rationalization.

This consciousness of ill desert, then, is not to be taken as the accurate measure of the guilt of sin. This is true with reference to one's own sin or to another's. Our moral judgments are no more infallible than are our judgments in other realms. In fact, it is often the case that the reverse is true, namely, that the greater one's guilt, the less he is conscious of it. This is true because of the blinding power of sin. Sin darkens the spiritual vision and warps the moral judgment. Consequently, probably the most dangerous condition that one can be in spiritually is to have no consciousness of sin and no sense of danger. For one to have no sense of ill desert is not a sign that one is without guilt; it is a sign that he is spiritually blind and in great spiritual danger. The closer one gets to God, the more conscious he is of his own unworthiness. On the other hand, if we say that we have no sin, we deceive ourselves and the truth is not in us (1 John 1:8). Self-conscious goodness is always sham goodness. It is rotten at the core. This was one of the outstanding characteristics of the Pharisees. They thanked God that they were not like other men. They turned up their noses at "publicans and sinners." They despised Jesus for associating with such human driftwood. But these self-righteous Pharisees were the men that Jesus denounced most bitterly. He scorched them with the fires of his righteous indignation. On the other hand is Paul who in his old age called himself the chief of sinner, (1 Tim. 1:15), and counted not that he had attained perfection (Phil. 3:12-13).

The ground of guilt, however, is the relation of man as ill deserving to the holiness of God. Man's sin is ill deserving because it is against God as holy. If God were not holy, sin would not be ill deserving. The conception of any religion as to the character of sin is determined primarily by its conception of the character of

God. It is against the background of God's spotless
character that the blackness of sin is to be seen. This
is why the saintly man sees his own sin so clearly, because he sees his sin over against the character of God.
The prophet sees Jehovah high and lifted up, the exalted
and Holy One. Then he sees himself and the people
among whom he lives as sinful. The perfection of God's
character is probably the fundamental conception of the
First Epistle of John. God is light and love. In contrast to the perfection of his character the writer sees
with distinctness man's sin. If any man says that he
has no sin, he deceives himself and the truth is not in
him.

Men are not equally guilty before God. In the Old
Testament there were sins of ignorance and sins of presumption; sins that could be atoned for by sacrifices and
sins that put one outside the covenant relation to God.
Jesus recognizes this principle. The people of Sodom
and Gomorrah will not have as heavy condemnation as
the cities which had the benefit of his ministry and teaching (Matt. 11:20 ff.). The servant who knows not his
master's will shall not have the same punishment as the
one who knows but does not (Luke 12:47-48). Paul
also recognizes the same principle. Men are held responsible for the light they have, whether that light be the
light of nature, of the heart and conscience, or of the
Old Testament law (Romans 1-2).

It seems, then, that light and privilege are elements
that enter into the determination of the degree of one's
guilt. The degree of one's guilt might be said to be
determined by the measure of wilfulness that enters into
one's sinning (Heb. 10:26 ff.). To the extent that one
sins wilfully, to that extent is one guilty and his character fixed in sin.

It is sometimes said that ignorance is no excuse, and
the implication is that the ignorant are as guilty as
those who have greater light and privilege. But this will
not hold. The case of Paul is sometimes cited to show

that one may act ignorantly and yet be guilty. Paul does seem to imply here that he was conscientious and yet guilty. But Paul also says that because he did what he did ignorantly in unbelief, God had mercy on him. This clearly implies that his ignorance modified his guilt (1 Tim. 1:13).

This principle is recognized in the social relations of life. The man with light, privilege, opportunity, ability, is held to a stricter account by his fellow men. Courts of law take into account the element of deliberateness in a man's crime in assessing his penalty.

(6) *Sin as depravity*

Another phase of sin is described by the term depravity.

a. By this term is meant that state or condition of man's moral nature that makes it not only possible that he may sin on account of his power of choice, but certain that he will sin on account of his moral weakness and inherent tendency toward evil. This depravity of man's nature is inherent and universal. These two ideas —the idea that depravity is inherent and that it is universal—seem to be inseparable. Certainly, if sin is inherent, it is universal; and, on the other hand, if it is universal, there is a strong presumption that it is inherent. By saying that sin or depravity is inherent we do not mean that sin is a constituent element in human nature, or that sin and human nature are inseparable. Human nature was not created sinful or depraved. Christ did not have a depraved human nature. Besides, if sin were a constituent element in human nature, man could not be saved from sin. But in saying that depravity is inherent in human nature is meant that man as fallen is born depraved; that since Adam's time and on account of the Fall all men are born with such a moral tendency toward sin that it is a moral certainty, that it is morally inevitable, that when they come to make moral choices, they will commit sin.

b. That depravity is inherent is evidenced by the following facts:

(a) The direct teaching of the Scriptures. In Psalm 51 the writer says: "In sin did my mother conceive me" (Psalm 51:5). Jeremiah says: "The heart is deceitful and desperately wicked; who can know it?" (Jer. 17:9.) Paul says that we are by nature the children of wrath (Eph. 2:3). Some claim that Paul is not here referring to the inborn disposition inasmuch as in the context he is discussing the course of life as sinful. Hence it is said that he is not talking about an inborn depravity, but a course of actual transgression. As a matter of fact, he is talking about a course of life, but it is a course of life as growing out of and as expressing the inborn disposition. It is the native disposition developing in its natural course into a life of sin. The life of sin is explained by referring it to the native moral disposition. Men are by nature the children of wrath in the sense that their lives of sin, which incur the wrath of God, are the natural outgrowth of their native disposition.

(b) Another fact that shows that depravity is inherent in the sense indicated above, is the fact that it is universal. That sin is universal is clearly taught in the Bible. In Genesis, following the sin of the first man, there is the intensive and extensive development of sin until the race soon became so corrupt that God sent a flood and destroyed the race except Noah and his family. While Noah was a man of faith, he was a very imperfect man. It is made clear that no man in biblical history was sinless, except Jesus himself. The very best men of both Old and New Testament times were weak and sinful. The psalmist represents God as searching the earth, but finding none without sin (Psalm 14:1 ff.). Jesus regarded all men as sinful. He says: "If ye then, being evil" (Luke 11:13). This expression shows that he regards all men as evil and sinful. He teaches, as one of the fundamental things in prayer, that men should pray for forgiveness (Matt. 6:12). They need forgiveness as universally as they need daily bread. Paul explicitly teaches that all men are sinners. All have sinned (Rom. 3:9 ff.). This presupposition underlies his argument in Romans 5:12 ff.

Experience, observation, and human history show that sin is universal. The best of men confess themselves sinners. Nor is this to be interpreted as the result of an abnormal or morbid consciousness on their part. Men who, like Paul, Luther, and John Bunyan, stand at the center of spiritual Christianity, cannot be regarded as wholly misinterpreting their own relation to God. Then the consensus among men is that no man lives above moral and spiritual blame. The course of human history indicates that there is something fundamentally wrong with mankind.

The best explanation of the universality of sin is to explain it by referring it to the corruption of human nature in the beginning of human history. The Bible gives us to understand that the first man violated God's expressed will and by doing so the stream of human history was corrupted at its source.

c. The question has been discussed as to whether man is totally depraved. That depends altogether on the definition of total depravity. If by total depravity is meant that man is as corrupt as he can be, then certainly the doctrine is not true. But in the sense that man is totally helpless, because of his natural inheritance, outside the provisions of God's saving grace, the doctrine is true. The matter might be summed up by saying that man is totally depraved in the following sense:

(a) In the sense that man's whole nature, every element and faculty of his being, has been weakened and depraved by sin. Body, soul, and spirit have passed under its power. Man's mind has been darkened, his heart depraved, his will perverted by sin.

(b) It means that man is totally unable to deliver himself from the power of sin. Here is the crux of the matter. The truth for which the term total depravity stands is the total inability of man to save himself, his entire helplessness in the grasp of sin.

(c) Without divine help man becomes worse and worse. Instead of total depravity meaning that man is as bad as he can be, it means that, without the redeeming power of God's grace, he will forever sink deeper and deeper into sin.

Much of the dispute over the term total depravity has been aside from the mark, because it was based on the preconception that the thing that made sin deadly was the extent to which man was affected by it. Sin was regarded as ruinous provided the sin was big enough. But it is not the extent of sin that makes it deadly; it is the nature of sin. Sin kills because it is sin, not because it is big. The very nature of sin is such that it would dethrone God and introduce moral and spiritual anarchy into God's universe. It is in direct antithesis to God's nature as holy. Therefore, no sin can be tolerated in man. The very nature of sin is such that it poisons man's moral nature and ruins his spiritual life. It cuts man off from God.

(7) *Sin as bondage*

We have noted that sin produces a state of moral weakness from which man is totally unable to deliver himself.

Jesus and Paul emphasize the servitude of sin. Jesus says that the man who commits sin is the slave of sin (John 8:34). In one place he says that the truth will free from this bondage; in another, the Son (John 8: 32, 36). Paul sets forth in Romans 6 that man is either the servant of sin or of God and righteousness. In chapter seven he gives a vivid account of his own struggle with the power of sin, of his utter inability to deliver himself, and of his finding deliverance in Christ. There seem to be three distinct stages in Paul's experience as set forth in this chapter. The first is a state which he speaks of as being alive without the law (v. 9a). He had no consciousness of condemnation and death, because he had not been awakened by the law to a knowledge of its demands. The second stage is one in which he becomes aware of the righteous demands of the law, but cannot live up to its demands. "The commandment came, sin revived, and I died" (v. 9b). This leads to a sense of utter helplessness and then to despair. Finally comes the realization of deliverance through Christ (v. 25). This reigning principle of sin Paul recognizes as being universal, as shown in chapter five. It is a pathetic description that Paul gives us in Romans 7 of a man divided against himself. He recognizes the good, he has aspirations after the good, but he cannot attain it. He is pulled apart. Such a man can never attain the good until his personality is united in reaching out after the good. And his personality cannot be so unified in reaching after the good until it is unified around a person, Jesus Christ. Until Christ comes in and takes possession, sin reigns. A greater power must drive out sin, and Christ alone is that greater power.

Such a case as Paul describes in this chapter is pathetic, but not the most pathetic by any means. He describes the man with a high standard of right and wrong (the law), with a sensitive conscience and a keen desire to do the right and win God's favor. But he does not have the ability to achieve what he aspires to be and do. He fails and becomes conscious of his failure. There are other men who have no such keen sense of right and wrong, no high moral and religious standards, and no urgent desire to do the right as they do see it. They are the ones who, if they recognize the good, do so only in a kind of dumb fashion. Perhaps every human being recognizes the good to some extent, but some seem to do so only dimly. And this recognition becomes more and more blurred. Of course, we have to recognize that many times there are stirrings in the human heart of which we see no outward sign. But there also seem to be many people who give themselves over more and more unrestrainedly to sin. They become increasingly the slaves of sin. Evil more and more rules the inner life as well as the outer. In fact, as Jesus teaches us, it is the dominance of evil over the inner life that is the most pathetic part of the picture. The tree is bad, and hence the fruit is bad. Some men are taken possession of by evil until, as Paul says, they come to "work all uncleanness with greediness" (Eph. 4:19).

(8) *Sin as an evil heart*

Thus Jesus emphasizes sin as being an inner matter of thought and motive. When the Pharisees criticized his disciples for eating with unwashed hands, Jesus told them that it was not that which enters into a man that defiles him, but that which comes from within, from the heart (moral nature) of the man. He then enumerates evil thoughts and all kinds of wickedness (Mark 7:1 ff.). He makes sin to be both inner and outer. It is a matter of the whole man, the outer deed, but the deed as revealing and expressing the inner life. The man is then as a whole more and more dominated by evil. Man in judging his fellow man is largely limited to the outward act; God judges the heart.

Here as everywhere human life must be judged from within to be judged truly. To look only on the outward act is to miss the significance of the matter. Sin is a deed; but it is more than an act seen from without; it is a personal deed, and a person acts from within. Sin is a deed committed by a person, and a person acts from within prompted by a moral motive. The moral quality of the deed lies in the quality of the motive. So Jesus interprets murder and adultery (Matt. 5:21 ff., 27 ff.). The moral quality of the deed belongs rather to the person than to the deed as an act considered simply as an act. The moral quality of the man determines the quality of the deed rather than that the deed determines the quality of the man. Of course, the deed indicates the man, but the man determines the deed. The tree determines the fruit, and the fruit marks the tree as good or bad.

So the inner and outward life of the man constitute a unity. One cannot be separated from the other. Of course, a bad man may simulate the virtues of the good man; but, even so, his simulation is the expression of a hypocritical and wicked heart. To make the fruit good, the tree must first be made good. A man, then, may be a murderer at heart without actually killing anybody. He that hates his brother is a murderer (1 John 3:15). John is talking about hatred as a settled and governing principle in one's life. If hatred becomes the governing principle of one's life so that he would kill his brother if opportunity arose, then he is a murderer whether he commits the deed or not. The same applies to adultery, to stealing, to lying, and to all other forms of sin. The wickedness of the man makes the deed wicked. Sin is more than an act; it is a state of character. Committing the deed will confirm and fix the character in evil; but it is the evil heart (whole, inner moral life of man) that makes the deed wicked.

III. Original Sin

1. *A preliminary survey*

The question of original sin has been much discussed. The facts to be accounted for are in general two: man's inborn moral depravity, and, secondly, the universality of sin. These are the facts of vital moment to man. These facts do not depend upon any particular explanation as to how they came to be. They are not two facts, but two aspects of one dark and awful fact—the reign of sin in human life and history. Paul in Romans 5 connects the universal reign of sin and death with the transgression of Adam. Many theories have been invented as to how we are related to Adam's sin in such a way as that his sin became the means or ground of our condemnation and death. Paul himself offers no theory of the matter. He simply asserts the fact. The most simple and natural explanation is that, since Adam was the natural head and source of the race, the race as a whole inherits a depraved nature from him. In other words, the fact of sin and death as a universal phenomenon in human life is traced back to Adam's sin as the cause or source. The connection between Adam and his descendants is simply that of head of the race and members who spring from him. As to the imputation of Adam's sin as an act of sin to the individual members of the race, no theory of such imputation is needed, for the simple reason that there was no such imputation. The idea that Adam's sin as an act of sin is charged to his descendants and on that account they are guilty and hence condemned, is an idea too preposterous to be seriously entertained.

2. *The Augustinian and Federal theories*

The Augustinian theory is that because men were seminally present in Adam, or present as to the substance of their being, they, therefore, shared in his sin, and on that ground the sin was charged to them. They are, therefore, guilty of Adam's sin, because they shared in it. Since the sin is imputed to them and they are guilty of it, they are born depraved and condemned. To say the least of it, this theory regards in a very crude and materialistic way the idea of Adam's descendants being present in him. There is no sense in which Adam's descendants can be regarded as having been present in him so as to justify the imputation of Adam's sin to them.

The Federal theory is no better. It says that God made a covenant with Adam, the terms of which were that on condition of Adam's obedience to God his descendants should have eternal life; on condition of his disobedience his sin should be charged to them, and hence they would be guilty and condemned. There is not a shred of evidence from the Bible that any such covenant was ever made with Adam. Somebody has well said that the covenant originated in Holland rather than in the Garden of Eden. Such a charging of the sins of one human individual to another on the ground of a covenant, with which the one to whom sin is charged had nothing to do, would be the height of injustice.

3. Race unity

There is, however, an organic unity of the race which inevitably results in the members suffering with and for one another. God created the race as a race, not as detached and isolated units. Original sin means that the race as a race, and all its individual members have fallen. Every man is born into a fallen race and shares its fallen state. If one objects to this on the ground that one member should not suffer for another's wrongdoing, the answer is that this is a law of life, no matter what we may say about it. It is not a question as to whether we think it should have been that way or not. As a matter of fact, it is that way. And it must be that way if there is to be any social life for man. An arrangement according to which every man would suffer only for his own wrongdoing would be an arrangement in which every man stood out as an isolated, detached unit. There would be no social life in such an arrangement. Nor could there be any such thing as one man enjoying the benefits of another's labor or goodness. Not only would there be no social evil; there could be no social good. Every man would suffer with inexorable, mathematical precision the exact desert of his own deeds and nobody could help him.

The best social thought of our times emphasizes this aspect of both sin and righteousness; namely, that others are affected by either. No man can draw himself off into a corner and live to himself in such a way that nobody else is concerned as to the kind of life that he lives. Others are concerned, vitally concerned. While sin, as before stated, is primarily against God, this truth has sometimes been interpreted in such a one-sided way as to make the impression that only God and the individual soul are concerned in one's sin. But sin is a social affair. There is no such thing as an individual in the sense of a detached and unrelated unit. No sin in its consequences is ever limited to the soul that commits it. Sin is against God. But God has established a social and moral order. This order in which men live together is violated by man's sin.

The doctrine of original sin means that man is not only a social being, but that the race is an organic unity, and as an organic unity it was affected by the sin of the first man, the head of the race. Through the law of natural generation, the whole race has inherited the evil effects of that first transgression. All men have been born on a lower moral and spiritual plane than they would have been if Adam had not sinned.

This evil entail of sin has been passed down by social influence as well as by natural inheritance. Sin is self-propagating. It has corrupted the whole social environment of the race and has penetrated every phase of the life of man. No part of man's life is untouched by it. All human relations and all social institutions have been pervaded by the power of sin and the corruption produced by it. If anybody challenges the idea that depravity can be a matter of natural inheritance, one thing is certain: namely, that the corrupting power of moral evil is found throughout the whole extent of man's life. This is true irrespective of particular means as to how it came to pass.

4. *Individual responsibility in relation to race unity*

(1) Most of the difficulty in this question has grown out of the effort to solve the theoretical question as to whether the individual was guilty on account of that first sin and to what extent and on what ground. So far as individual responsibility and guilt are concerned, there can be no such responsibility and guilt for an act committed thousands of years before one was born and with which he had nothing to do. I am no more indivi-

dually responsible, and hence guilty, for what Adam did than I am for what Julius Caesar did. But I am affected in my life by what both did. Organic, social, and historical influences have bound my life up with what they did. As to the justice of an order of things in which that should be true, I may not be able to work that out. There are theoretical difficulties. It may be difficult to understand how I should be responsible for deeds which grow out of and express a nature which I inherited. If I am not responsible for the nature, how can I be responsible for the deeds which inevitably grow out of it?

(2) In answer to this difficulty some things may be said:

a. The first is that whatever theory one may hold as to Adam's sin and our relation to it, the fact seems to stand that, when we come to the age of moral consciousness and moral activity, we find ourselves so identified with evil impulses within us and evil social forces around us that we are already practical slaves to them. These evil forces did not originate in acts of our own will. This may seem like a fact of dark and ominous aspect, but we cannot get rid of it by denying its existence. Unpleasant facts are not disposed of by denying their right to be or by calling them by euphemistic names. Men have tried long enough to heal the world's moral corruption by this kind of word jugglery.

b. The second fact to be observed is that both the Scriptures and moral consciousness bear testimony to our responsibility for our lives in spite of our inherited natures. In fact, this evil inheritance is regarded in the Bible as constituting a part of our awful condition, calling for divine grace and help. The testimony of our moral consciousness on this point cannot be doubted. As evil and sinful, we acknowledge our deplorable state and renounce the sinful self. One must deny this sinful self, take up one's cross, be crucified with Christ, in order to live.

c. In the third place, there is general agreement among all classes of evangelical theologians, justified by principles drawn from the New Testament and from our Christian consciousness, that all disability up to the point of positive transgression and deliberate rejection of moral light is provided for in the redeeming work of Christ. There is race redemption as well as race sin. No man, therefore, will be lost merely because of original or race sin. Up to the point of positive transgression or rejection of moral light, the individual is provided for in the grace of God without personal repentance and faith. Someone may be unsatisfied at this point on the ground that it leaves a borderland in which we cannot tell as to the condition and destiny of the individual. That is true. It does leave a borderland. But it makes reasonably clear the principles upon which God deals with men. As to deciding the destiny of the individual, we need not give ourselves any undue concern about that, since it is not our business. It is made plain in the New Testament that the man who rejects clear gospel light is lost. The man who definitely accepts the grace of God is saved. As to those who fall in between, we can very safely leave them in the hands of God. Since that is where their destiny finally rests, that is what we will likely do, whether we will or not. The only relation we have to the matter is to carry the light of the gospel to all men, so that their responsibility in the matter will be as definite as possible. As for deciding matters which rest in the hands of God, he can probably do that better than we can. The best way for us to clear ourselves in the matter is to do what he has clearly revealed as his will. As to deciding who is lost and who is not, even if we cannot decide in the case of every individual, it is clear as to the difference in standing before God of those who reject clear gospel light and those who accept it. As has been well said, although we cannot thrust in a knife blade at the exact point that separates day and night and say that here one ends and the other begins, still the difference between light and darkness is fairly clear.

5. *Conclusion as to the moral condition and salvation of the infant*

As to the question of infant salvation, then, it is generally agreed among evangelical theologians that those dying in infancy are saved. This is not held so much on the ground that there is specific Scripture teaching to that effect as it is because of certain general principles in gospel teaching as to God's dealings with men, and because of the general view of the character of God as revealed in Christ. There are several positions on this question of the condition and destiny of the child that may be summed up in brief statements.

One position may be put in the statement that the child is an angel. But the child is not an angel, using that term to symbolize an innocent, unfallen being. The child is depraved in nature and potentially a transgressor of God's law.

Another position may be summed up in the statement that the child is a devil. But that is not true. The idea of a devil or demon is a being wholly determined toward evil, and so without impulses to good that even the grace of God could not change its character.

Another statement that summarizes the position of many is that the child is an animal. The child is an animal, but much more. If the child were only an animal, it would never become capable of moral life and character. The child has the capacity of developing into a moral personality. It does not have the powers and capacities of personality at first, but normally these develop. In that sense the child transcends the animal. It does not have the developed powers of personality, but its normal destiny is to grow into personality. In that sense it is personal.

Moreover, there are such seeds of evil tendency in the child's nature, and such social influences for evil in the world in which the child lives that it inevitably commits transgressions when it comes to the age of moral responsibility. In that sense the child is a sinner. It does not have personal guilt. That is impossible where the conditions of personal responsibility are lacking. These are absent in the child's life until the powers of self-consciousnes and self-determination arise. There can be no personal guilt except in the case of a personal agent.

In view of these considerations we believe that we are justified in holding that the child dying in infancy is saved. In other words, where there has been conscious and positive identification of oneself with evil, there must be also, under the grace of God, conscious and positive repudiation of evil and identification of oneself with right before there can be deliverance from evil. Up to the point of positive identification of oneself with right or wrong, there is only the potentiality of moral life. In the case of the child, that potentiality is evil except for the positive influence of the grace of God in redeeming from this evil potentiality or the life of transgression that grows out of it. So far as the bent of the child's nature and the social influences of the world order are concerned, these are toward evil. To save the child from this evil inheritance requires the grace of God, which transcends nature and the world order.

If anyone should raise the objection that this makes gospel light a dangerous thing, in that it may be the means of heavier condemnation, we not only grant the objection, but urge that it is true. But all moral light is dangerous. The most benevolent forces in the world, when properly used, become the most dangerous when we are ill-adjusted to them. The life-giving forces of air, water, and light become life-destroying unless wisely controlled and directed. Intelligence wrongly directed becomes darkness and death. The grace of God, when rejected, becomes eternal death and irretrievable destruction. To be a person with moral opportunities and responsibilities is itself a dangerous thing. But who would, therefore, care to sink to the level of the brute? Consequently, the forces that make for the development of personality are hazardous forces. The highest of these is the grace of God that saves from sin. But so far as we can see, even God cannot make and develop personality without running the risk involved. He cannot present his grace to man with a view to his salvation without running the risk of having men reject that grace and thereby incur condemnation.

IV. The Results of Sin

Some of the things treated here as results of sin might as well perhaps have been considered as being of the nature of sin. But whether they be considered as results or of the very essence of sin, they are inseparable from it. In the moral order of the world, sin and the things here discussed belong together. Some of them are more clearly of the nature of results, but others might be considered more nearly as of sin's very essence.

1. *Sin alienates from God*

It is of the very nature of sin to alienate man from God. In the parable of the prodigal son (which might better be called the parable of the loving father), Jesus tells us about the younger son who gathered all together and departed for a far country. Here we have a vivid picture of sin and its ruin. Sin is a going away from God. It is going into a far country. Sin turns man's whole being against God and shuts God out of man's life.

This going away from God, or alienation from God, is not, however, a passive attitude; it is positive hostility to God. Paul talks about the carnal mind of man. By this he means man's mind as unrenewed by the Spirit of God. He says that this mind is enmity against God. It is not subject to the law of God; it cannot be. To be thus subject to the law is contrary to its moral nature (Rom. 8:7). In the Garden of Eden, after Adam disobeyed God, in his shame, he hid himself from God (Gen. 3:8 ff.). Man has been acting thus ever since. Sin shuts man out from God's presence and drives God out of man's life.

One of the most instructive passages in the New Testament on sin is Romans 1:18-32. Paul tells us there how the invisible God reveals himself to men through the things that are made. Then he indicates that men, "knowing God, glorified him not as God, neither gave thanks." He indicates that they "refused to have God in their knowledge."

But they did not give up religion. Their religion rather was degraded. They became idolaters. They worshiped the images of corruptible man, of birds, of four-footed beasts and creeping things. They worshiped the creature rather than the eternal Creator of all things. This might be an indication of what Paul means when in Ephesians (2:12) he speaks of men as "without God in the world" (literally, "atheists in the world"). Perhaps he means that they are without a knowledge of the true God. He is speaking here as in Romans 1:18-32 of the condition of the Gentile world. They do not know the true God. But in the vanity of their minds (Rom. 1:21-22) they invent substitutes for him, and false religion takes the place of true. Paul did not seem to think that one religion was as good as another. History proves that religion may be a degrading power in human life as well as an elevating power. Sin lays its slimy hand on the altar of man's worship and befouls it.

2. *Sin degrades the sinner*

Paul tells us that no man lives to himself (Rom. 14:7). This is often taken to mean that in what we do we are related to others and should, therefore, be careful about such relations. Paul does teach that a man should have a mind to his relations to others and especially as to the influence of his life on others. He makes that point in this chapter, but that is not his point when he says that no man lives to himself. He goes on to say that no man dies to himself. So he says that whether we live or die we are the Lord's.

Man's life and personality are grounded in God. We have just seen that sin alienates from God. Since sin cuts the roots of man's fellowship with God, it causes his personality to shrivel and die. In popular language, when we speak of man's personality or of his personal power, we are thinking of his social qualities. We have schools that claim in a few easy lessons to tell one how to develop his personality so as to be able to influence other people and get them to do what he wants done. But all this is rather superficial. Sometimes what it amounts to is learning how to cover up one's selfish intentions and make oneself pleasant enough to be able to hoodwink the other fellow. The roots of one's personal being are in one's fellowship with God, the Creator and Sustainer of us all. To nourish one's fellowship with God, therefore, is the best means of developing one's personality. And whatever breaks that fellowship will cause one's personality to shrivel and die. Fellowship with God is as necessary for the development of personality as air and sunshine are for the growth of flowers. And let us not deceive ourselves here. We are not to seek fellowship with God for the sake of developing personality. There may creep in here a form of subtle spiritual selfishness that will be self-defeating. God is not to be degraded into the position of being used for our selfish ends—even so-called spiritual ends. We must find our end in God, not seek to make him the means of carrying out our ends.

By what was said above, we do not mean to say that the disturbance of social relations caused by sin is not degrading to personality. The rupture of such relations due to sin does degrade man's personal powers. What we were affirming is that personality is grounded in God, and to be cut off from God dwarfs personality. But it is also true that personality is begotten in a social matrix, is developed in social relations and must be maintained in social activity. Consequently sin degrades personality, both because it cuts man off from fellowship with God and disrupts his relations with his fellows.

It is easy enough to see how sensual sins destroy man's personal powers, but it is not always so evident that this is true in the case of more refined and so-called spiritual forms of sin. But whether evident at once or not evident at all, all forms of sin are degrading to personality. All forms of sin tend to close one up in a casing of selfishness that shuts out God and one's fellows. Self-centered personality dies. It can live only in an atmosphere of fellowship—fellowship with God and with one's fellow men. Turned in on itself it dies. The first demand of discipleship is self-denial. One must renounce self-mastership. He must give himself over to Another. One cannot come to himself until he comes to Christ as Lord.

It is instructive to take a passage (one out of many such in the New Testament) like Ephesians 4:17-19 and note some of the expressions Paul uses to describe the course of the sinful life. Notice some of these expressions: "the vanity of their mind"; "darkened in their understanding"; "because of the ignorance that is in them"; "because of the hardening of their heart." Here we have expressions that describe accurately the disintegration and degradation that come to personality because of a life of sin.

Some people seem to think that unless some external calamity befalls a man when he sins, he is not being punished for his sin. But the most terrible punishment does not come in the form of external calamity, but in the form of the internal collapse of his personal powers and capacities. The most awful calamity that comes to a man is what happens in the man himself. Emerson argues, in substance, in one place, that many people circumnavigate the globe to get away from their misery but cannot do so because they cannot get away from themselves. "Myself am hell."

One phase of this degradation of the sinner's personality is the self-deluding power of sin. Whatever form one's sin may take, it tends to turn the sinner in upon himself so that he becomes infatuated with his own ideas, plans, and purposes.

We have seen that temptation always appears in the guise of a good. Otherwise it would be no temptation. And when one yields to temptation and indulges in sin, as a rule, he does not learn wisdom from the experience and renounce his evil course. Usually the opposite is true. The sinner becomes blinded and deluded. Some men have argued that experience in sin would be the remedy for sin; that by experiencing the bitter results of sin, men would renounce sin and follow after righteousness. Sometimes, by the grace of God, this has been true. But it should be noted, that, when this takes place, it is due to the grace of God, and not to wisdom that came from indulging in sin. Indulging in sin does not give wisdom; it only generates folly. It does not open one's eyes to truth; it blinds so that one cannot see the truth. What men sometimes take for wisdom learned from a godless life is only blind conceit that means folly and ruin. Professing themselves to be wise, they became fools (Rom. 1:22).

Thus sin is self-defeating. This is exemplified in the lives of those who make their chief purpose in life the pursuit of material goods. One who strives after material goods as his chief object becomes more and more engrossed in the pursuit of things and loses the sense of the value of spiritual things. His heart becomes more and more set on things. Where one's treasures are, there will his heart be (Matt. 6:21). If one thus engaged in the pursuit of material wealth as his chief end fails in acquiring wealth, he becomes disappointed and miserable, because he fails to acquire that which he most desires in life. He fails in his chief aim in life and dies defeated. On the other hand, if he succeeds in acquiring wealth, he will find, as Jesus taught, that life does not consist in the abundance of the things that one possesses (Luke 12:15). Such a man had thought that the possession of things would give happiness and abundance of life. Now he finds that it does not. What he thought he wanted he may still want. Like the miser gloating over his gold, he may still cling to his idol, but it brings only disillusionment and misery. And it needs to be kept in mind that such disillusionment is much more apt to produce worldly cynicism than it is to lead to spiritual insight and wisdom.

This same thing results whenever man sets his heart on any thing less than, and other than, God. Augustine says: "By my own sin Thou didst justly punish me. For Thou hast commanded, and so it is, that every inordinate affection should be its own punishment."[8] Only God gives ultimate satisfaction. Man may set his heart on pleasure, wealth, personal ambition, even family, country, or friends. None of these can take the place of God. Anything else put in the place of supreme affection and esteem that rightly belongs to God becomes an idol and will let one down in the end. Man was made for God and can find life and satisfaction in nothing other than God.

3. *Sin disrupts social relations*

As already stated, sin is against God and alienates man from God. But while sin is primarily against God, it also perverts and disrupts all the relations of man with man. These social relations are meant to be a blessing to man and are, except as they are perverted. Man finds in these relations much of the joy and blessedness of life. In fact, outside of these relations nothing resembling a human life could be lived. A normal human life depends, first, on right relations with God and, second, on right relations with man. If the theistic interpretation of the world is right, then, everything depends on being right with God. But if a man is not right with God, he cannot be right anywhere. So the sin that perverts man's relations with God perverts his relations with his fellow man and with the whole creation.

---

[8] *Confessions*, Book I, (XII), 19.

Accordingly, we find that the first sin told about in the Bible after the fall of Adam and Eve was the murder of Abel by his brother Cain. From that day to this, all human relations and institutions have been under the curse of sin. The very relations and institutions that were meant to bless man have often proved a curse.

On the other hand, Paul teaches that man is reconciled to God through the cross of Christ and thus finds peace with God. But more than that, he teaches that through this cross, Jew and Gentile are reconciled to each other, and Christ becomes the ground of peace between man and man as well as between man and God (Eph. 2:11 ff.). In Christ God is creating a new humanity by removing the hostility and alienation that separates them.

This explains the relation between religion and ethics in the teaching of Jesus. Jesus has sometimes been reduced to the role of an ethical teacher, but he never taught ethics *for ethics' sake*. Jesus knew too much about man to think that man could be made right with man simply by dealing with human relations alone. He knew and taught that man's fundamental relation is with God, and that so long as man is wrong with God he could never be made permanently right with man. Trying to set man right with his fellows without first making him right with God would be like treating a sick man for surface symptoms when he is being eaten up by an internal cancer. In the teaching of Jesus, ethics are grounded in religion and religion expresses itself in ethics. As a matter of fact, it is not ethics *and* religion; it is rather religion that is fundamentally ethical in its nature. In the teaching of Jesus, true religion is ethical, and ethics are grounded in religion. Man cannot be right with man without being right with God, and getting right with God includes getting right with man. The central principle of religion is love to God. The central principle of ethics is love to man. These are not two but one. Love to man is rooted in love to God. Love to God bears fruit in love to man.

Sin blights man in his own personality by alienating him from God and perverting his relations with his fellows and cursing all human institutions.

4. *Sin causes suffering*

One question that arises here is with reference to the relation of natural evil or suffering to moral evil or sin. There can be no strict separation between the two. The distinction has been pointed out as being, in general, the distinction between that which man suffers and that which he inflicts.[9] One is imposed upon man by the weakness and infirmity of his own nature and by the disorders of the natural world with which his life is inextricably bound up. The other he is responsible for as being the perversity of his own will.

To hold that there is no connection between the two would be an untenable position. That would bisect the world and destroy its unity. We cannot agree that our world is thus divided. Two things that are so intimately interwoven in life must bear some causal connection.

Nor could we say that the connection is that sin is the outgrowth or expression of natural evil or human weakness. This is practically the view already discussed, that sin is human finiteness or limitation. Undoubtedly there is a close relation between man's physical and mental weaknesses and limitations as purely natural and much of his moral weakness and sin. But to make sin nothing but natural weakness or the result of it would contradict the clear voice of conscience and the plain teachings of the Scriptures. This would not explain sin; it would explain it away.

We know that much of human suffering is directly and indirectly due to man's sin. Both the man who sins and others as well suffer because of his sins. The connection is not always easy to trace, but often it is obvious. If all the suffering of mankind due to its own perversity were taken out of the world's history, that

---

[9]Fairbairn, *Philosophy of the Christian Religion*, p. 134.

history would make quite different reading. Here the connection is so obvious that we do not have any trouble tracing it. We cannot always trace the connection in detail, but the broad outlines are plain.

But what about the suffering due to the disorders of nature herself, the cyclones, floods, earthquakes, volcanoes, etc? There is an indication in Genesis and other places that there is a connection between natural evil and the sin of man. In Genesis work or labor is to be a part of man's penalty. This does not mean that work or activity as such is a part of the penalty, for man was to keep the garden even before the Fall. And after redemption there is to be activity. God's servants will serve him (Rev. 22:3). Heaven is to be no place for inactivity. But the fact that man is to earn his bread in the sweat of his brow indicates that the element of burdensome labor came in because of sin (Gen. 3:19). Then it is said that the earth should bear thorns and thistles for man (Gen. 3:18). This may be taken as a particular statement indicating that natural evil in general came because of man's sin and as a consequence. Paul's statement in Romans 8:18-22 may indicate that the whole physical universe is to be renovated and renewed as a part of God's redemptive plan. (Cf. 2 Peter 3:13.)

Some have concluded because of the statement in Genesis that there was no suffering, no animal death, no natural evil of any kind in the world before man sinned. But this is a precarious position for several reasons. In the first place, there is no clear teaching anywhere in the Bible to the effect that all suffering, animal death, and all natural evil, are the consequence of man's sin. This is rather an inference from such statements as we find in Genesis 3:17-19, Romans 8:19-22, and 2 Peter 3:13. These statements do not clearly and unmistakably teach the position under consideration. And we must distinguish between the clear teaching of Scripture and our own inferences from some more or less general statements of Scripture. Where the statements are not clear and definite, it becomes us to practice a modest reserve in our affirmations.

Then another thing to remember is that even if one holds that natural evil, in whole or in part, is the consequence of man's sin, still it is not necessary to hold that man's sin preceded in the order of time the appearance of natural evil in the world. The order in which things come in the purpose of God is not necessarily the order in which they appear in the temporal order. The disorder and natural disturbances of the world may have been intended, whether meant strictly as penalty or not, to remind man of his own sin and need of redemption. Perhaps the disorder of the physical universe is intended as a reflection of the disorder of the moral universe. Unless we are going to hold to a form of dualism, or make the physical universe the primary factor of which the moral is simply a reflection, then it seems that the physical is in point of purpose and intention a reflection of the moral and spiritual. Yet this would not necessitate the reconstruction of the physical world at the time of man's sin, with a reversal of the laws of the physical world. The imperfections and disorders of the physical may have been of the nature of "anticipative consequences." God could have made the physical universe to correspond to the foreknown condition of the moral world. If God could not do that, he did not have as much foresight and power of adjustment as does a man who builds his house with reference to conditions of weather that he knows will come in the climate in which he lives. So the statement in Genesis (3:18) does not necessitate that thorns and thistles began to grow only after man sinned. It is no more necessary to hold that thorns and thistles first began to grow after man sinned than it is to hold that God changed the laws of the refraction of light after the flood so that the rainbow should first appear. In each case it is probable that the divine wisdom selected certain natural phenomena already in existence as a sign to man. The history of the natural world would indicate that animal death was operative before man appeared in the world, and there is no good reason for holding that the Scriptures teach differently.

But whatever may be said about natural evil in general as being in whole or in part due to man's sin, there is no question that specific forms of suffering are at times the direct or indirect result of man's sin. Nor is there any good reason for denying that this suffering is of the nature of a penalty for man's sin. Sometimes these evil results come to the one who commits the sin; sometimes they fall upon others. Such evil consequences sometimes come as the result of the violation of moral or spiritual law. The Old Testament especially emphasizes that sickness and death as the shortening of life came as a result of sin and disobedience to God (Ex. 20:12; Prov. 3:1;10:27).

This cannot be made an inexorable law—at least not to the extent of saying that one's condition of worldly prosperity is an infallible index to one's spiritual condition; i.e., that misfortune is always a sign that one is a great sinner, or that prosperity is a sign of righteousness. (See book of Job and John 9:1 ff.) Still it is true that righteousness promotes good health and prosperity, both in the nation and the individual, and also that sin tends to shorten life and bring unhappiness and woe. Experience and observation also justify the conclusion that specific evils often follow immorality and sin.

To a limited extent, at least, then, natural evil or suffering may be regarded as the penalty of sin, or as a punishment for sin.

When we come to the doctrine of providence as related to grace, we will see that suffering or natural evil serves another purpose in relation to sin; that is, it is used as a means under grace for the development of Christian character; it serves a redemptive end. This we know both from the teachings of the Scriptures and from Christian experience. This is involved in the saying of

Jesus about the blind man in the ninth chapter of John. He says in substance to the disciples that they will never understand suffering and misfortune so long as they try to interpret these exclusively as the infliction of penalty for sin; they must see them as related to God's benevolent purpose toward mankind. We must remember that every phase of life is to be interpreted from the point of view of God's redemptive purpose in Christ. Law and penalty do not speak the final word. They speak a true word, but the final word is spoken by grace and truth as revealed in Jesus Christ. There is a penal aspect to suffering or natural evil; but there is also a redemptive aspect. For the man who rejects grace, suffering is primarily penal; for the redeemed man, it is primarily remedial and disciplinary. For society in general, in proportion as sin reigns, it is primarily penal; as grace reigns, it is redemptive. We know that the race has got much of its development, mental, social, and moral, by striving to overcome natural evil.

We said further back that sin is the perversion of the good. Something of the same kind might apply even to suffering and natural evil in general. Suffering and death could have been a part of the natural order purely as natural. In a sinless order they could have served a good purpose. This does not mean that within themselves they would have been good, but they could have served good ends. But the incoming of sin could have perverted the moral order so that these good ends were perverted and the good became evil. Suffering, then, becomes evil except as the grace of God intervenes to bring good out of natural evil.

In a moral order, uncorrupted by sin, suffering and natural evil might serve morally good ends. Sin perverts this order, and natural evil becomes a curse instead of serving good ends. The grace of God introduces the principle of redemption into the working of the natural order and makes the whole natural order, including natural evil, to work for redemptive ends.

5. Sin brings death

There are places in the Bible where the penalty of sin is summed up in the word "death." God said to Adam: "In the day that thou eatest thereof thou shalt surely die" (Gen. 2:17). Paul said: "The wages of sin is death" (Rom. 6:23). Speaking of an unrighteous life, he says: "The end of those things is death" (Rom. 6:21). He says again that the mind of the flesh is death (Rom. 8:6). James says that sin brings forth death (1:15).

The question arises as to whether this includes physical death, or is the penalty here spoken of spiritual death? There are places in the Bible where death clearly means spiritual death; for instance, when Jesus said: "He that liveth and believeth on me shall never die" (John 11:26). He certainly does not mean that one who believes in him shall never die physically. But at times death includes physical death. This is certainly so at times in the language of Paul. This is evident in 1 Corinthians 15, where he discusses the resurrection over against death. He also means to include physical death in Romans 5 when he talks about the universal sway of death as the result of Adam's sin. When the Scriptures speak of death as the penalty for sin, they do not mean either physical or spiritual death to the exclusion of the other, but they mean death as a totality, both physical and spiritual, the death of the whole man. There may be places where one aspect is emphasized, but neither phase of death is excluded.

There is no necessary inconsistency between this interpretation of death as related to sin and the idea that death is a law of life in the natural world. The biblical writers were not writing natural history. They were not writing as scientists. They were giving a spiritual interpretation of the facts of the world in which we live. Death is a law of the natural world. This law of the natural world is seen by the biblical writers as meaning that there is a fundamental rupture in man's life in his relation with God.

What was said in the preceding section about natural evil as related to sin will apply largely to physical death, because death is the summation and consummation of natural evil. We can sum the matter up, then, by saying that for the Christian physical death is primarily redemptive and disciplinary; for the unredeemed man it is penal.

ELECTION: GOD'S PURPOSE OF REDEMPTION

I. Background of the Doctrine

1. God as personal and purposive
2. God's plan in relation to the world order
3. God's plan in relation to Christ and his church
4. God's knowledge and control of nature and history
5. God's purpose and his praise

II. God's Purpose in Its Racial Aspects

1. As indicated in man's religious history
2. As indicated in the Old Testament
3. As indicated in Christ and the New Testament

III. God's Purpose in Relation to the Salvation of the Individual

1. God brings the sinner to repentance and faith
2. He does so in pursuance of an eternal purpose
3. All credit for man's salvation belongs to God
4. God's purpose includes the good we do

IV. Objections to the Doctrine of Election

1. That it makes God partial
2. That it is unjust to the non-elect
3. That it is inconsistent with man's freedom
4. That it discourages effort on the part of Christians

CHAPTER II

ELECTION: GOD'S PURPOSE OF REDEMPTION

We have seen something of the nature and ruin of man's sin. To think of all men as resting under the curse of sin would be a disturbing thought if that were all that we could see. In considering sin we found that it has significance only in relation to a holy God. The fact that makes sin such an awful reality is that it is against a God of holy love. Sin would not be what it is unless it were sin against God, and against such a God; nor would it appear in its true character unless seen in contrast to him.

But if seeing sin in relation to God brings out the blackness of sin, on the other hand, seeing a God of saving grace in relation to sin brings out the glorious character of his grace that saves. Paul brings out the contrast in the character of the two in Ephesians 2:1 ff. In verses 1-3 he shows the awful blackness of sin. Then he says: *"But God . . ."* He then brings out the glorious character of God's grace that saves. Sometimes when we speak of man's sin, we then turn and say that men are not all bad, or that they are not altogether bad, or at least that they are not all as bad as they might be. But Paul shows greater wisdom. He finds relief from the blackness of the picture in the God whose character makes the blackness of sin so black. Our refuge from the despair of sin is not in any goodness found in man, nor in any power of man to save, but in the God against whom man has sinned. Man's only hope lies in the goodness of the God against whom he has sinned.

I. Background of the Doctrine of Election

What one believes about God's purpose as related to our salvation will likely depend, to some extent at least, on what he believes about some other things.

What does one think about God? What does he think about the universe and about its relation to God? Who and what is man? What is his place in the universe and what is his relation to God?

It is evident that what one thinks about such questions as these will help to determine what he thinks about election. Here as everywhere else in religion the all important question is what one thinks about God. What one believes about God will largely determine what he believes about everything else.

Consider a few questions that will have a specific bearing on this problem of election.

1. In the first place, we are to remember that God is personal and purposive.

Of course, if one thinks of God as an impersonal principle or power in or over the universe, he will not believe in anything like election. Neither will he believe in any other purposive activity on God's part. In that case, the Power that we call God may effect some results (they could hardly be called ends or purposes) that will prove beneficial to man, but they could hardly be considered as having been intended or purposed as beneficial. They just turn out to be beneficial by chance or fate or in some way that we do not understand.

But it was not so that Jesus and Paul—the whole Bible, in fact—regarded God. Clearly they regarded him as personal in a very definite sense and as working out specific purposes in the world. Jesus regarded himself as having a specific mission in life. He regarded himself as having been sent of God into the world on such a mission. Paul's whole life was revolutionized and dominated by such a conviction concerning himself. That such was the conviction of Jesus and Paul is hardly questionable on the basis of what we see in the New Testament.

One has a perfect right to differ with the New Testament on this matter. But it is very questionable whether a man would have a right to regard God as simply the tendency toward integration, or something of that kind, and call that the Christian doctrine of God. The Christian conception of God is definitely that God is personal and purposive. The whole Bible favors such a view of God, and so does Christian experience. Especially is this true in the experience of a man who has felt the call of God to some specific form of Christian service. In that respect the experiences of Jesus and Paul run through the lives of thousands in Christian history and in the present day. If some present-day armchair philosopher denies that he has had such an experience, the simple answer is that nobody said that he had. But that is no proof that nobody else has. If the objector says that nobody can have such an experience, the answer is that his denial cannot offset the positive testimony of thousands of good and reliable men and women that they have had such an experience and that they have found the key to the meaning of their lives in the experience.

2. In the second place, the historical world order is the scene of the working out of a plan of God.

If somebody wants a scientific demonstration that this is true, there is only one answer: namely, that no such demonstration can be given. This is not a matter of scientific demonstration; it is a matter of faith. From a scientific point of view, one might review all natural and human history and not be able to establish any conclusion of this kind. Some such conclusion, however, is a necessity for a theistic view of the world. If there is a God who is the Creator and Sustainer of all things, then it inevitably follows that he created and sustains the world for purposes of his own and that the world is the scene for the effecting of his purpose. Some such assumption was clearly in the minds of the biblical writers. In Genesis 1:31 the writer says that God saw all that he had made, and, behold, it was very good. Evidently the author means that, with reference to the ends or purposes that the Creator had in mind for the world and for man, they were well adapted to carry out his purposes.

Otherwise stated, in the finite and historical order the infinite and eternal God is becoming immanent for purposes of his own. This does not mean that there are in the historical order no elements that resist his purposes. The Genesis account indicates that there are such elements. So does universal human experience. But the claim of faith is that this purpose will be carried out in spite of these intractable elements. In fact, the presence of these intractable elements helps to emphasize the necessity for the carrying out of such a purpose on God's part.

3. In the third place, Christian faith holds that God is working out through Christ and his church a redemptive program in the world.

This is to be joined up with what has just been said. Creation and redemption form one plan with God. Creation was for redemptive ends. Redemption was not an afterthought on God's part. He did not make the world, and unforeseen to him have his plan wrecked by sin, and then go to work to salvage something out of the wreck. His was a unified plan from the beginning. Creation looked toward redemption, and redemption is to be the goal and climax of creation. In Romans 8:18 ff. Paul seems to indicate that, in the consummation of redemption, the creative order comes to the realization of a teleology immanent within that order. Supralapsarian Calvinism was right in the sense that there was nothing deeper in the mind and purpose of God than his purpose to redeem.

4. A fourth thing to keep in mind is that the processes and forces of both nature and history lie open to God's mind and are under his control.

As previously stated, this is not to deny that there are certain forces, especially in man's will, that can and do oppose God and his purposes. But with reference to these, one of the paradoxes of faith is that God works out his purpose in spite of the opposing forces in the world, and often through them.

We might take two instances in which this paradox is exemplified. One is the history of Israel. God chose Abraham and his descendants for a worldwide mission. In Abraham and his seed all the nations of the earth were to be blessed. But Abraham's descendants forgot this. They repudiated their worldwide mission. They became so thoroughly centered in themselves that they forgot the world beyond. They did not feel that they had any mission to the Gentile world. They considered that God had chosen them for their own sakes and not for the sake of the world.

But in spite of Israel's repudiation of her worldwide mission and obligation, and through Israel's rejection of her Messiah, God brought in a new religious order that is truly universal in principle. All the nationalistic and limiting elements were sloughed off, and Christianity supplanted Judaism. The only completely spiritual and universal conception of God and of worship that the world has known thus came into being. Through Israel's failure God succeeded.

The other instance is just another phase of this one. Christ came to save. But his people to whom he came repudiated him. His own received him not. But it was through their repudiation and rejection of him that he carried out his redemptive work. With wicked hands men crucified him, but in doing so they carried out what was in the determinate counsel and foreknowledge of God (Acts 2:23).

This suggests the place where one of the sharpest issues is drawn in regard to this matter. Does God foreknow all things, including the free acts of men, even their most wicked and diabolical deeds? This has been the usual theistic and Christian position, even the position of those who did not hold to any definite doctrine of election and predestination. But some men today deny that God foreknows man's free acts. This is the position taken by Dr. A. E. Garvie in his absorbing book, *The Christian Doctrine of the Godhead.*[1] He rejects both foreordination and foreknowledge on God's part. This, he thinks, is necessary if man is to be free. He says that no one can conceive how an act could be both foreknown and free.

The consequences of denying foreknowledge on the part of God are quite serious. Dr. Garvie says that, though God does not foreknow the free acts of man, yet he does know the limits within which man's acts may affect the fulfilment of his purpose and he knows his own resources to meet the emergency.[2]

But the denial that God foreknows the free acts of man is not a matter of a superficial limitation. If God does not foreknow the free acts of man, then, for all practical purposes, he does not foreknow the future at all. When we speak of the future, we mean the future for man. If you take away the life of man, there is no future for the world. Only to a rational being do past, present, and future mean anything. And all development in time is largely determined by the choices and creative activities of men. If such choices and activities of men cannot be known by God until after they have taken place, that, in effect, leaves God trailing the procession rather than leading it. Men have intuitively believed that somehow God exercised a providential control over the affairs of men. But providence means to *see before.* If God cannot foreknow the free acts of men, however, then his power of providence is only a very dim one. He can see ahead only very indistinctly. Hence his control of the future would be very questionable.

This undoubtedly is not the view of either the Old or New Testament. This is so manifest that it seems superfluous to argue the point. According to this denial, God himself did not foreknow the betrayal and crucifixion

[1]See pp. 240 ff.
[2]Ibid. p. 243

of Jesus. Jesus says, speaking of the end, that no one, not even the angels in heaven, neither the Son, knows, but the Father (Mark 13:32). But according to Dr. Garvie Jesus should have added that not even the Father knows. If he does not foreknow the free acts of millions of men preceding the end, it is hardly to be expected that he foreknows the time of the end. Evidently Jesus believed that he did.

Besides, the position that foreknowledge on God's part excludes freedom on man's part is wholly gratuitous. On the day of Pentecost, Peter puts side by side the fact that Jesus was delivered in the counsel and foreknowledge of God and that men slew him with wicked hands (Acts 2:23). Instance after instance could be found in both Old and New Testaments where such matters are treated in the same way.

Another instance was that of Paul on the way to Rome to be tried before Caesar. They were caught in a great storm on the Mediterranean and it seemed that they would all be destroyed. In the midst of the storm Paul was given assurance from God that he and the whole company would be spared (Acts 27:21 ff.). But a little later, when they were stranded on the shore of Melita, Paul told the military captain that, if the sailors were allowed to escape in the lifeboats, they would all (the prisoners and soldiers) perish. So in Paul's mind the matter was certain or fixed from the divine point of view and yet contingent so far as man was concerned.

How can a thing be fixed or certain in God's mind and contingent so far as man is concerned? No man can tell. But that does not mean that it cannot be. We must remember that the infinite mind of God may have ways of knowing that transcend the operation of our finite minds. The whole temporal order, including man and all his activities, is grounded in the will of God. That involves a directness of relationship between man's mind and God that is entirely different from anything known in human experience.

So we shall discuss election on the assumption that all the events of the world order are known to God and that its forces are under his control. If this be not so, of course, to talk about election would be out of order. But we refuse the assumption of those who deny his foreknowledge and his power.

5. For a right approach to the doctrine of God's purpose as related to our salvation, we remind ourselves of another thing: namely, that this doctrine as presented in the Scriptures is not proposed as the solution of an intellectual riddle; it is rather set out as an expression of praise to God for his grace in saving us.

When Jesus finds himself and his message despised and rejected, he says: "I thank thee, Father, Lord of heaven and earth, that thou didst hide these things from the wise and understanding, and didst reveal them unto babes" (Matt. 11:25). Then he adds: "For so it was well-pleasing in thy sight." Paul begins the Epistle to the Ephesians on the note of praise: "Blessed be the God and Father of our Lord Jesus Christ" (Eph. 1:3). He blesses God because he blessed us with every spiritual blessing in Christ Jesus, and this he did in accordance with the fact that he chose us in him before the foundation of the world. In Romans 8:28 Paul gives us that wonderful statement that all things work together for good to those who love God. But he goes on to ground this in the fact that he foreknew us and predestinated us to be conformed to the image of his Son.

It is in the atmosphere of adoring praise for his goodness that we find the idea set out in the New Testament, not in the atmosphere of speculative curiosity. The doctrine always becomes a dangerous thing when considered in any spirit other than that of humble praise to God for his grace that saves.

Election is a doctrine for the elect. It is meant to cherish in them the spirit of humility and praise. For others it cherishes the spirit of haughtiness and exclusiveness. If it does develop such a spirit in one, he thereby

shows that he is not of the elect. If one becomes puffed
up with pride over being of the elect, he thereby shows
that he does not belong to the elect. Election is meant
to emphasize the fact that God saves helpless sinners as
a matter of grace on his part. It is not meant as a speculative interpretation on a rational basis of God's activity
among men.

II. God's Purpose in Its Racial Aspects

We shall first look at God's purpose of redemption in
its more general aspects. We have seen how the race as
a whole fell under condemnation and death. Is there any
evidence that, with reference to mankind as a whole, God
is working out a purpose? We believe there is.

1. *The religious history of man*

The general religious history of man would indicate
that God has planted in man an insatiable thirst for God
so that man can never rest until he rests in God. Man's
entire religious history is a record of man's search for
God. But this search for God is the result of a disposition that God has implanted in man's soul. Surely this
search is not all in vain, and man's religious history is
moving some whither.

2. *The Old Testament*

We get clear indications of a redemptive purpose of
God in Old Testament teaching and history. As soon as
man sinned, there was a gleam of light that broke
through the lowering clouds in the form of a promise to
the woman—a promise that has its fulfilment only in
Christ (Gen. 3:15). There was also a bow of promise
that lighted the destruction of the flood with its light of
hope (Gen. 9:9-17). The call of Abraham marks a new
era in the development of God's purpose of grace (Gen.
12:1 ff.). God entered into a covenant with Abraham
and his descendants by which they were made his special
people for a great purpose in the world. They were not
made his people, however, to the exclusion of the other
nations. They were rather to be a blessing to the other

nations (Gen. 12:2-3). Israel was to be Jehovah's missionary to the nations (Isa. 42:1 ff.). Israel, however, as a nation misinterpreted her mission. She took her call to mean the exclusion of the other nations, and, therefore, she became proud and arrogant in her spirit. Yet it is the great paradox of history that Israel did not fail, because out of her came the Redeemer, the one through whom God's redemptive purpose should be accomplished and who is, therefore, the fulfilment of all that was involved in God's ideal for national Israel. Old Testament history and teaching moved to their purpose and goal in Jesus Christ.

3. *Christ and the New Testament*

Beginning with Christ, we have further evidence of a worldwide purpose of God. We have the evidence of this in the doctrine of the kingdom of God in the New Testament. That kingdom was initiated with the coming and work of Christ (Matt. 3:2; Mark 1:15). He tells that the kingdom that began in such insignificant smallness is to become a mighty affair (Matt. 13:31-33). Many shall come from all directions (Gentiles) and shall sit down with Abraham, Isaac, and Jacob in the kingdom while the sons of the kingdom (Jews) will be cast out (Matt. 8:11-12). The aged Simeon greets the babe Jesus as the one who should bring a salvation which God had prepared before the face of all peoples. He was to be a light for revelation to the Gentiles as well as the glory of Israel (Luke 2:31-32). Jesus commands that his gospel be preached to all nations (Matt. 28:19; Luke 24:47; Acts 1:8). The book of Acts narrates how the gospel broke through Jewish bounds and began to lay hold on the Gentile world. Paul carried the gospel to the very center, even to Rome. Others had even preceded him there, for there was a church in Rome before Paul went there. It is made clear in Acts that the preaching of the word to Gentiles was done under divine guidance. Paul went to the Gentile world under a special call from God (Acts 13:1 ff., and many other passages). The book of

Revelation gives us a graphic picture, mostly in symbolic language, of the final and complete triumph of God's kingdom. The struggle is long and hard, but complete and final triumph comes at last with the coming of the New Jerusalem down to earth from God.

III. God's Purpose as Related to the Salvation of the Individual

The Scriptures teach not only that God has a general plan that is being carried out in human history, but also that God's purpose applies to the individual. When a man is saved, he is not saved as a matter of chance or accident or fate; he is saved in pursuance of an eternal purpose of God. God saves men because he intends to. He saves a particular man, at a particular time, under a given set of circumstances, because he intends to.

Election does not mean that God instituted a general plan of salvation and decreed that whosoever would should be saved and, therefore, the man who wills to be saved is elected in that he brings himself within the scope of God's plan. It is true that God has decreed that whosoever will shall be saved; but election is something more specific and personal than that. It means that God has decreed to bring some, upon whom his heart has been eternally set, who are the objects of his eternal love, to faith in Jesus as Saviour. The general meaning of the doctrine of election might be summed up in two statements. The incarnation and cross of Christ mean that God became immanent in a sinful race to found a kingdom of redemption. Election means that, of his own free grace, God becomes redemptively immanent in the life of an individual sinner, and that he does so on purpose.

This doctrine might be analyzed and summarized as follows:

1. *In the first place, when a sinner repents of his sins and believes in Christ to the saving of his soul, he does so because God has brought him to do so.*

Men do not turn from sin to God on their own initiative. God must move them to do so if ever they turn. This includes all good influences, all gospel agencies, all circumstances of environment, all inner dispositions and promptings of heart and conscience that enter into one's decision. It includes the whole historical order in which one is so situated as to have gospel privileges, and this order is viewed as being providential. Especially does it include the inner promptings and leadings of the Holy Spirit.

To regard one's conversion from sin to Christ as the work of God is the spontaneous impulse of the Christian heart. When a Christian hears of someone's turning from sin, the first expression to come to his lips is, "Thank God." But if this is not the work of God, then he should not be thanked. He does not deserve credit for what he does not do. This is the view of Scripture as well as the spontaneous impulse of the Christian heart. In the Bible salvation is everywhere attributed to God. To save is the work of God. But to save includes bringing about this change of mind and heart that we call conversion. It is not true that the sinner within and of himself repents and believes and then God comes into the process in forgiveness. No, God was in the process from the first. He works to produce repentance and faith. He works to bring about the conditions upon which he can forgive. He seeks the sinner. We yield to a God who draws us to himself. We seek him because he first sought us. The gospel of Christ is the gospel of a seeking God. He seeks worshipers (John 4:23). The Son of man came to seek and to save the lost (Luke 19:10). The seeking of the Son of man is a revelation of the heart of God. Drawing men to Christ is the work of God. Without this drawing power men cannot come to Christ (John 6:44).

Paul talks about God as calling men (Rom. 8:28-30; 1 Cor. 1:24, etc.). By this calling he seems to mean more than a general gospel invitation to men to be saved by the grace of God. Paul's use of the term seems to correspond rather to what Jesus speaks of as the drawing of God in John 6:44. It is a dealing of God with the hearts of men that results in their coming to Christ and being saved. This efficacious call does not come to all, not even to all who hear the gospel. Some are called; to them the gospel is the power of God. To others the gospel is a stumbling block or foolishness (1 Cor. 1:23). This call gives one a spiritual mind that enables him to get an insight into the meaning of the cross.

This drawing power of God is necessary, because man's natural inclinations are so opposed to God and righteousness that without it man will not come to God. Paul tells us that the carnal mind is enmity against God. It is not subject to the law of God. Its nature is such that it cannot be (Rom. 8:7). Man must be born again, because that which is born of the flesh is flesh (John 3:6). Hence one must die to sin (Rom. 6:2). The old man must be crucified (Rom. 6:6). One must deny himself and take up the cross to be a disciple of Jesus (Matt. 16:24).

2. *In the second place, what God thus does in bringing men to himself and in forgiving and saving them, he does in pursuance of an eternal purpose.*

He does not suddenly make up his mind to save. From all eternity he has moved in the direction of saving men. All his activities in creation, in preservation, and in providence have led toward redemption. Redemption has been in the heart of God's purpose and activity from before the foundation of the world.

Election is affirming the self-consistency of God. It says that God's nature, purpose, and activity are in conformity with one another. It is God's nature to redeem. The incarnation and cross of Christ came out of the very heart of God. Moreover, it is God's purpose to save. His nature and his will are one, and both are redemptive.

What God does in time is the revelation of what God is in his eternal being. His nature and purpose are objectified in his redemptive activity. Election is affirming both the self-consistency and the unchangeableness of God. God may and does initiate new lines of activity. He may do things in the world or in the life of an individual that he has not done before, but he does not do what he had not contemplated or purposed. To deny election is to affirm that, when God saves a man, he does so without having planned to do so. If God can do nothing new, if he is unchangeable in the sense that he never initiates anything new, then God is the slave of his own immutability, and his immutability, as Dr. Mullins says, would mean his immobility. In that case, God would be an impersonal principle or power without the ability to act as a person. On the other hand, if God saves any person without having planned to do so, he acts impulsively, without deliberate foresight. The wisest activity among men is that which is most carefully planned.

To say that election would be an arbitrary thing is to say that planned activity is arbitrary activity. This is rather the opposite of truth. Activity that is planned by a wise mind has the least element of arbitrariness in it; activity that is planned by an omniscient mind has no arbitrariness in it.

If election means that God's activity in time is grounded in God's purpose in eternity, then it means that in planning our salvation, he took into account all the factors that entered into the actual situation. Election does not mean that God arbitrarily chose this man and that one and passed over this one and that one. It means rather that, foreseeing the man and his total environment and situation, taking into account all the factors that enter into the making of the man and his situation, God out of his own goodness planned to save him. He planned all the good influences and all the means that helped to accomplish the end. With this explanation of what election means, the only way that one could maintain that election was an arbitrary purpose of God, would be to maintain that God saves people in an arbitrary manner. If there is nothing arbitrary in the way that God saves a man, then there is nothing arbitrary in his purpose to save him that way.

When God elects a man to salvation, does God take into account the man's faith? As said above, God takes into account every factor entering into the situation. He does not elect a man to be saved apart from faith but through faith. But this does not mean that faith is the ground of election. Faith is not the ground of salvation but the condition. Faith responds to grace, it apprehends grace, it does not produce grace. Grace evokes faith, produces faith. Faith is the consciousness that we do not deserve salvation; it renounces all claim on God and his grace. But while faith renounces all claim on God and his grace, it embraces God and his grace and rests in his goodness. Grace precedes faith and is the ground of faith. Election is of grace; it is to faith.

What about reprobation? Is there a double predestination? Does God choose some to eternal life and consign others to eternal death?

God does not choose some for destruction in the same sense that he chooses some to eternal life. We might remember again that election is the working out in time of an eternal purpose of God. Those whom God saves he saves in pursuance of an eternal purpose. In his actual dealings with men in time, does God pass over some without saving them? To ask that question is to answer it. We must say that God passes over some without saving them, unless we are going to maintain that God saves all men. The next question, then, is this: Did God in eternity plan to pass over those whom he actually does pass over in time? Here again we must say that he did unless we are going to maintain an inconsistency between God's purpose and God's activity. If God's activity is grounded in his purpose, then all that God does he planned to do. If this is not true, then we would have to maintain that God did not know his own mind beforehand. He would be a changeable God. He would not only change at times in his activity, but also in his purpose or plan for men.

But another question needs to be examined. When God passes over men and leaves them in their sins, does he have good ground for doing so? The New Testament makes this point clear. Men are cast off because of their unbelief and their perversity in sin. They are not cast off as an arbitrary matter, nor are they rejected because God does not want to save them. The New Testament makes it clear that God's love is for all men, that salvation has been provided for all, that we can sincerely offer salvation to all. Man's own perverse will is the only thing that keeps any one from being saved. God goes as far as he can, consistently with his own nature and with his moral government of the world, to save any man and all men. In dealing with men God has limited himself by man's will, by man's sin, and by the moral order of the world. In some respects God has made himself dependent on men. God is limited by the material with which he deals and through which he works. God cannot do just anything. We are insisting all the way through this discussion that God is consistent with himself. He will not make man a free and responsible agent then deal with him as a thing. To do so would be the height of inconsistency on God's part.

God rejects men, then, only on the ground of their perversity, particularly their unbelief. This means that God shuts out only those who shut themselves out. He will not force them to come in. He could not consistently do so. God predestinates to destruction, then, only those who will not come in. In the sense that he purposes to leave to their own destruction those who will not be saved, and in that sense only, he predestinates some to destruction. For their destruction all the blame is on them, none on God. He cannot save those who will not be saved.

3. *In the third place, then, we point out that election means that all the credit for man's salvation belongs to God.*

God takes the initiative. God thought and planned before man did. God moves before man. Man yields and accepts what God plans and works.

Perhaps there will still be lingering in somebody's mind the idea that if all the credit for salvation belongs to God, then all the blame for the destruction of the lost is his also. This does not follow.

Paul says that God works all things after the counsel of his own will (Eph. 1:11). This is true in the sense that the whole universe is under law to him, that all things and all men must operate according to the methods ordained by him, and in the end will all contribute to his plan and purpose for the world. But it is not true in the sense that God directly and efficiently produces all things. God does not work evil in the same way that he produces the good. All the good (the morally good) in the universe has its source and efficient cause in God. He produces the good—all good. This is not to deny that finite wills may have to work with him to produce some forms of good. But it is to say that God and his will are the inspiring and guiding power in it all.

This is true in man's salvation. Salvation from beginning to end is God's work. He plans, provides, and effects salvation. All credit for salvation is his.

On the other hand, the lost man is lost because he will not let God have his way. Where God has his way man is saved. But if the sinner will not yield, if he insists on turning God out of his life and on having his own way, then he is doomed. Letting God into control means salvation; shutting God out means damnation. If the sinner shuts God out, he cannot blame God.

4. *We need also to keep in mind that God's purpose concerning any man includes, not only the man's salvation, but also the good that God may do through him.*

He chooses us for salvation, but also for service. He has chosen and appointed us that we should go and bear fruit (John 15:16). In choosing us he had regard for others as well as for us. He purposed beforehand good works that we should walk in them (Eph. 2:10). We are chosen in Christ, Paul says (Eph. 1:4). He is the sphere within which God contemplated us in ordaining us to eternal life. It is only in him that God could contemplate us with any pleasure. But in choosing us in Christ he had in mind for us all that union with Christ could mean to us and for us. It means salvation, holiness, service to God and man. All that God calls us to do in the world he had in mind for us in Christ when he foreordained us to be Christ's.

IV. Objections to the Doctrine of Election

Most of the difficulties and objections with reference to election grow out of misinterpretations of the doctrine and hasty inferences from it. The answer to the objections, therefore, will take the form mainly of clearing up the difficulties by correcting the false interpretations of the doctrine and showing that the hasty inferences are not proper conclusions from the doctrine. In other words, the way to answer the objections to the doctrine is to set forth the doctrine more fully and correctly.

1. *One objection to this doctrine is that it makes God partial.*

People often quote in opposition to this doctrine Peter's saying that God is no respecter of person (Acts 10:34). But the context, especially the rest of Peter's sentence, makes it clear that what Peter meant is that God does not accept a man because he is a Jew or reject him because he is a Gentile. God has respect to the state of the heart rather than national or artificial distinctions in his dealings with men.

Most likely there is in the mind of the one making this objection the assumption that God is under obligation to bestow equal privileges, opportunities, and blessings on men. But, as a matter of fact, God does not bestow equal blessings on men with reference to natural gifts. Men are not equal in looks, in physical or mental ability, nor in moral and spiritual endowments. He gives to one five talents, to another two, to another one. The Spirit bestows his gifts on men, to each one severally as he will (1 Cor. 12:11). When one thanks God that he was born in a Christian land or of Christian parents, or for good health, he is recognizing the fact that God has given him blessings that he has not given to many others. The same is true if he thanks God for salvation. But the objector might say that, so far as natural blessings are concerned, these could not be equal because they come to us through natural means and in a social order that necessarily makes a difference among men. We reply, may not the same thing apply in regard to religious blessings and opportunities? These also are mediated to us through natural, social, historical means, and it might be as impossible for God to reduce men to a common level of privilege and blessings here as in the case of natural gifts. Religious blessings themselves come at least partly through natural means. To put all men on a level of privilege and blessings might necessitate that God take men out of the natural, historical, social connections in which they live. So the fact that God bestows more blessings on some men than on others does not mean that he is "partial" in an arbitrary way.

One thing we can say is that God bestows more blessings on every one than he deserves. His blessings all flow to us out of his goodness and grace. What God is under obligation to do is, not to bestow equal grace on all men, but that he do no injustice to any. It will be shown in the next section that he is not unjust to any.

2. *Another objection is that it is unjust to the non-elect since it makes his salvation impossible.*

If man is unable to come without the special drawing power of the Spirit and this is not given, then why is the sinner to blame? This, the objector says, would hold the sinner responsible for not doing something which he could not do.

But this objection misconceives the matter. It assumes that, if God deserves the credit for the salvation of the saved, he, therefore, is responsible for the condemnation of the lost. This is not true. The following things need to be kept in mind:

It must be remembered that God does not put anything in the way of the salvation of any man. He does not prevent the coming of any man. God wills not the death of any man, but desires that all should come to repentance (Ezek. 18:23-32; 33:11; 1 Tim. 2:3-4; 2 Peter 3:9). The doctrine of election is not contrary to this, but it goes further. It says that, not only does God desire the salvation of all, but he also positively purposed the salvation of some. He has good reasons for what he does. The fact that God does not save all is evidence that there are limitations on God that constitute sufficient reason why he should not save all. We can safely say that God does all that he can consistently with his own nature, the nature of man, and the moral order of the world to save all men.

No injustice is done any man. Whatever God does for him is a matter of grace. God desires the salvation of all. He has provided salvation for all in Christ. He gives every man the invitation. He brings influences to bear to bring him into the way of life. All this is grace. If in spite of these things the sinner will not come, he has nobody to blame but himself. So long as he is unwilling to receive the grace that God offers him, he cannot complain because God does not give him more grace.

The sinner's inability is an inability only so long as the sinner refuses to recognize his dependence on God. If he wants to come, he can come. The difficulty is on his part, not on God's. The barrier is in the sinner. The only difficulty is in the sinner's attitude toward God. For that attitude he is responsible.

There were limitations placed on God in the matter that prevent him from carrying out his desire to see all men saved. Man's freedom and perversity have much to do with it. We would be safe in saying that whatever aspects of the situation God takes account of in saving men, these he took account of in electing men to salvation. If this be not true, then God is inconsistent with himself. Perhaps we make a mistake in thinking of the matter as if God elected a man to salvation as an isolated individual, without reference to the moral and historical connections in which the man lives. Evidently this is a mistaken idea. Whatever God's purpose concerning any man may be, that purpose must relate to him in the total environment in which he lives. He is not elected simply as a detached individual. He is elected as a member of the race living in a certain moral and historical environment. God's purpose with reference to any man's life is a part of his purpose for the race.

It does not seem that one man is elected to salvation and another not, on the ground that the man elected is morally more deserving than the one not elected. All men are under condemnation. All are sinners. God's purpose to save any is a purpose of grace. God purposes to condemn the sinner on the ground on which he does condemn him; namely, because the sinner's attitude is such that God cannot consistently save him. God gives him over to his own doom because he would not be saved.

But it may be asked: Does not the fact that God purposes to condemn one man because of his foreknown unbelief, carry with it the idea that he elected another because of his foreseen faith? No; election means more than that. It means that God purposed to produce the faith that is the condition of salvation. There is no faith to foresee except the faith which God produces. He does not produce man's unbelief. God deserves credit for man's faith; man deserves the blame for his unbelief.

3. *Another objection to election is that it is inconsistent with the freedom of man.*

The objector says that as some men were elected to salvation and others not, this would put man in the hands of an inexorable fate, things would be fixed beforehand and there would be no use for any man to seek to be saved.

But we must remember that God's purpose of election is not to the effect that a man shall be saved irrespective of whether he repents and believes. Rather it is a purpose on God's part to bring this man to repentance and faith. And God does not compel the elect to believe. He so leads and persuades them by the gracious influences of the gospel and the wooings of his Spirit that they choose to come to Christ.

As Dr. Strong[3] points out, if anything interferes with the freedom of man, it would not be God's purpose concerning our salvation, but what God does in carrying out his purpose. If God's dealings with us in saving us do not interfere with our freedom, certainly his purpose formed in eternity to do what he does would not interfere. The question then becomes: Does God's work in saving us from sin interfere with the autonomy of the one who is saved? The answer of every saved man is that in his experience of salvation his moral self-determination was not interfered with. On the other hand, he feels that in the experience of salvation he was lifted to a plane of freedom that he had not known before.

Let us remember that God's purpose of election was God's purpose to do in saving a man just what he does when he saves him. Therefore, if saving the man does not interfere with his freedom, the purpose in God's mind in pursuance of which he was saved certainly would not do so.

This question is simply one phase of the relation of man as finite and free to God as absolute and sovereign.

---

[3] *Systematic Theology,* section on election.

This question has already been discussed. The religious consciousness, particularly Christian faith, holds tenaciously to both the sovereignty of God and the freedom of man.

4. *A fourth objection to election is that it discourages effort on the part of Christians for the salvation of others.*

The objector says that, if the matter is fixed in one way or another, then effort on our part is useless since we cannot change what is fixed.

This objection also is founded on a misunderstanding. The doctrine of election does not hold that the salvation of any man is fixed as a matter of fate, or even rendered certain irrespective of conditions. God does not decree that he will save a certain man whether he ever hears the gospel or not, or whether he repents and believes or not. Rather it is God's purpose so to direct the providential factors of the man's life as to bring him under gospel influences and so to incline his heart that he will turn from sin to God.

This doctrine, on the other hand, is an encouragement to Christian effort, if the doctrine is properly understood. One of the values of the doctrine is that it assures us not only that God desires the salvation of men, but also that his heart has been eternally set upon that very thing and that he planned the world with reference to it and so directs it in his providence that men shall be saved. It assures us that the purpose to redeem men from sin is the deepest thing in the mind and purpose of God from all eternity. What better encouragement than that could one wish to encourage him to work at the task of saving men from sin? If this is God's eternal concern, it should be our concern and task. We can work at it with the assurance that we work in line with his eternal purposes and that he works in us and through us.

The "Hardshell" philosophy on this point was that, if God purposes that a thing should be done, we should leave him to do it. But a truer philosophy says that, if

God purposes that a thing should be done, we should for that very reason undertake to see that it is done. And if God purposes that it should be done, that is our assurance that we can do it and our encouragement in doing it. If God calls me to preach, I have the assurance that my work will not be in vain. He will give me fruit from my labor. Wherever he directs me to work, I have the assurance that he has a work there to do and I can do it with his help. Paul's assurance as he labored at Corinth was that the Lord had much people in that city, and, therefore, the Lord would be with him and no man should harm him while he labored there (Acts 18:10).

We have seen that unless God took the initiative in our salvation and drew us to himself, no man would be saved. We have just seen also that the doctrine of election is an encouragement to us in doing Christian work in that it assures us that our work will not be in vain in the Lord. Later on we will see that it is the basis of the doctrine of providence and of the safety of the believer. Election is the basal idea in the doctrine of salvation by grace.

THE REDEMPTIVE WORK OF CHRIST

I. The Cross as a Deed of Redemption
1. Our salvation Christ's achievement
2. The death of Christ his redemptive act

II. The Cross and the Person of Christ
1. The gospel of the Son of God
2. Incarnation and atonement

III. The Cross and the Character of God
1. The moral necessity for the cross
    (1) In relation to sin
    (2) In God's purpose to save
2. The cross and the righteousness of God
    (1) The cross as vindication of righteousness
    (2) Redemptive righteousness more than retributive justice
    (3) The governmental theory
    (4) The penal theory
        a. Development and meaning
        b. Weaknesses
        c. Strong points
    (5) A difficulty considered
3. The cross and the love of God
    (1) Love the motive of redemption
    (2) The moral influence theory

IV. The Cross as Victory over Sin
1. The ransom theory
2. Sin as opposition to God
3. The conflict in the life of Jesus
4. The cross as the climax of this conflict
5. Victory manifest in the resurrection
6. The risen Christ and the Spirit

V. The Cross and the Christian Life
1. The Christian as sharing the cross
2. Some repects in which the Christian shares the cross
    (1) Self-denial
    (2) Evangelistic and missionary activity
    (3) Intercessory prayer
    (4) Overcoming evil with good
3. The cross and blessedness

CHAPTER III

THE REDEMPTIVE WORK OF CHRIST

We have seen something of the extent of sin in the human race and the ruin wrought by it. We have also considered God's purpose of grace, both as to the race and as to the individual. This purpose of God to save finds its revelation and means of accomplishment in Jesus Christ. Christ is Saviour. "Thou shalt call his name Jesus; for it is he that shall save his people from their sins" (Matt. 1:21). "The Son of man came to seek and to save that which was lost" (Luke 19:10). "Faithful is the saying, and worthy of all acceptation, that Christ Jesus came into the world to save sinners" (1 Tim. 1:15).

One difficulty in theological discussions of the saving work of Christ has been abstract processes of thought. One example of this is found in the use of the term atonement. Christ's work on the cross has usually been discussed under that heading, and theologians have meant by it what Christ did in his death to make possible our salvation. One theologian has said that the atoning work of Christ "was only Godward, and only removed all the obstacles in the way of God's pardon of the sinner."[1] This is the meaning usually given this term. But it is doubtful if this adequately represents the view of what Christ accomplished for us on the cross. The New Testament rather contemplates the matter from the standpoint of the result accomplished in the actual reconciliation of the sinner. Moreover, the word atonement is not a proper translation of any word found in the Greek New Testament.[2] Dr. Mullins warns against such abstract processes of thought.[3] He points out that law

---

[1] *Abstract of Theology*, by Jas. P. Boyce, p. 297.
[2] The King James Translation wrongly used it for reconciliation in Romans 5:11.
[3] See his *The Christian Religion in Its Doctrinal Expression*, pp. 311-312, for an excellent statement on this matter.

has been considered as some vague abstraction that Christ satisfied; that the ideas of penalty and wrath of God have been treated abstractly; that salvation has been viewed as if it were a matter of bookkeeping; that the Persons of the Trinity have been set over against one another; that justice and mercy in God have been viewed as in conflict with each other, and on and on. Dr. Mullins discusses this subject under the title of "The Saving Work of Christ," rather than calling it atonement. Dr. John B. Champion reminds us that the term atonement is an Old Testament term and that it is not adequate to express Christ's work on our behalf. He therefore entitles his work on Christ's redemptive activity *More Than Atonement.*[4]

We will make small use, therefore, of the term atonement. We consider it better to use New Testament terms to express New Testament ideas. Our purpose is to try to unfold what we find explicitly set out or implied in the New Testament. We will use mainly New Testament terms to do this.

Both in the New Testament and in Christian history, the most distinctive symbol of Christ and his saving work is the cross. We will center, then, our discussion in this chapter around the cross. We mean to include in the term all that Christ accomplished by his death on our behalf.

I. The Cross as a Deed of Redemption

1. *In the first place, it is made clear that Christ did something on which man's salvation depended.*

Our redemption was his achievement. This is shown by such statements as that of Jesus when he said that the Son of man came to give his life a ransom for many (Mark 10:45). Whatever else this may mean, it shows that he did something that was necessary for our liberation from sin. Another statement is that of Paul when he says: "Christ redeemed us from the curse of the law,

---

[4] A worthy and stimulating treatment.

having become a curse for us" (Gal. 3:13). The following quotations from the book of Hebrews make this point clear: [Christ] "entered in once for all into the holy place, having obtained eternal redemption" (Heb. 9:12); "but now once at the end of the ages hath he been manifested to put away sin by the sacrifice of himself" (9:26); "By which will we have been sanctified through the offering of the body of Jesus Christ once for all" (10:10). "but he [Christ], when he had offered one sacrifice for sins for ever, sat down on the right hand of God" (10:12); "For by one offering he hath perfected for ever them that are sanctified (10:14). In Revelation we find this language: "Unto him that loveth us, and loosed us from our sins by his blood" (1:5).

Other passages could be given, but these are sufficient to show that the New Testament teaches that our salvation depended on something that Christ did for us. Christ saves, and he saves by virtue of something that he accomplished. Our redemption was his achievement. He did something that makes possible for us a new relationship to God.

It is made clear that Christ's work for us was a deed of redemption. He revealed the attitude of God toward us, but his saving work was more than that. He came to make known to us that God was favorable toward us, but his work was more than didactic. It has sometimes been represented as if Christ saves us by revealing God's attitude toward us. It would be more accurate to say that he revealed God's attitude by achieving redemption for us. In Christ God himself entered the contest on our side and did something for us. In the farewell discourse to his disciples, as given in John's Gospel, Jesus tells them that they will be left in a world of tribulation. But he said: "Be of good cheer; I have overcome the world" (John 16:33). No doubt he was speaking here prospectively. He contemplates the victory of the cross. Anticipating it by faith, he speaks of it as already accomplished. To his vision it stands as an accomplished fact. Then on the cross, he said: "It is finished"; and John says that he gave up his spirit (John 19:30). Perhaps it was at this juncture, that, according to Luke, he said: "Father, into thy hands I commend my spirit" (Luke 23:46). Both John's account and Luke's seem to be intended to make the impression that the act of giving up his spirit in death to God was a deliberate act and the completion of a process or transaction leading up to that moment. Something was consummated, a task had been finished. Then Jesus *gave up* his spirit. The term is the one used for the betrayal of Jesus by Judas. It suggests almost a formal transaction in which a process is brought to a formal end. He deliberately gave himself up in death to God. He yielded his life back to the Father who gave it.

There is an expression used several times in the Acts and Epistles that agrees with this idea. It is said that Jesus sat down at God's right hand *after completing a task*. He sits at God's right hand reigning as Lord of the universe. The promise of Jehovah to David has been fulfilled and David's Son now is crowned as Christ and Lord (Acts 2:33 ff.; 5:31). He is waiting for all his enemies to be put beneath his feet (Heb. 10:13). But he was not seated there until a definite phase of his work was finished. He sat down when he *had made purification of sins* (Heb. 1:3). When he had made *one sacrifice* for sins *forever*, he sat down on the right hand of God (Heb. 10:12). The author emphasizes that it was *one* sacrifice *forever*, because he wants to impress the idea that one was enough. It was something completed. It was a task finished.

From the days of early gnosticism down to the present there has been a tendency in Christian thought to deny the historical as the real in Christianity. The tendency has been to identify Christianity with general and necessary principles of truth. Christianity would thus be reduced to a form of idealistic philosophy, more or less true, and separable from the person and historical work of Jesus. It was over against this tendency that the so-called Apostles' Creed emphasized historical facts of our religion. Jesus was born of a virgin, lived, died, rose from the dead. Those were not general truths of philosophy; they were facts of history. And they are in line with the New Testament. The New Testament is no textbook of religious philosophy; it is first of all a record of facts. The Ritschlian theology was right in emphasizing that Christianity was founded on facts of history.

In regard to the redemptive work of Christ, this idealizing process has tried to identify the atonement with the eternal suffering of God. It has been summed up in the statement that the cross of Christ did not make atonement, but revealed the atonement.[5] Here is the same insidious tendency to make Christianity an ethereal philosophy—a tendency that came from Greek or Oriental influences—and divorce it from facts.

Christian theology can readily agree that Christ and his cross reveal God's eternal love for man. In fact, it must and does affirm this. It cannot live without this affirmation. Christianity consists of Christ and what he did for men. What he did involves certain facts with their meaning. But theology is first of all a practical discipline, not fundamentally a speculative one. And it must insist that we cannot have the meaning *apart from the facts*. The redemptive significance of Christ and his mission lies first of all in *something that he did*. It was a deed in time. It stood for the coming of the Eternal into time, but the Eternal came in the form of a Person and a deed that he performed.

2. *Another thing that comes out in the passages quoted above, and in many others, is that it was the death of Christ that constituted his redemptive act.*

It is significant that from the time of the great confession at Caesarea-Philippi Jesus laid great emphasis

[5] See *Systematic Theology*, by A. H. Strong, Vol. II, p. 715.

in teaching his disciples on his approaching death. (See Matt. 16:21; 20:17-19; Mark 8:31; 9:31; 10:33; etc.) Up to that time Jesus had been waiting for the disciples to recognize him as the Messiah and become firmly convinced of his Messiahship. When they announce their acceptance of him as Messiah, he turns his attention then to teaching them the kind of a Messiah that he was to be, namely, a suffering Messiah. Is it an accident that so much of the space of the Gospel records is taken up with the last week of the life of Jesus, his death and resurrection? He was put to death as a malefactor, crucified between two robbers. But this death of shame and ignominy is the thing that the evangelists put the emphasis on as the climax of a life of glorious service to God and man. This was the goal toward which his whole life moved.

This was true in the thought of Jesus. He deliberately moved toward the cross as the place where his mission of redemption should be brought to consummation. As he faced the cross there seemed to be something that was urging him on. After Peter's confession at Caesarea-Philippi, Jesus began to teach his disciples that it was necessary that the Son of man should suffer and die and be raised from the dead (Mark 8:31 ff.). Since the disciples now had it fixed in their minds that he was the Messiah, Jesus seems to be chiefly concerned in teaching them that his messianic mission could only be carried out by suffering and death. From here on he returns to this idea over and over again. (See Mark 8:31 ff.; 9:31; 10:32 ff., and parallels.) Once Mark uses the imperfect tense to express the idea (9:31). Jesus kept on saying to his disciples that the Son of man is betrayed into the hands of sinners and they will kill him. During this period it was the constant theme of his teaching.

Especially informing is Mark's account in 10:32-38. They were on their way, going up to Jerusalem. Jesus was pressing on ahead. His disciples followed, amazed and afraid. They could not understand his attitude and his conduct, and he could not explain it to them. He tried, going somewhat into detail, and they could not grasp it. His spirit and theirs were far apart.

The account in Matthew follows pretty closely Mark's account in this period, but Luke's seems to be independent. Luke's account, however, reinforces the impression that we get from Mark. Luke comes back again and again to the idea that Jesus is facing toward Jerusalem. In his several references to the matter it is difficult to tell whether he is talking about one journey to Jerusalem or more than one. But there is one thing that is not difficult to understand; namely, that Luke means to tell us that through this period of his activity Jesus is consciously facing toward Jerusalem with the certainty that death awaits him there. He knows what going to Jerusalem means; yet he faces Jerusalem with full determination to go there and fulfil his mission. He is conscious that he cannot fulfil his mission outside of Jerusalem and the inevitable clash that is bound to come there with the authorities and the death that must come from this clash. (See Luke 9:51; 13:22; 17:11; 18:31; 19:11, 28.) In this situation Jesus said: "I have a baptism to be baptized with; and how am I straitened till it be accomplished!" (Luke 12:50). He was looking forward to the cross as the consummation of his work.

He taught his disciples that the Son of man must suffer (Mark 8:31). He regarded his death as a necessity. It was not necessary in the sense that he could not avoid it. He said that he could call on his Father and he would send twelve legions of angels to deliver him (Matt. 26:53). His death was not necessary in the sense that he was the victim of circumstances which he could not control. His death was necessary in a higher sense—in the sense that his mission could not be fulfilled without it. He must die in the sense that he could not do God's will without dying and for him to do God's will was more important than to avoid death. He prayed in the garden to be delivered from death, but only within the will of God. He died rather than refuse God's will.

Early in the ministry of Jesus there are evidences that he was conscious of the necessity of suffering to fulfil his mission. The Voice at his baptism said: "Thou art my beloved Son, in thee I am well pleased" (Mark 1:11). The latter part of this saying is taken from Isaiah 42:1. The indication, then, is that Jesus at his baptism is recognizing himself as the Suffering Servant of Isaiah. Perhaps he was there beginning to see that identifying himself with this motley crowd of sinners that John was baptizing meant suffering. The first part of the statement identifies him as the messianic Son of God, the second, as the Suffering Servant.[6] The temptations in the wilderness are based on the assumption that Jesus was conscious of messiahship and that the fulfilment of his messianic mission involved suffering. Apart from this assumption the temptations are without meaning. This temptation to avoid suffering by taking the easy and popular way continued with Jesus all the way through his ministry and came to its climax in Gethsemane. When Jesus early in his ministry went back to Nazareth, he went to the synagogue on the sabbath (Luke 4:16 ff.). When he read the Scriptures, he selected a passage from Isaiah (61:1-2) and read about the Servant of Jehovah. Then he told them that this Scripture was being fulfilled before their eyes. Thus he identifies himself with the Suffering Servant of Isaiah. As we have seen, Jesus said on the cross: "It is finished" (John 19:30). His redemptive work in the aspect of suffering and death was now accomplished.

II. The Cross and the Person of Christ

So far, our discussion has set out that our redemption was a definite achievement on the part of Jesus Christ,

---

[6]Cf. Jas. Denney, *The Death of Christ*, pp. 8 ff.; A. T. Robertson, *Epochs in the Life of Christ*, pp. 17, 22; and *The Divinity of Christ in John's Gospel*, pp. 47-48.

and that the thing that achieved our redemption was his death.

1. *The gospel of the Son of God*

We turn now to another idea: namely, that the one who thus achieved our salvation was Jesus Christ the Son of God. This is fundamental to any consideration of this matter. The gospel of the New Testament is the gospel of the Son of God.

We mean by this, not a gospel preached by the Son of God, but a gospel concerning the Son of God. We mean a gospel in which Jesus is the object of faith, not simply one in which he is the subject. Some men have maintained that Jesus was the example of faith, that we are to believe in God after his example. They say that Jesus was the first Christian. His mission, so we are told, was to teach by precept and example, that God loves men, that he is our Father, and that we should trust him as Jesus did. To be a Christian is to believe in God after the pattern set for us by Jesus.

We do not propose to discuss this whole question here. We do mean to say that this does not give Jesus his rightful place in the gospel. We maintain that in the gospel of the New Testament Jesus is the object of faith, not simply the exemplar of faith. Of course he believed in God, worshiped God, prayed to God; but the New Testament also teaches that he sustained a relation to God that was more intimate and fundamental than that, a relation that no other has ever maintained or can maintain. He was the primal, archetypal Son of God. His relation to God as Son was fundamental to all other aspects of his being and causative in relation to all phases of his mission. We maintain that this is the position, not simply of John and Paul, but also of the whole New Testament, and that it is fundamental to historic Christianity.

Paul speaks of the Son of God, "who loved me, and gave himself up for me" (Gal. 2:20). When we begin to speak, then, of one who died to bring us redemption from sin and its curse, it needs to be distinctly understood that we are not talking about something done for us by another mere man. Our salvation is not the work of man; it is the work of God. It is not man's achievement; it is God's. Here is the distinctive feature of the New Testament gospel of redemption. It is not a gospel that tells us about something achieved for us by a great and good man, nor a gospel that inspires us to attempt to throw off sin for ourselves. It is the good news of something that God in Christ has achieved for us and offers us as his gift, something to be received by man, not something to be achieved by him.

The suffering of Jesus, then, was more than the suffering of a good man who endured the opposition of men as he fought for truth and righteousness in the world. It was that. The New Testament abundantly witnesses to the fact that his sufferings were exemplary for us and that we should therefore suffer after his example. But to say that this is the full or even the main significance of his sufferings would not be true. Jesus was more than a martyr to a righteous cause. What is sometimes called the example theory of the atonement fails.

This theory holds that Christ was only a man, a great religious teacher and genius. He died as a result of fidelity to truth and duty. He gave up his life rather than yield what he conceived to be his duty to God and man. We are saved, if we should use that term at all, by following his example. He was the first Christian. He was *primus inter pares*. He was not different in kind from us. He was the subject but not the object of faith. We do not trust in him for salvation; we have faith in God after his example, as he went even to death trusting God to take care of him. What we need is not someone to expiate the guilt of sin, but an inspiring example to stimulate us to be true to the highest and best we know. That is what Jesus does for us. It is in this sense, and this sense only, that he saves us.

Whatever else may be said of this theory, it is not the Christian view with reference to Jesus and his saving work for us. Jesus is our example. We are exhorted to suffer after his example. (See 1 Peter 2:19 ff.)   His spirit in this respect should be ours. We are to deny ourselves and take up the cross (Matt. 16:24). But this does not state the full view with reference to Jesus and his redeeming work. We are not only to follow his example, we are to trust him as Saviour also. We are to obey him as Lord. He made demands upon men that would have been absurd if he were not the object of faith as well as the subject (Luke 14:33). We are to imitate the example of Jesus in his sufferings. We are to bear the cross. The cross is to be the moral dynamic of our lives. As he loved, so are we to love. But the cross cannot be imitated by us, we cannot love after the example of Jesus, unless the cross is more than an example for us, unless it is a redemptive power that delivers us from the bondage of sin. So long as I in my moral consciousness am enslaved by the sense of guilt and condemnation, how can I follow the example of the sinless Christ in his life of love and sacrificial death? The cross cannot be my example unless it is first my redemption. To be my example it must be more. This is true for the simple reason that I am a sinner, while Jesus was not a sinner. I must be made different from what I am by nature before I can imitate Jesus.

The redemptive value of the suffering of Jesus may very well turn on the question as to who he was. Was he the Christ of God or was he only a man? Did he suffer as one man among many or did he suffer as the Lord Christ?

We will not get the Christian view of the work of Christ unless we get the Christian view of his person. His person and his work are inseparably linked. The person is to be adjudged in terms of what he does for men, and his work for men is to be understood in the light of who he was. If Jesus was only a good man, albeit the highest and best, then his death had redemptive significance only as any good man's suffering and death may influence other men for good. But if Jesus was the Christ of God, sustaining a unique relationship to God and man, then his death might have also unique significance for men in their relation with God. The New Testament does not present Jesus as only a great and good man who died for a unique purpose. It presents him as a unique Person whose death had exceptional significance for man's relationship with God. His death could have exceptional value for us because he was an exceptional Person.

2. *Incarnation and atonement*

This means that the ideas of atonement and incarnation in Christianity stand or fall together. Whatever else may be said about Anselm's book, *Cur Deus Homo?* his argument in one respect was sound. He undertook to answer the question, "Why God Man?" That is, he was trying to tell us why God became man in the person of Christ. His argument was that incarnation was necessary to atonement. Only God could meet the situation caused by man's sin. If Christ's death was only that of a martyr to truth and goodness, it has no saving significance for us. God became incarnated in a human life that he might meet the situation caused by man's sin.

Sometimes the view is advanced that the incarnation, rather than the cross, is the center of Christianity. Christ, we are told, stands for the union of God and man. Man needs to find his true destiny in God, and Jesus Christ as the incarnation of God saves us by helping us to find our destiny in God. In this view the main function of Jesus Christ was to exemplify the union of God and man and to enable us to find our unity with God. John and Paul have been contrasted here—John as centering everything in the incarnation, Paul in the cross.

This, however, is a false contrast. John does center everything in the incarnation, but he also tells us that this incarnate One is the Lamb of God that **takes** away the sin of the world (1:29). He was lifted up that men might not perish, but that they might have eternal life (3:14-15). He tells us in the First Epistle that the incarnate Son is the propitiation for our sins and for the sins of the whole world (1:2; 4:10). Paul magnifies the cross, but it is the cross of the incarnate One. With Paul the cross and the incarnation go together.[7]

A passage in Hebrews 10:5 ff., "Sacrifice and offering thou wouldest not, but a body didst thou prepare for me," has been misinterpreted. The author is giving the meaning of Psalm 40:6 ff. Then over against the statement that in burnt offerings and sacrifices for sin God has no pleasure is put the statement: "Lo, I am come; . . . to do thy will, O my God." The inference is drawn from this that the thing that counts was the coming of Christ in the incarnation and his doing the will of God in a life of ethical obedience. But if we read a little further we find that the doing of the will of God spoken of is the will of God by which we were "sanctified through the offering of the body of Christ once for all." The contrast the author is making is not the contrast between the incarnation and an ethical life of obedience on one side and Christ's dying for sin on the other. The contrast the author is making is between the Levitical sacrifices and offerings for sin and the once-for-all offering of himself by Jesus Christ. The former could not redeem from sin and were not pleasing to God; the latter was in accord with God's will and brought eternal redemption. This author, then, joins the incarnation and a redemptive sacrifice for sins, and knows nothing of an incarnation apart from such a sacrificial death of Christ.

The incarnation known to New Testament Christianity, then, is the incarnation of a God of grace who came into human history to identify himself with a sinful race for its salvation. That salvation could not be achieved without a sacrificial deed of redemption. The cross of Christ stands for that deed of redemption.

---

[7] See, e.g. Philippians 2:5 ff.

Neither the incarnation nor the cross means anything for man's salvation apart from the other. In the New Testament the two go together. What God has joined together, let not the speculative religious philosopher put asunder. Bishop Westcott[8] talked about the idea that God would have been incarnated in a human life, even if man had never sinned. Man's true destiny, we are told, could only thus have been realized, for man cannot realize himself apart from God. We can readily agree that only in union with God can man's true destiny be realized; but as to how that union would have been realized in a sinless world we might as well leave wrapped up in the silence that belongs to the realm of things that the Almighty has reserved to his own wisdom. The business of Christian theology is to discuss and set out as accurately as possible how God saves men in this actual sinful world, not to speculate about what God would have done in a totally different kind of world.

III. The Cross and the Character of God

It needs to be kept in mind that theology is concerned, first, last, and all the time, with the character of God. Strictly speaking, theology is concerned with nothing else.

We come, now, to the question as to how the cross of Christ and the character of God are related. Even a casual acquaintance with the history of Christian thought will reveal to one that in theology these two ideas have been vitally related. What one believes about God will determine what he believes about the cross. At least these two ideas are vitally interrelated. What one believes about either will help to determine what he believes about the other.

What necessitated the death of Christ? How does the cross of Christ save us? What did he accomplish in his death by virtue of which we are saved?

In discussing this matter, we are assuming that the cross was a necessity. It was neither an accident of his-

[8]See, e g., his *Christus Consummator*, pp. 99 ff.

tory, something occurring in a meaningless world, nor an arbitrary appointment of the divine will. We are assuming that there was a deep necessity in the moral universe for the cross.

Modern theology has been divided over the question as to whether this necessity for the cross lay in God or in man. Theories of atonement have been divided on this line—some being classed as holding that the atonement was for satisfying God with reference to man's sin and thus making it possible for God to save man, other theories being classed as holding that this necessity for the cross lay in man and his attitude toward God rather than in God and his attitude toward man. Whatever one holds about this will go back ultimately to what one believes about the moral nature of God.

1. *The moral necessity for the cross*

(1) In relation to sin

The necessity for the cross lay in the moral nature of God in relation to man's sin.

The cross of Christ was not meant to affect either God or man except as related to the other. It affects either God or man only as God is related to man or as man is related to God. It is not true, therefore, to say that the cross was meant to affect God but not man, or man but not God. Either statement would be meaningless. We would agree that it was meant to affect God primarily provided it is understood that we mean God in relation to man's salvation. In that case it would mean nothing to say that it did not affect man. God is the primary factor in religion, but man is also involved in any matter touching religion. To talk about anything as affecting God but not man would be to say that it had nothing to do with religion or God's relation to man. Why discuss it, then?

God could not simply pass over sin as if it did not exist. Much of our present-day thought treats sin very lightly; it hardly recognizes such a thing and even wants to discard the term. Such thought is marked by moral shallowness. So far as it recognizes sin, it tends to regard it as a bad dream—the quicker one forgets it the better. Even some professedly Christian thinkers look on God as a good-natured Somebody (or Somewhat) who never holds anything against anybody. His main concern is to keep everybody in a good humor with him and with everybody else.

The God of the Bible is a God of moral earnestness. He cannot disregard sin. Nor can he treat the righteous and the unrighteous alike. There is a necessary reaction of God as moral (or holy) against the sin of man. If God should simply disregard sin, then he would not be a moral God. In the last analysis, this would mean that sin is not sin. In that case God would not be God and we would be living in a nonmoral universe.

The question arises, then, as to how God should deal with sin. If God cannot disregard sin, what can he do about it?

One conceivable thing that he might do, if he is not to disregard sin, is to mete out exact punishment to every individual sinner. That is, he could deal with men on the plane of exact retributive justice. This, however, would exclude the possibility of salvation. On that plane, there could be no salvation. Every man would suffer the penalty of his own sins, God's justice would be vindicated, and the whole human race would be left in its lost condition.

(2) In God's purpose to save

Our question must be stated a little more definitely. It is not sufficiently defined if we talk about the relation of God's character to sin. Before we can come to grips with our problem, we must bring into the discussion the fact of God's purpose to save man. We are not dealing with the problem of the cross until we view it as God's method of carrying out his purpose of redemption. Until we thus view the matter, we are dealing largely in hypothetical abstractions, which is rarely a profitable exercise in theology.

How does the cross of Christ save man?

Taking the record as we have it in the New Testament, interpreted in the light of Christian experience and Christian history, we believe that certain things can be affirmed. These ideas, no doubt, cannot be considered a complete theory with reference to the redeeming work of Christ. Perhaps no such theory will ever be formulated. Certainly none has so far. But we can at least interpret to ourselves some of the fundamental moral realities involved in our salvation through the cross of Christ. This will add to our mental assurance and spiritual strength and satisfaction as Christians and will help us to interpret our religion to others.

In dealing with the cross as related to the character of God, theologians have usually considered the redemptive work of Christ as related either to the righteousness (justice) or to the mercy of God. Some have viewed the cross mainly as a demand of God's justice and some as an expression of God's love. Practically every man tried to consider Christ's saving work in relation to both God's righteousness and his love, but a proper balance has not always been maintained.

2. *The cross and the righteousness of God*

(1) The cross as vindication of righteousness

Our fundamental proposition here is that the cross vindicates the righteousness of God in our salvation.

We mean by this that the cross shows that God saves us on principles of righteousness. The cross makes it clear that in saving man God did not compromise with sin. The cross of Christ is the most uncompromising condemnation of human sin to be found in either history or experience. Human selfishness and sin stand utterly condemned before that cross as nowhere else in God's world.

This condemnation of man's sin in the cross is not just man's condemnation; it is God's judgment on man and his sin. This is made clear in the Gospel of John. In this Gospel, it is made plain that man's condemnation of Christ became God's judgment on man. It became God's judgment on the whole historical order to which we belong. The cross condemns this order as a fallen order. God's judgment rests on it as a whole. The whole world lies in the wicked one and is condemned by the cross. This historical order as such cannot be redeemed. God can work out a program of redemption within this historical order and on the basis of it; but our American liberal theology that regards this historical order as only slightly ailing and as needing only a little doctoring to be turned into the kingdom of God is doomed to disappointment in view of the cross. In the New Testament as a whole, the cross condemns the whole religious, civil, and social setup of the historical order of the world. The Christian is not to love the world, neither the things in the world (1 John 2:15). He is not to lay up treasures on this earth. If he does, he is in danger of setting his heart on the earth and its treasures (Matt. 5:19 ff.). He is to be in the world, but not of it (John 17:14 ff.).

(2) Redemptive righteousness more than retributive justice

The righteousness of God manifested in the cross is of a higher type than retributive justice. Sometimes theologians have contrasted righteousness in the sense of retributive justice with the love or mercy of God and have set them over against each other in sharp contrast. One theologian has said that mercy and justice are represented (in the Scriptures) "as antagonistic; mercy pleading for the sinner, and justice demanding his punishment."[9] According to this way of viewing the matter, the cross of Christ is a manifestation of righteousness, because on the cross Christ met the demands of justice in paying the penalty of our sins. Thus the cross was a

---

[9] See *Abstract of Theology*, by Jas. P. Boyce, pp. 287-288.

manifestation of the inexorable demand of divine justice that sin be punished. Not even the mercy of God could avert the demand of justice that penalty for sin be exacted.

It seems to me, however, that instead of saying that the cross of Christ was the infliction of penalty on Christ for our sins and thus an exhibition of divine justice, it would be better to say that it was an exhibition of righteousness of a higher type than retributive justice. When sin is condemned in retribution, it is condemned without hope: it is a condemnation unto despair. When sin is condemned by the cross, it is condemned savingly: it is a condemnation that is gracious in its character and is the ground of hope.

The condemnation of sin in the cross is more than an exhibition of retributive justice. It is a condemnation that grows out of an exhibition of grace that saves. It results from a manifestation of the mercy of God toward the unworthy. Retributive justice measures out to every man rewards and punishment in accordance with his deserts; mercy deals with men better than they deserve.

Grace transcends law. The gospel of Christ transcends the law method of dealing with sin. The law method of dealing with sin is the method of retributive justice. Penalty is executed against the sinner. Righteousness as retributive justice is thus manifested and vindicated. But grace transcends this method. Grace also manifests and vindicates righteousness, but it is righteousness that transcends retributive justice. It is redemptive righteousness. Retributive justice vindicates itself in penalty; redemptive righteousness vindicates itself in the cross of Christ. Suffering under law is penal; Christ's suffering was redemptive.

The theologians have been right who distinguished justice (or holiness, whatever term they might use) and grace or redemptive love. But they have been wrong in making justice (holiness or righteousness in that sense) superior to love or grace and in interpreting them as opposed to each other. Justice was thus made the ruling attribute in God and love had to bow to its demands. The writer remembers hearing a preacher say that God never forgives sin; he may forgive the sinner, but the sin must be punished. This may be true; but if so Jesus was wrong. He speaks repeatedly of God's forgiving sins, debts, trespasses, etc., and he makes sin (debt or trespass) the direct object of the verb and the sinner the indirect object. This making of justice supreme tends to make our salvation something that God owed to Christ as a matter of debt.[10] It also tends to take away the element of grace in God's dealings with us. In that case, Christ would be gracious; God would be just. Christ bought our salvation from God and made a gift of it to us. Thus we would be obligated to Christ but not to God.

It is really the other way around. Grace transcends justice or law. It transcends the law method of dealing with man. Law was only a partial revelation of God. Grace transcends law and takes its values up into itself. Law is not a false revelation of God; it is incomplete. It is completed (fulfilled) in Christ.

Paul indicates that this legalistic method of dealing with man has been abrogated. The ordinances of the law were nailed to the cross (Col. 2:13 ff.). There has never been a greater travesty in theology than the interpretation of Paul's doctrine of justification as legalistic. Paul is not reducing the gospel to a form of legalism. As Dr. Mullins points out, he was combating legalism.[11]

The grace of God reveals a higher type of righteousness in God than does the law and calls for a higher righteousness in man. And what it calls for it produces.[12] This is the reason that Jesus says that he does not abrogate the law but fulfils it (Matt. 5:17). Paul says that faith fulfils the law (Rom. 3:31). (*See also*

[10]See, e.g., Boyce's *Abstract of Theology*, p. 289.
[11]*The Christian Religion in Its Doctrinal Expression*, p. 398.
[12]For a further development of this point, see division V, this chapter.

Rom. 6:1 ff.; 8:1 ff.) The thing which the law failed
to do grace accomplishes. It produces righteous men.
But it is a righteousness that transcends legalism. It
has the element of grace in it. This is shown by the
teaching of Jesus that God will not forgive us if we do
not forgive our fellow men (Matt. 6:12, 15, et al.). Unless the grace of God produces a gracious character in
us, it does not do much for us. The righteousness of the
gospel transcends legalistic justice: it is justice raised to
the plane of grace.

The cross is the highest manifestation of the holiness
of God, and holiness includes both the severity or justice
of God and his mercy or grace.[13] Grace is not indifferent toward sin. It is love with the element of righteousness at its heart.

The mercy of God, then, manifested in Christ does
not mean that God relaxes the demands of the moral law
and excuses men in their sins. Nor does it mean that
God merely relieves men from the punishment due to
sin. Such an interpretation of mercy is the Mohammedan rather than the Christian interpretation. In the
Mohammedan conception of mercy, God relaxes the demands of the moral law, and excuses those whom he thus
favors. It is God's method of arbitrarily releasing his
favorites from the moral consequences of their evil deeds.
No kind of a god can do such a thing except one who
is a moral despot. The God and Father of our Lord
Jesus Christ is not that kind of a God. He is not an
arbitrary despot, but a God of grace toward the sinful.
But grace is not moral indifference nor moral laxity. It
is mercy, but mercy with moral integrity at its center.
It is love but it is holy love. It wills to save, but on
principles of righteousness. Paul had a hard time keeping men from interpreting the grace of God as meaning

[13]It is doubtful, however, if justice in the Bible is used in as narrow a
sense as it usually has been in theology; that is, as the principle of retribution in giving man only what he deserved. It means rather fair dealing,
sometimes including the element of grace.

such moral indifference on God's part as would allow
men to continue in sin.

Two of the most influential theories of atonement dealt
with the matter from the standpoint of vindicating the
righteousness of God.

(3) The governmental theory

One of these, the governmental theory, interpreted
Christ's death from the point of view of God's government of the universe. The theory was formulated by
Grotius, a Dutch lawyer. It was set forth in elaborate
form in his treatise called *The Satisfaction of Christ*.
He wrote in answer to Socinus, who denied that any satisfaction was necessary as a condition of the forgiveness
on sins.

Grotius maintained that there was necessity for satisfaction. That necessity lay in God's government of the
world. The satisfaction was not made to God as a private person but as Governor of the world. So far as
his own personal interests or nature were concerned, God
could afford to forgive without satisfaction. But God
acted, not as a private person, but as the Governor of
the world, and as such a Governor he must require satisfaction for the sake of the interests of moral government.
It was not God's nature as such, but rectoral justice that
demanded satisfaction. The necessity for satisfaction
lay in the fact that, should God freely forgive without
requiring satisfaction, sin would not be restrained properly and the interests of his moral government would be
imperiled.

Grotius freely used such terms as penalty and punishment in discussing the matter, but the satisfaction that
he insisted on was not the strict infliction of penalty as
usually understood or as set forth in the penal theory.
It was not a strict *quid pro quo* transaction. It was
rather the idea that the death of Christ was such a manifestation of God's displeasure toward sin that God could
forgive without encouraging the idea that he was lenient

toward sin. It stands for an important element of truth. One of its great weaknesses is in regarding the moral law as rather an arbitrary enactment and too much in abstraction from the moral nature of God. The law is considered too much as a pure enactment of will rather than as a matter of moral necessity. Hence the law was regarded as something that God could relax at will. The death of Christ was such a manifestation of God's displeasure toward sin that God could safely forgive; that is, remit the penalty of the law.

(4) The penal theory

a. Development and meaning

The other theory that seeks to interpret Christ's redeeming work from the standpoint of God's righteousness is the penal theory. This theory is not the work of any one man; it developed over a considerable period of time. It is a legitimate development from Anselm's view and is the rightful heir and successor to his view. One of the main differences is that Anselm said that it was the satisfaction of God's honor as offended by man's sin that necessitated the death of Christ, while the penal theory says that the necessity for his death lay in the demands of God's justice in relation to sin. The theory has received many typical statements in theological literature, some of them set forth with great logical acumen and learning and some more popular and evangelistic in their appeal. The theory has insisted on the substitutionary aspect of Christ's work and has sometimes carried this so far as to try to interpret his substitution in quantitative terms. This led in the stricter forms of Calvinism to the idea of a limited atonement. Sometimes, in interpreting the matter under the analogy of a debt, it was said that it would not be just for God to collect the debt from both Christ and the sinner. God, it seems, was almost regarded as being under obligation to save the man for whom Christ died.

b. Weaknesses

It can be easily seen how this view at times tended to introduce antithesis within the Godhead, the Father being regarded as the embodiment of justice requiring the sinner's punishment and the Son regarded as the embodiment of mercy seeking to save the sinner. No respectable system of course ever quite said that, but it was almost implied at times. The view also—at least, in its more rigorous forms—tended to run a line of cleavage between the justice of God and the mercy of God. Not only so, but justice was also looked on as primarily, if not exclusively, penal in its nature, and was exalted to the supreme place among the attributes of God. This was true, whether the term used was justice, righteousness, or holiness. The chief characteristic of holiness (righteousness or justice) was its demand for meting out exact punishment to sin; and this must be done whatever else might come to pass. God's chief function came to be regarded as the meting out of rewards and punishments to the subjects of his moral government according to their deserts. This was in accord with the emphasis on justice as the chief or supreme attribute in God. It was often said that God *might* exercise mercy, but he *must* punish sin. Mercy on God's part was optional, punishment was obligatory. This method of interpreting God and redemption had difficulty with John's statement that God is love (1 John 4:8).

This theory, then, can hardly be regarded as an adequate interpretation of the redeeming work of Christ. Every theory worked out has had an element of truth in it, but no complete theory has yet been propounded. The penal theory has been subjected to criticism for over a century. Its weaknesses have been pointed out, and its inadequacy exposed. While many of the opponents of this theory have been found outside the ranks of evangelical Christianity, many have also been found inside those ranks, and the theory in its more rigid features is untenable.

As already pointed out, this theory tends to set the attributes of God over against each other in an unjustifiable manner, even if not to set the Persons of the Trinity in opposition to one another. To regard the suffering of Christ as the literal payment of a debt, so that it could be measured in quantitative terms, is wholly beside the point. To regard sin as a literal debt and the death of Christ as the literal payment of a debt is to literalize language that seeks to set forth spiritual truth in the language of an analogy. The same thing is true if we seek to interpret the work of Christ as literal bearing of penalty. According to the fundamental principles of this theory itself, penalty as such vindicates justice and nothing more. Penal suffering, therefore, is not redemptive in its nature. It could not save. It is thought of as canceling the guilt of past transgression; but it does not provide for the revolution of character nor furnish an adequate dynamic for Christian living. The cross of Christ as presented in the New Testament does more than cancel the guilt of past sin; it is the one and only source and dynamic of the Christian life. It is not one of the sources of salvation and Christian living; it is the one and only source and power of salvation and the Christian life.

The cross of Christ stands, then, not for the bare endurance of penalty. The opponents of this theory are perhaps correct when they insist that penalty (or guilt) as such is not transferable. If we mean by guilt personal ill desert, then Christ was not guilty. As Dr. Mullins says, he could not have borne penalty in the ordinary sense of the term.[14] He did not suffer the personal displeasure of God. He died in loyalty to God's will and in his death he was executing the redemptive good pleasure of God on behalf of man. When he is represented as coming to do God's will, it is God's will in making an offering for sin that he was executing (Heb. 10:5-15). His sufferings were redemptive rather than penal.

---

[14]*The Christian Religion in Its Doctrinal Expression*, p. 323.

Sometimes the idea of substitution has been carried to the point of insisting that Christ suffered in quality and quantity what the redeemed would have suffered had Christ not redeemed them. Such a position can hardly be defended. It is not unreasonable to think that one element in the suffering of the unredeemed in the next life, as well as in this, will be remorse. Surely Jesus suffered no remorse after having given his whole life in unbroken service to God and man and while dying in loyalty to God's will. Surely Jesus did not die spiritually in the sense in which the sinner does. Sin kills in that it separates from God. Jesus did not die spiritually as the sinner does who drives God out of his life. Jesus died to sin (Rom. 6:10), on account of or for sin (Gal. 1:4), and for the sinner (Rom. 5:6, 8), but he did not die in sin and to God as the sinner does. The penalty of sin as suffered by the impenitent is to be cut off from spiritual life in God. Jesus did not suffer penalty in that sense.[15]

If we might use an analogy to throw light on the nature of the suffering of Jesus on our behalf, we might think of a criminal being executed for his crime. The suffering of Christ for us would be more like the suffering of the criminal's Christian mother as she would give her life for her son than the suffering of the hardened criminal himself. It would likely be true that his career of crime would have so hardened him that he would be incapable of suffering as she would suffer. Her suffering would be more intense than his and of a different order.

Moreover, the penal view tends to regard God as delighting in suffering as such. It looks on him as demanding so much suffering for so much sin. Suffering is of value only when related necessarily to moral or spiritual ends. God is not revealed in the New Testament as an infinite Shylock demanding his pound of flesh before he will exercise mercy.

---

[15]See a pamphlet by John B. Champion entitled, "Did Christ Die Spiritually?"

c. Strong points

This view has some points in its favor.

In the first place, it had the advantage of giving a clear and understandable explanation of the necessity for Christ's death as related to the nature of God on the one hand and to man's salvation on the other. Since God as just was bound to punish sin, the penalty must be borne on the part of the sinner or somebody who took his place. He could be saved only in case somebody should suffer the penalty for him. Among the historic theories of atonement, it stands at the top of the list, when it comes to giving a logical account of the necessity for Christ's death.

Again, the theory is in a strong position in its appeal to those Scriptures, in both the Old and New Testaments, that represent the saving value of the sacrifices or of the blood of Christ as depending on the idea of substitution or the vicarious feature of the offering. Undoubtedly that feature of the sacrificial work of Christ is presented as of its very essence. The ground for this is laid in the Old Testament sacrificial system. The saving work of Christ is represented as saving us from God's wrath and in some real sense as propitiatory and substitutionary. One of the great weaknesses of the example and moral views was in evading or denying this feature of Christ's work. Even the governmental theory was weak at this point, although in a stronger position than these other two views.

The third respect in which this view was strong was in its appeal to the sinner who was under a sense of failure and guilt. A sinner with an acute sense of failure and guilt needs a gospel that assures him that someone has made adequate provision for a free pardon for his sins. Other theories were weak at this point.

While the penal theory falls short as a sufficient account of Christ's redeeming work, we see that it does stand for some elements of truth. Christ's work for us was truly substitutionary in the sense that he took the curse of death on himself that we might be saved. He tasted death for every man (Heb. 2:9). He was made to be sin for us in order that we might become the righteousness of God in him (2 Cor. 5:21). He redeemed us from the curse of the law by being made a curse for us (Gal. 3:13). What was the curse of the law? Dr. Burton says that it was the law itself; that is, that Christ by his death delivered us from the law as a legalistic system, which was a curse.[16] Dr. Burton makes it still more definite as to what is meant by the curse of the law. That curse was the curse of conceiving God after a legalistic fashion as one who holds men to strict account for their sins. To be redeemed from the curse of the law means to come to a better understanding of God and realize that the law as a legalistic system misrepresents God. He says: "From this it follows further that redemption from the curse of the law is not forgiveness of sins, but deliverance of the mind from a misconception of God's attitude toward men." That is, the law in holding that God holds men to a strict account for their sins misrepresents God, and we are redeemed from the curse of the law when we come to understand that this conception of God in relation to sin is not true. Jesus, too, then must have misconceived God when he tells of how strict an account men must give. He says that one who says to his brother, "Thou fool," shall be in danger of the hell of fire (Matt. 5:22).

Paul does hold that Christ delivered us from the law as a legalistic system. But it is almost certain that this is not what he means here by the curse of the law. The curse was the curse of death. That curse came on us because of our sin. The law pronounced that curse of death upon us because of our failure to live up to its requirements. (See Gal. 3:10-12.) Christ redeemed us from that curse by taking the curse of death upon himself. Thus he redeemed us from the curse.

---

[16]See *Atonement*, by Burton, Smith and Smith, pp. 182 ff.

The death of Christ was a vicarious work. It was substitutionary. He did something for us which we could not do for ourselves.

Jesus said that he came to give his life a ransom for (*anti*, instead of) many (Matt. 20:28; Mark 10:45). The preposition used here denotes substitution. The prepositions usually used do not within themselves denote substitution (*peri* and *huper*). It is said that he dies for, or on behalf of, sinners. But this does not exclude the idea of substitution. A thing may be done for, or on behalf of, one by being in his place or stead. So when it is said that Christ dies for our sins (1 Cor. 15:3), or on behalf of us (Rom. 5:8), this may be done in the way of substitution (*huper, peri* would have about the same meaning). But when it is said that he gave his life a ransom in the stead or place of (*anti*), many, it can hardly be anything but substitution.

Christ, then, in his redeeming work was propitiatory. In classic Greek, to propitiate means to render favorable. Christ did not render God favorable, but he so dealt with human sin as to make it possible for God to show his favor in salvation. Paul says that God set him forth as propitiatory in his blood (Rom. 3:25). John says that he is the propitiation, not only for our sins, but also for the sins of the whole world (1 John 2:2). The book of Hebrews says that as a faithful high priest he makes propitiation for the sins of the people (Heb. 2:17). The Christian idea is not that God has to be satisfied before he will have mercy or love the sinner, but it is rather that God's holy character reacts against sin and that sin interposes a barrier between God and the sinner so that God cannot be consistent with his own moral character and save the sinner until the barrier is removed. God is not vindictive, but he does have regard to his own moral consistency. The propitiatory work of Christ is the revelation and expression of God's love.

It is doubtful, however, if Paul means to say that Christ in his death was propitiatory in the sense that

God was pleased with his death as such apart from its result in saving man. The usual interpretation has put the emphasis on the blood as propitiatory. But Paul says that God set forth Christ as propitiatory, *through faith*, in his blood. John does not say that Christ's death was a propitiation. He says rather that Christ was such a propitiation. He did not die to purchase God's favor. He came rather as the revelation of God's love. Nor should Paul's expression, *through faith*, be passed over, as it usually is, as if it were incidental, almost an afterthought. Christ in his blood opened up the way for man to come to God through faith, and the result, that is, man's coming to God, was pleasing to God. God was propitiated in the sense that when the sinner exercises faith, God can bestow mercy instead of wrath.

(5) A difficulty considered

The difficulty is often raised as to the justice of one person's suffering for another's sins. Here we meet a difficulty that often arises in life, one that we cannot entirely clarify, but some things can be said that will relieve the difficulty.

The objector needs to remember:

a. That ours is a fallen world. All men, the whole world order, rest under the curse of sin. In our race, there are only relatively innocent men, none who are entirely so. This curse represents the judgment of God. God's judgment is on the whole human order of life. One who identifies himself with man for his redemption must share this curse. This curse on man and his world represents the reaction of God's holy character on human sin. This helps us to understand what is meant by the propitiatory character of Christ's death. Man's moral judgment approves the idea that the guilty should suffer. Man's moral judgment would also approve the idea that those who would deliver the guilty from the curse of sin should share in the suffering of the guilty.

b. It is a law of life that men should suffer for the wrongs of others. No matter what we may say about the justice or injustice of it, this is a fact. And it is difficult to see how it could be otherwise in a social world. An arrangement by which one would suffer the exact deserts of his sins and nobody else suffer for them would hardly be a social world at all. And it is true that the innocent suffer for the guilty. Instances are too numerous to need mention. This is one of the great disciplinary laws of life. Men are often restrained from evil by the consciousness that others will suffer if they sin. Also, it is true that much of our moral development comes from suffering on behalf of others. It is a law of the Christian life that one should be willing to follow the Saviour's example in doing this.

c. The highest expression of love is found in this Christian law of willingness to suffer on behalf of others. This was the crowning glory of the life of Christ and is the thing that marks a man as a follower of Christ. If any man hath not the Spirit of Christ, he is none of his (Rom. 8:9). It is love that moves one to share the sufferings of others. It was love that moved Christ to give himself for us. If it is held that one could not bear the sins of another, that would be equivalent to saying that love in that respect was limited. That is to say, in the very realm where one most needs help, in the moral and spiritual, the realm of our sins and failures, love is impotent to render service.

d. Besides, this objection is based on a false assumption. The objection says that it would be unjust for God to lay the sins of one man on another man. But there are two things to be said in answer to this. One is that God did not take our sins and lay them on an unwilling victim. Christ took our sins on himself. As a matter of love, he voluntarily assumed our obligation. He laid down his life of himself (John 10:18).

Again, the objection assumes that Christ is only one human individual among other human individuals. Perhaps the objector would be right in saying that one human individual could not bear the sins of countless other human individuals. The relation of Christ to any man or to the race as a whole is entirely different from the relation of one who is only a human individual to his fellow men or to his race. The race exists in Christ. It was in and through him that the race was created and is preserved (John 1:3; Col. 1:16-17). He is, therefore, the author of the whole moral order that has been violated by man's sin.

The death of Christ for our sins does not mean that God laid the burden of our sins on a helpless human individual, but rather that in the person of Christ God himself got under the burden of our sins to save us. The work of Christ is the work of God.

Our faith in Jesus throws light on his redemptive work. We trust him as Saviour from sin. We come to him confessing ourselves morally and spiritually bankrupt. We recognize that we have no standing of our own before a holy God. For such standing we must trust ourselves into his hands. We acknowledge ourselves dependent upon him in the most important of all realms, the moral and spiritual; and in the most fundamental of all relations, our relation with God. We confess ourselves disqualified to deal with God as holy in our own name; our sins have disqualified us. Christ is qualified to deal with God for us. And the New Testament makes it clear that the thing that qualifies him to deal with God on our behalf is his death for us. This sets his death as the ground of our acceptance with God over against our sins as the ground of our rejection. Our sins constitute our moral disqualification; his death constitutes the basis of our moral standing before God.

3. *The cross and the love of God*

One thing stands out clearly in the New Testament, and must never be obscured; namely, that Christ's death grew out of, and expresses, God's love for us. Any view that denies this is anti-Christian, and any view that obscures this lacks that much of being fully Christian.

(1) Love the motive of redemption

The motive of redemption is the love of God. "God so loved the world, that he gave his only begotten Son" (John 3:16). "God commendeth his love toward us, in that, while we were yet sinners, Christ died for us" (Rom. 5:8). Christ did not die to win for men the love of God, but as an expression of that love. It is a travesty on the New Testament view of this doctrine to represent it as meaning that God was the embodiment of justice and Christ the embodiment of love and that Christ died to win for man the love of God. The love of Christ for sinners was the love of God. The death of Christ was the love of God in action, seeking to redeem men from sin; it was love going to the limit of suffering and agony to redeem the lost from the ruin of their own sin. The cross of Christ is the pledge of God's love for a sinful and ruined race. As such the cross represents an act of grace. It stands for God's gracious love going out to redeem man as sinful and unworthy.

This is one reason that we must insist that the death of Christ was more than a martyr's death. His death represents something more significant than the deed of a man for us. Athanasius and those who stood with him in early Christian history for the idea that the Son was of the same substance with the Father contended that only God could reveal God and only God could save man. The cross, therefore, in Christian history has always symbolized something God did for man and not what man did. One who was only a man could not do something that would reveal the love of God. This is also contradictory to the idea that it was only the human nature of Christ that suffered, not his divine nature. In that case, the cross stands for what humanity did, not what God did for man.

(2) The moral influence theory

So far, those who have advocated the moral influence theory would agree. This theory denies that Christ's death was substitutionary. There was nothing of the nature of penalty in his sufferings. There is nothing in the way of wrath in God to be satisfied before God can forgive sin. Christ died only as a revelation of love for the sinner. The only difficulty in the way of the sinner's salvation is on the sinner's part, not on God's. If the sinner will only repent, God stands ready to forgive. The purpose of the death of Christ is to manifest the love of God and thus lead the sinner to repent.

It has much in common with the example theory. Along with that view, it objects to the idea that one person should die in the place of another. One may suffer sympathetically with and for another, but one could not suffer in the place of another. Especially does it insist that this is true with reference to the penalty of sin. There is a strong tendency among those holding this view to make love the controlling attribute in God, to the neglect or denial of anything like retributive righteousness. Suffering is regarded as primarily, if not exclusively, remedial.

One objection to this theory is that it tends toward a psychology of religion that reduces the guilt of sin to a guilt consciousness that has no objective ground. It says that the only difficulty in the way of the sinner's salvation is in the sinner, not in God. That amounts to saying that man's guilt consciousness is an illusion. His sense of ill desert is morbid. The kind of religious experience that we find in Bunyan, Luther, Carey, or Paul is abnormal and interferes with the development of the right type of Christian character. What men need is not salvation from guilt and condemnation, but salvation from their consciousness of guilt and condemnation.

But if man's religious consciousness is illusory in respect to guilt and condemnation, why may it not be also with reference to God's love and mercy? Why should our religious consciousness be trustworthy in regard to one and not in regard to the other? The consciousness of guilt and condemnation has been as thoroughly embedded in the experience of Christians as the consciousness of the love of God. In fact, in experience the two go together. This is the teaching of Jesus in Luke 7:40 ff. At least it is involved in what Jesus says. He shows that one who is most conscious of sins forgiven will love most. He is speaking to Pharisees who had no sense of need of forgiveness. He says in substance: "You do not love because you have not had any sense of sins forgiven." It is only as we have a consciousness of sin and guilt that we will have such a consciousness of the grace of God in saving from sin as to call out our love to God. The love of God is not magnified then, but minimized, by minimizing the guilt and condemnation of sin. This has its bearing on practical Christian activity. The men that have had a deep sense of guilt, followed by a consciousness of salvation through the grace of God, have been the great evangelists, missionaries, and builders in the kingdom of God. They have been the men who have initiated new eras in the advancement of Christianity in the world.

This consciousness of condemnation is too vitally related to the consciousness of the love of God to explain the former as subjective and illusory while holding that the latter is true to reality. It is easier to explain the experience of those who do not have a distinct consciousness of guilt as due to a lack of spiritual perception on their part than to explain the consciousness of guilt on the part of those who do have it as being merely subjective and illusory. We hold that the sense of guilt is so vital a factor in the Christian consciousness that to reduce that sense of guilt to illusion means to invalidate the Christian consciousness altogether and land us in religious agnosticism.

Another objection to the moral influence theory of the atonement is that it furnishes no rational connection between the death of Christ and the end to be accomplished by it. The vicarious or substitutionary view does furnish a clear explanation of the connection between the two. The end to be accomplished according to the substitutionary view is our deliverance from the condemnation that comes upon us because of our sin. Christ accomplishes that end by taking on himself the curse due to our sin. He died in our place. According to the moral influence theory, the end to be accomplished is such a revelation of the love of God as will turn sinners from their sins. But the question arises: How is the death of Christ a manifestation of the love of God? What is the connection between his death and our sin that makes his death a manifestation of God's love to us? The vicarious view answers this question by saying that Christ's death was the bearing of our curse; it was such a manifestation of the wrath of God against sin as to make it possible that God could be righteous and yet justify the penitent sinner. The moral influence theory has no answer to the question. In other words, this theory can show nothing in the moral connections to necessitate the death of Christ as the ground of our salvation. The illustrations of Dr. Denny's *Death of Jesus* and of Dr. Mullins' *The Christian Religion* are in point. If a father should plunge himself into the water and drown himself, or thrust his hand into the fire and burn it off, this would not be a manifestation of love to the father's child unless the father incurred the loss to save the child from a danger of drowning in the one case or of burning in the other. It would rather be a manifestation of folly. So unless the sinner rests under a condemnation that endangers his spiritual welfare, how is the death of Christ a manifestation of the love of God to the sinner?

This view, however, does have the advantage of emphasizing one of the main things in the New Testament: namely, that Christ died because of God's love for men lost in sin.

We must never forget, however, that the love of God manifest in the cross of Christ is holy love. It is love that is eternally opposed to sin, actively opposed to sin. As such it is righteousness. Righteousness and love, then, are not antithetical or opposed to each other. Both

denote the moral perfection or holiness of God. Love
is never mere amiability nor moral indifference; moral
integrity is the heart of it. And righteousness always
has love at its center. Whether we consider the moral
nature of God as love or righteousness, it is opposed to
sin. It seeks to overcome sin, and the cross is the method
used to conquer sin.

IV. The Cross as Victory over Sin

1. *The ransom theory*

One of the earliest views with reference to the saving
work of Christ was known as the ransom theory. It was
never formulated in any very definite manner and could
hardly be spoken of as a definite theory. It prevailed
more or less generally for something like a thousand
years. It had associated with it such outstanding names
in Christian history as Origen and Augustine. Since
many of the names of the early church fathers were associated with the view, it is sometimes spoken of as the
"patristic" view. It was the nearest thing to a definite
theory of the atonement in Christian history until
Anselm's day.

The view had for a scriptural background or foundation such passages as the saying of Jesus that the Son
of man came to give his life a ransom for many (Mark
10:45) and numerous other passages in which his work
is spoken of as a ransoming or redeeming from sin and
its power. When the question arose as to whom the ransom was paid, many of the early fathers said that it
was paid to the devil. In general outline, with variations, the view was that the devil in the Fall acquired a
right over mankind; God redeemed man from his enslaved condition by delivering Christ in death to the
devil, according to terms of an agreement. But in the
resurrection Christ overcame the devil and he was left
despoiled of both Christ and mankind. Sometimes an
element of deceit and trickery was introduced into the
theory, in that the devil was offered Christ in death in

exchange for the race. The devil was unaware of Christ's divinity. Christ, however, being divine overcame the devil and thus robbed him of his victim.

2. *Sin as opposition to God*

Crude as this view was, it truly represents sin and salvation as a conflict between God and the devil. It is a conflict that is more than human and more than individual. It is a conflict between a kingdom of light and one of darkness, between God at the head of the forces of righteousness and Satan at the head of the forces of evil.

Some recent writers have indicated that a true view of Christ's saving work would need to follow this line rather than the lines of the "moral" or "penal" views.[17] As I understand them, they mean to say that we should think of Christ's saving work as being the overcoming of spiritual opposition to God and the death of Christ as the means by which this was accomplished. It seems to me that this is a true insight. From the beginning of human history sin has been opposition to God. Moreover, it has been more than a human conflict. Man fell, under temptation from a superhuman source. We wrestle not with flesh and blood alone. Sin is diabolical in its nature.

Moreover, sin develops over against righteousness. The higher the manifestation of righteousness the more subtle and intense does the opposition become. Paul speaks of "the passions of sins which were through the law" (Rom. 7:5). The law becomes an occasion for the development of sin. Most of the rest of the chapter is an exposition of what the apostle means by that statement. He indicates that before we come into possession of moral light sin is a slumbering principle in us. When we come to have moral light (the law) and learn what is right, we do not perform the right. Instead of that, sin awak-

---

[17]See *The Doctrine of the Work of Christ*, by Sidney Cave, especially pp. 292 ff., and *Christus Victor*, by Aulen.

ens to energetic action and man is enslaved by its power. Only Christ can deliver from its power.

Jesus indicates that the condemnation of the people to whom he ministered would be greater than that of the people of Sodom and Gomorrah or of Tyre and Sidon. This was true because the people of Chorazin, Capernaum, and Bethsaida had greater light and privilege, and hence greater guilt. In John's Gospel Jesus says: "If I had not come and spoken unto them, they had not had sin"; and, "If I had not done among them the works which none other did, they had not had sin" (John 15: 22, 24). Now, he says, they have no cloak or excuse for their sin. The thing that made their sin so terrible was that they had seen both him and the Father (v. 24). His presence in their midst as the light of the world meant that they must accept that light and turn to God or else turn irrevocably to sin and death. It is doubtless along this line that we are to understand the warning in Matthew 12:31. He was in their midst doing the works of God under the power of God's Spirit. They were blasphemously saying that his works were the works of the devil. They could not deny his mighty works, but they were saying that they were devilish in character. Anybody who would thus deliberately call white black was in danger of putting out his own spiritual eyes and so perverting his own moral nature that it would be a moral impossibility for God to save him. He would forever fix his own character in sin.

So we see that the character of sin is such and the character of God's holiness or righteousness is such that there is an inevitable conflict between the two. This conflict has been going on since the beginning of human history and will go on to its end. The Fourth Gospel refers to this conflict when it says: "The light shineth in the darkness, and the darkness did not apprehend [or better perhaps, overcome] it" (John 1:5). This conflict is represented in John's Gospel as a ceaseless struggle between light and darkness.

This view, of course, would be inconsistent with an absolute monism. It is based on the assumption that man has moral freedom and responsibility and that sin is real opposition to God. It is monotheistic in its interpretation of the world but not monistic. Sin is more than weakness or immaturity: it is voluntary rebellion against the will of God.

3. *The conflict in the life of Jesus*

The life of Jesus was one of conflict with evil all the way through. During his infancy the forces of evil were seeking to destroy him, so that his parents had to flee with him to Egypt. From his entrance into his public ministry, he was beset with trial and temptation, but was always victorious. So far as we are given light on his temptations and struggles, they centered in his mission and how he should fulfil that mission. His messianic mission was not a part of his life; it was all his life. He lived for the one thing of fulfilling his mission. His meat was to do his Father's will and complete the work that God had given him to do. The big question in his life was not whether he should do the work assigned him, but how he should do it. What method and means should he use to do the work assigned him? How should he proceed to inaugurate God's kingdom on earth? Should he appeal to spectacular methods, perform miracles that would astound the multitude and win a popular following? Should he appeal to military or physical force and subdue his enemies with irresistible power? Such questions as these formed the center of his struggle in the wilderness and in the great crises of his life, even up to Gethsemane.

He had come to establish the righteous reign of God among men. The question was what the nature of the reign should be and how it should be established. Evil must be dethroned; but how could that be done? The methods used to establish the reign of God must conform to the nature of the kingdom to be established. A spiritual reign could not be established by spectacular and military methods. God can reign in the lives of men only by their free consent and by their active co-operation. Hence the means used must be such as would secure that result. This could not be done by military or political power. God can use military power to destroy military power, but he cannot use military or political power to establish a spiritual kingdom. The history of Christianity is a demonstration of the futility of the use of carnal means and methods for promoting spiritual ends.

Jesus saw that love was the only power that would be effective in establishing a kingdom of love. He made love, therefore, the central principle in religion. But Jesus saw another thing. He saw that love in the kind of world in which he lived would be crucified. He warned the disciples that following him would mean persecution. He knew how the Old Testament prophets had been treated, and he knew what living a life of love would do to him and what it would mean to those who followed him. There is a significant statement about Cain in 1 John 3:11-12. It says that Cain slew his brother for the reason that his own works were evil while his brother's were good. The nature of sin is such that it fights the good. It would not be evil if it did not.

So Jesus was put to death because of his goodness. The evil forces of his day were bound to kill him. They could not live with him. What else could they do? They must kill him or cease to be evil. On the other hand, if Jesus had ceased using the method of love and had adopted the method of worldly force, he would have ceased to be righteous and would have lost the power of righteousness, the power of love. When the devil tried to get Jesus to compromise by worshiping him, Jesus saw that this was not the way to win but to lose. By compromising with evil Jesus would have lost all. His mission would have failed and evil would have triumphed.

John tells us that God is love (1 John 4:8, 16). This makes love the essence of God's being. The penal view tends to make retributive justice the fundamental or controlling attribute of God. The New Testament makes nothing more fundamental than love in God. Since God is love, to say that love and evil are in conflict with each other is to say that God and evil are in conflict. This was the guarantee that, in the case of Jesus, love should triumph over evil. When Jesus was executed as a malefactor, crucified between two criminals, it seemed that evil was definitely and finally victorious over righteousness and truth. He was hounded by envy, jealousy, and malice, accused by false witnesses and put to death as a criminal. Yet it is to be noted that the Jewish Sanhedrin condemned him to death on the ground of his own confession that he was the Messiah, the Son of God. The paradox seems to be that in pretense, on the surface, he was put to death as a malefactor and a criminal, but in reality he was condemned as the Messiah of God, the Saviour of the world. It was sin that put him to death, and he was put to death as God's Messiah.

4. *The cross as the climax of this conflict*

This conflict thus came to its climax in the cross of Christ. Here light and darkness, holiness and sin, God and the devil came into deadly combat. One side or the other must forever be conquered. Holiness and truth here forever conquered sin and evil. God could oppose sin in one of two ways. One is by punishing the sinner; the other is by redeeming him.

The former method gives a partial but true revelation of God. It reveals the element of retributive justice in God. The second method gives a final revelation of God's character as grace that saves. We do not come to the Christian conception of God until we know God as grace. In the future we may know more about God's grace, but we will never know him in any character that is higher than grace. Such is a moral impossibility. This gives finality in the revelation of God's character as grace.

The method of redemption nullifies sin; punishment only suppresses it. An evildoer may be restrained by justice; grace changes him into a saint.

In this view the cross was inevitable if the incarnation is granted.[18] If Christ is God come as a sinless man into a fallen race, the cross was inevitable. In that case, the sinless Christ is sure to live a life of service to men and they are sure to crucify him. Each acts his part. This view not only brings the incarnation in line with the cross. It also makes redemption the work of God all the way through. It has been customary among advocates of the penal view, from the days of Anselm on, to regard the atonement as man's work, not God's, in the sense that it was held that it was the human nature of Christ that suffered, not the divine. It is true that Anselm and his followers held that Christ was divine, but they held that he suffered only in his human nature. His divine nature, it was said, gave added dignity to his person and hence gave increased value (infinite or practically so) to his sufferings. These sufferings had to be of infinite value to counterbalance the infinite indignity suffered by the honor (or justice) of God. But while the divine nature of Christ gave infinite value to his person and hence to his sufferings, it was held that the divine nature did not suffer, since God was impassible. He could not suffer.

The idea that Christ acted according to his two natures, either one governing his action according to the situation independently of the other while the other gave value to what he did, amounts to denying the reality of the incarnation. We are not here trying to solve the mystery of the incarnation, but we are arguing on the assumption of its reality. But if the natures lay side by side in his person and he could act according to either nature independently of the other, then God did not become man, he only took human nature as a kind of coat

[18]Cf. *The Christian Religion in Its Doctrinal Expression*, by Mullins, pp. 320-321.

which was only a garment he wore, not a part of him. In that case God came near to man; he did not become man. This would not be a real incarnation.

Besides, if there was no divine suffering, there was no divine sacrifice for sins, and the redeeming death of Christ was a human act, not a divine achievement. This is not the New Testament view. The New Testament view is that in Christ God became man and that his work in saving us—all his work in saving us—is God's work. God himself got under the burden of our sins. He achieved our redemption.

The revelation of God as love contradicts the idea that God cannot suffer. A God who loves must suffer when his world is invaded by sin and men are destroyed by it. To say that God does not suffer is to say that he does not care.

5. *Victory manifest in the resurrection*

When Jesus died on the cross it appeared that sin and death had conquered. But not so in reality. He triumphed over sin and death. He conquered death because he conquered sin. Peter was right when he said that he could not be holden of death (Acts 2:24). He seemed to be conquered by sin, but he had conquered sin and therefore rose victorious over death.

Thus the conflict between Christ and sin that culminated in death issued in resurrection. Sin and death go together. They are parts of one whole. Death is not something that God arbitrarily inflicts on the sinner. Dr. Mullins talks about the sin-death principle.[19] This is in line with the New Testament. Paul closely links sin and death in all his discussions. This comes out clearly in such passages as Romans chapters 5-8. "The wages of sin is death" (6:23). Those who live according to the flesh are about to die (8:13). The justified man is not under condemnation, because the law of the Spirit of life (the control of the Spirit that produces life) has

---
[19] *Ibid.*, p. 319.

freed him from the law (control) of sin and death. Sin and death are Siamese twins. They are inseparable.

The reason Christ conquered sin and death was because he was the incarnation of God. This conflict was not between man and sin. Sin had won that contest throughout history. But now God, in the person of Christ, entered the contest on behalf of man, and won in the conflict. The resurrection was the complete defeat of sin, death, and the devil. Jesus did not die as a victim; he died as a victor. His victory was manifest in the resurrection. He said that no man took his life from him. He laid it down of himself, and of himself he took it again (John 10:18). The penal theory treats Jesus as a victim, but he died as a conqueror. In dying he conquered death and Hades. The resurrection of Jesus is the watershed of New Testament Christianity. It marks the continental divide. To change the figure a little, it marks the point where we go up onto a higher plane, but we do not come down again.

The resurrection of Jesus was the elevation of his whole personality to a higher plane of being. It gives us a universal, spiritual Christ instead of a local, limited Christ. Many people look back with longing to the Christ of the Lake or the Galilean hills. It was evidently wonderful for the disciples to have Christ present with them in the flesh. But we today have something more wonderful than that. We have a Christ who in his resurrection was raised above the limitations of time and space.

The author takes the liberty of quoting at some length here what he has said on this point in another book:

Let us look at some specific New Testament passages on this matter. One is a statement from Matthew in which Jesus is represented as saying, "All authority hath been given unto me in heaven and on earth" (Matt. 28:18). After giving to his disciples the great commission on this basis (notice the "therefore" of verse 19) he says again, "And lo, I am with you always, even unto the end of the world" (Matt. 28:20). This is a post-resurrection statement of Jesus. Notice the universal sweep of the authority here claimed as given him. It is authority that came to be his. Evidently it is authority given to him in the resurrection. It represents his supreme victory over sin and death. Then he promises his spiritual omnipresence with his people as they carry out his command. In a pre-resurrection statement he promises to be in their midst whenever two or three are gathered in his name (Matt. 18:20). Evidently Jesus is looking forward to his post-resurrection state and his relation to his disciples in this promise.

Another significant statement is found in Acts 2: 36. Peter says, "Let all the house of Israel therefore know assuredly that God hath made him both Lord and Christ, this Jesus whom ye crucified." Peter is here explaining to his hearers the significance of what has just taken place on the day of Pentecost. He explains that the Holy Spirit has been poured out by the risen and exalted Christ. In fulfilment of Psalm 110:1, God has raised Jesus from the dead and exalted him to a position of authority and power at his right hand. Jesus who has been thus exalted, having received from the Father the promised Holy Spirit, has poured forth this which they now see and hear. Then he says that the significance of the whole thing, so far as Jesus is concerned, is that God has made this Jesus whom they have crucified both Lord and Christ. God did this in the resurrection and ascension. This is evidenced by the coming of the Holy Spirit.

What does he mean when he says that God has made Jesus both Lord and Christ? The name Jesus denotes the person whom they have known as living in their midst and whom they have put to death.

Now Peter announces to them the startling fact that God has reversed their judgment of condemnation upon Jesus and exalted him to a position of authority and power that rightly belongs to him as Lord and Christ. The position he occupied before in their midst was not the position that was rightfully his. He was present as one limited in power, as one characterized by humility, even by weakness as shown in his being put to a shameful death. This position is his no more. God has exalted him. God has clothed him with universal authority and power. This power is spiritual in its nature as shown by the outpouring of the Holy Spirit. It is moral, not physical or military, in character. That is guaranteed in the fact that it is the same Jesus whom they had known and who had died rather than allow his disciples to use force in defending him or rather than call upon supernatural spiritual power as represented in the angels to defend him.

The book of Acts is written to set forth the activity of this exalted Christ. Luke's first treatise was about what Jesus began to do and teach (Acts 1:1). The program of the risen Christ is set forth in Acts 1:8. The rest of the book is to show how the evangelistic and missionary activity of the early disciples was the carrying out of this program as the ascended Christ worked by his Spirit through his people. From Pentecost on in the New Testament, the presence and activity of the Spirit are always regarded as the spiritual presence and activity of the glorified Jesus. By his Spirit he is present with his people and works in and through them to establish his kingdom on earth.

Does not Paul in Rom. 1:4 mean the same thing as Peter in Acts 2:36? Not simply, as the translations would indicate, that Jesus by the resurrection was declared or demonstrated to be the Son of God, but rather that God in the resurrection instated

Jesus in a position of power that was in accordance
with his higher spiritual nature (according to the
spirit of holiness). He has just indicated that on
the human side (according to the flesh) he was born
of the seed of David. But the position that he occupied while living among men on earth did not correspond to his higher nature, the spirit of holiness.
But when God raised him from the dead he brought
him into a position of power that corresponded to
his higher nature. During his earthly life his higher
nature was limited, cramped, one might say, in a
state or condition of humiliation into which he voluntarily came for man's redemption. The resurrection was his release. It was his emancipation day.
The limits were removed. The everlasting doors were
lifted up and the King of Glory marched to his
throne. This interpretation is favored by the context
and fits in admirably with the conception set forth
by Paul in other places, and by the whole New Testament concerning the glorified Christ.

Essentially the same view is involved in what
Paul says in 1 Corinthians 15:20-28. Christ is the
first fruits from the dead. Having risen from the
dead, he now reigns at the right hand of God. There
he will remain until he has abolished all rule and
authority and power. That is, every rival or opposing power in the universe will be subdued. The
climax of this conquering reign will come when
Christ comes again to raise the bodies of his people
from the dead. All things will then have been subdued by Christ excepting God alone who has subjected all things unto Christ.

Perhaps the most outstanding passage in the New
Testament on this question is Philippians 2:9-11.
Here Paul says that God highly exalted Christ, and
gave unto him the name which is above every name.
He has the supreme place in the universe of God.
Every knee is to bow to him, of things in heaven, on

earth, and under the earth. Every tongue shall confess that he is Lord to the glory of God the Father. This absolute lordship comes to Christ as a moral reward for his voluntary humiliation and death. Because he emptied himself, God exalted him. This idea we tried to express above by saying that Christ won his supreme victory in submission to death.

In the book of Revelation John records his vision of the glorified Christ in the first chapter (vv. 10-20). He appears in his majesty and power. His feet that had been pierced are now feet of burnished brass. The strength of the sun is in his countenance. He holds the messengers of the churches in his hand and walks in majesty among the churches. A sharp two-edged sword proceeds out of his mouth. The Son of God goes forth to war. The book of Revelation gives us a view of the war that he conducts against darkness and sin. That war never ceases until sin is vanquished and righteousness and truth rule in God's world.[20]

Many other passages bearing on this subject could be given from the New Testament, but it is unnecessary to quote them. The whole New Testament from the Gospels on is written from the point of view of the risen, reigning Christ. He is no longer limited as he was during the days of his flesh. He is now the conquering Christ. He is himself the supreme example of the spiritual law that one wins life through death.

The Gospel of John speaks of his death as his being lifted up above the limitations that he experienced in the flesh. He was glorified in death. Through death he came to the glory and power that were rightly his as the Son of God.

When he conquered sin and death on the cross and manifested his victory in the resurrection, he brought life and immortality to light for all who believe in him. He became the source of eternal life to all who were

---

[20]*Revelation and God*, pp. 201 ff.

united to him by faith. He became the source and the head of a new humanity that is being created in the spiritual image of God. He is himself the active agent in the creation of such a humanity.

We call to mind again that expression occurring several times in the New Testament that Christ sat down at the right hand of God. He sat down as a victor. He had accomplished the task of making a complete once-for-all offering for sin. He sits down to reign. God has placed him on the throne of David to rule forever (Acts 2:29 ff.). All his enemies have not yet been put beneath his feet, but they will be someday (1 Cor. 15:24 ff.; Heb. 2:5 ff.).

6. *The risen Christ and the Spirit*

The cross and resurrection of Jesus constitute the ground of victory over evil on a cosmic scale. Yet that victory, while final in principle, must be extended. They did not consummate the kingdom; they founded it. The cross is the ground and foundation of every victory that God's people will ever win over evil until the completed and eternal kingdom of God shall come.

As victor over sin and death, Christ sends the Spirit on his people. He shed forth the Spirit on the day of Pentecost (Acts 2:33). He is now the living, super-historical Christ. As such he sheds forth his Spirit on his people. And the work of the Spirit is to make him Saviour and Lord in the lives of men. The Spirit is the Spirit of Christ (Rom. 8:9). The coming of the Spirit is the coming of Christ. The Spirit's presence is the presence of Christ. Pentecost was the extension in the lives of men of the redemptive power of the death and resurrection of Jesus.

The living Christ acts upon human life from above. He acts on human history in a perpendicular way, not simply in a horizontal manner. He pours fresh accessions of spiritual power into human life and history. He renews history. That is the only hope of the world.

With reference to this, notice two books in the New Testament. One is the book of Acts. This book is not telling of the acts of the apostles. Only two of the apostles have much prominence in the book. One of them was Saul of Tarsus, whom the living Christ conquered and commissioned as a missionary to the Gentiles. His missionary activities loom large in the latter half. In the earlier half Peter is the main human actor. John gets some mention, but not much. The rest of the apostles are hardly mentioned. If Christianity depended on apostolic succession, the author of this book hardly had the right point of view.

Luke tells Theophilus (1:1) that in his former treatise (the Gospel) he has recorded what Jesus began to do and teach. The real theme of the book, then, is the acts or deeds of the living Christ. He is the central actor. He works through his people, by his Spirit, for the coming of his kingdom.

The book of Revelation portrays the same idea. The living Christ appears in the first chapter with the strength of the sun shining from his face and a sharp two-edged sword proceeding out of his mouth. He is a militant Christ. The Son of God goes forth to war, and he continues to make war on sin and darkness until these are driven out of the world and the perfected kingdom of God has come.

We have some indications in this book as to how he is to work. He moves in the midst of the candlesticks, which are the churches. He holds the seven stars in his right hand. These are perhaps a symbol for the churches or their pastors. These two symbols would seem to indicate that the living Christ identifies himself with his people and that they are to be his agents in his work. The sharp, two-edged sword represents the gospel, or the word of God, which he is to use. We find also later that this Christ is pictured as the Lion of the tribe of Judah. Here is his omnipotence. But his omnipotence is spiritual in character, for as we behold the Lion of the tribe of Judah he becomes the Lamb slain. His power is the power of sacrificial love. It is by the blood of the Lamb and the word of their testimony that his followers overcome the devil (12:11).

V. The Cross and the Christian Life

1. *The Christian as sharing the cross*

If the cross of Christ is fundamental in our salvation, then we ought to find in the New Testament that the Christian life is interpreted in terms of the cross; and that is just what we find. Jesus repeatedly said to his disciples that they must renounce all, take up the cross, and follow him (Mark 8:34 ff.; Luke 14:25 ff.; et al.). In John's Gospel he said that unless a grain of wheat "fall into the ground and die, it abideth alone; but if it die, it bringeth forth much fruit" (John 12:24). Paul speaks of the Christian as one who has died to sin, been buried with Christ and risen to newness of life (Rom. 6:1 ff.). He says of himself that he has been crucified; yet he lives, in that Christ lives in him by faith (Gal. 2:20). Peter exhorts Christians to suffer, after the example of Christ, not as evildoers, but as those who are righteous (1 Pet. 2:20 ff.; 4:12 ff.). We believe that these passages, with others that might be taken from the New Testament, justify the statement that one cannot be a Christian unless the spirit of the cross is found in his life.

These passages make clear that the cross is something that the Christian is to share. Evangelical Christianity has emphasized that Christians reincarnate Christ. Christ was the incarnation of God, and through Christ God is being reincarnated in his people in the world. God's means of making himself known in the world today is through those in whom the Spirit of God dwells. They represent him, not in any externally official manner, but in that they are the living embodiment of his Spirit. This is one of the lines on which ecclesiology divides. Some hold that the church represents Christ because he committed to it his authority so that what the church does it does by the authority of Christ. Usually there is associated with this type of ecclesiology the idea of apostolic succession in some form. The Roman Catholic Church is a good representative of this type of ecclesiology. There is another type that holds that the church is the representation of Christ, because it embodies his Spirit, and that the activity of the church represents Christ and his authority only as the church is truly the spiritual body of Christ, embodying and expressing his will in the world; but that the church does represent the authority of Christ to the extent that it embodies and expresses his Spirit.

While evangelical Christianity has held that the church, as the body of Christ, was thus an extension of the incarnation, it has been slow to apply the same principle to the cross of Christ. There seemed to be a fear that, if this principle were applied to the cross, it would destroy the distinctiveness of Christ's saving work on the cross. It is true that, in either case, the distinctiveness of Christ's saving work can be lost. That has been done in the case of the incarnation by those who substituted for the evangelical doctrine of the incarnation the idea of an incarnation of God in humanity as a whole, denying that Christ was the incarnation of God in any peculiar or exclusive sense. Christ was looked on as the Son of God only in the sense that all other men were the sons of God. All men were regarded as divine. The result was that, by deifying every thing and every body, God himself was undeified. The personal and transcendent God of the Bible was lost in an indefinite pantheism.

It is entirely possible for a corresponding error to be made with reference to the cross. In fact, such an error is quite common. That is what takes place when the cross of Jesus is given only the significance of the martyrdom of a good man. In that case the significance of the cross is reduced to that of the suffering of a good man and that only. This method of reducing the significance of the meaning of the incarnation and the cross of Jesus is the error of liberal Christianity and modern idealistic philosophy.

With reference to the extension of the ideas of the incarnation and the cross to the people of God, there is an error also that belongs to the official or authoritarian type of ecclesiology, referred to above. The church is looked on as a divinely commissioned body. This divine commission (usually viewed as having been given to the apostles and passed on by them to bishops or their successors) is regarded as having given the church the authority of Christ himself, so that the church is regarded as the reincarnation of Christ and thus as being his authoritative body in the world. The authority of the church is the authority of Christ. Corresponding to this the eucharist is regarded as an actual sacrifice and as having divine efficacy for man's salvation. This makes the eucharist an extension or repetition of the value of the cross.

As over against these two types of view, the New Testament looks on renewed humanity as an extension of the principle of the incarnation. God dwells in his people, but no one of them, nor all of them together, is the incarnation of God in the same sense that Jesus was, but his indwelling in them is real and is based on God's incarnation in Christ. In a similar way the principle of the cross is reproduced in Christ's people. The cross as reproduced in them has not the saving efficacy for others that his cross has, but it is real and is essential for the extension of the cause of Christ in the world. If God's people embody Christ, it is the Christ who died for sinners that they embody. Thus they must embody the Spirit of the cross, if they embody Christ.

2. *Some respects in which the Christian shares the cross*

(1) Self-denial

The principle of the cross is seen in the Christian in that the Christian life is one of self-denial. Jesus said that one who would follow him should deny himself and take up his cross. To take up the cross is to die—to die to a selfish and worldly life and devote oneself to Christ and his service. The self-denial that Jesus here inculcates is not doing without this little pleasure or that. It is the utter and complete renunciation of self and self-mastership. It is recognizing that one does not belong to himself, but that he has been bought with a price. It is giving oneself up to Christ and his will as Christ gave himself up to God and his will.

The idea of self-denial here is not the idea that there is any value in suffering for suffering's sake. It is not the type of piety that imposes pilgrimages on oneself, or withdraws from the world to live in lonely self-examination and introspection. Such piety as this may easily become a species of self-seeking that is just the opposite of the spirit of the cross. The spirit of the cross is to give oneself to God and others. Such piety as we here speak of is mere self-repression. Self-repression is not Christian self-denial. A life of Christian self-denial means that one loses self in the service of Christ and one's fellows.

(2) Evangelistic and missionary activity

The spirit of the cross expresses itself in the evangelistic and missionary dynamic of the Christian life. Some people look on evangelistic or missionary activity on the part of Christians as a species of unworthy proselyting or as some pugilistic religionist trying to put his ideas over on somebody else. Such an interpretation shows that the one holding it has a very superficial view of what Christianity means in human life. Sometimes Christians are reproached for their missionary activity and are told that they have no right to try to impose their religion on somebody else. But the New Testament says that the gospel is good news. One wants to tell, one will tell, good news. He cannot suppress it.

Jesus died to bring to men in saving power the good news of the love of God. Missionaries around the world today are giving their lives to bring to men in the darkness of sin the good news of salvation through faith in his name. Men like Saul of Tarsus, David Livingstone, William Carey, Adoniram Judson, and thousands of others in the past and in the present, have sacrificed all the world counts worth while to carry to others the good news of Christ and his cross.

Spreading the gospel is always costly business. One cannot really do anything worth while at it unless he gives himself to it in the spirit of the cross. He must subordinate all else to Christ and his work. He must crucify self and earthly ambition. In fact that should be the spirit of every Christian and must be if his life counts for much in the service of Christ.

We get a view of what extending the gospel costs if we note the language of Paul in Romans 9:1-2. He says that he has great sorrow and unceasing pain in his heart. He could even wish himself accursed from Christ for his brethren, his kinsmen in the flesh, his Israelitish brethren. Here is the spirit of the cross, and that was the thing that sent Paul out over land and sea to tell men about the love of God in Christ. Present-day Christianity has little missionary power in it because it has little of the passion of the cross.

This is one indictment that can be brought against modern Unitarianism. It has very little missionary or evangelistic dynamic in it. It may do very well for swivel chair professors of theology who speculate on the "problems" of theology. But when such questions as the incarnation and cross of Christ become merely "problems" to speculate about rather than dynamics in Christian living, then they are no longer what they are in the New Testament. In the New Testament they are dynamic facts and factors in life, not simply something about which disinterestedly to theorize.

(3) Intercessory prayer

One phase of the Christian life that is an expression of the spirit of the cross is intercessory prayer. By intercessory prayer we mean prayer in which we come before God on behalf of another. It is prayer in which we seek the blessing of God on behalf of someone else. It may be seeking the salvation of a lost soul, or seeking for God's power on a Christian worker, or something different from either of these. In any case, we are intercessors if we seek to obtain God's blessing for another. We have numerous instances of such intercession in the Bible.

All such intercession is costly in a spiritual way. Perhaps this is one reason Christians do so little of it. It costs time, thought, effort, energy. It searches one's heart and helps to purify his life.

It expresses the spirit of the cross in that it reveals an unselfish concern for the welfare of another. One's prayers for himself may be selfish, even when he prays for spiritual blessings. One is not so likely to be selfish in praying for a blessing on someone else. The cross is the direct and absolute opposite of the spirit of selfishness. Intercessory prayer will help to develop and will bring to expression this spirit in the Christian's life, and as this spirit is developed in his life he will have power in intercession.

In Exodus 19:6, Jehovah says that Israel is to be a kingdom of priests for him. We find an expression like this several times in the book of Revelation. John says that God made us to be a kingdom, even priests, unto the God and Father of Christ (Rev. 1:6). Perhaps the idea in this peculiar expression is that, as God acquires spiritual sovereignty over us, he uses us to mediate his power to other people. God works through us. As we engage in intercessory prayer, we are not working against God. We are working with him against the sin and evil of the world. We are helping him to extend the victory of the cross in the lives of men around us.

(4) Overcoming evil with good

Another place where it is quite evident that the Christian life is a reproduction of the spirit of the cross is in the Christian method of overcoming evil. The way of the world is to overcome evil with evil. It is the law of retaliation. We find this law of retaliation embodied in the Mosaic legislation of the Old Testament (Ex. 21: 23-24; Lev. 24:19 ff.; Deut. 19:16-21). It is to be noted, however, that it is not endorsed in the Old Testament as something to be practiced between individuals as such. It is rather a principle embodied to a limited extent in civil law. For the purposes of civil government, at least in certain stages of moral and civic development, such a procedure is justifiable. It is a necessity. Force must sometimes be met with force. That is true in the dealing of society with criminal elements. It seems to be necessary, at least as things now are, in the dealing of nations with international brigands. Perhaps this is one of the places where, as Paul says, the civil authority does not bear the sword in vain (Rom. 13:1-4). Paul indicates that civil government is ordained of God and is justified in the use of force to accomplish its ends.

The New Testament distinctly forbids a Christian to manifest the spirit of retaliation in dealing with his fellow man. Jesus teaches instead of this to turn the other cheek, go the second mile, and give to the one that asks (Matt. 5:38 ff.). It seems hardly necessary to say that Jesus is not making up a rule book by which the Christian is to govern his conduct. He is inculcating a spirit, a spirit which he himself exhibited in his life. Nor was Jesus formulating laws to govern the state in relation to criminals, or society in relation to beggars and poverty, or nations in relation to international outlaws. If we could ask him about these things, he probably would say: "Man, who made me an economist or a lawgiver over you?"

But he was trying to instil a certain spirit into his disciples—a spirit they should manifest in all relations in life. That spirit has done much for human society and is destined to do more in the future.

In teaching them thus to act, Jesus cited the example of the Heavenly Father (Matt. 5:43 ff.). God is good to all men, good and bad. We are not to be good to those only who are good to us. After the example of the Heavenly Father, we are to do good to all men, even where they mistreat us and persecute us. When the Christian is persecuted and mistreated, he has a rare opportunity to manifest the Spirit of God in relation to other men.

Paul inculcates the same spirit in Romans 12:19-21. Instead of taking vengeance on our enemy, we are to do good to him. Leave the matter of taking vengeance to God. He reserves that prerogative to himself. We are to seek to overcome evil with good.[21]

If anybody should insist that the good is impotent to overcome evil, the answer is that good is the only thing that can overcome evil. Evil forces may counter one another, but evil can not overcome evil. The only way that evil can be overcome is to transform the sinner into a saint. So far as physical force is concerned, it may be used or overruled to good ends, but physical force as such cannot change man for the better.

What about those who will not be transformed into the good? Does the method of God's goodness or grace mean that those who will not be transformed are to be left free to work their evil will in God's world? This would be a false inference. Sinful men who will not yield to God's grace are not left free to work their evil designs in God's universe. The universe is so made that those with evil designs defeat their own ends. Evil is self-defeating. The Bible from beginning to end bears witness to this fact. The man who digs a pit for another falls into it himself (Psalm 7:15-16). The evil man who takes the sword against others will perish by his own sword (Psalm 37:15). This fact (that evil is self-de-

---

[21]So far as society (or the state) is concerned, it would seem that it has no right either to inflict punishment with the view of meting final and exact justice to men, but only to protect its members from evildoers. Something like that might hold in international relations.

feating) is not always evident at once, but in time it will infallibly prove true. The man who thinks that he can neglect or defy God, flout the laws of morality, pursue his own selfish ends and be happy will certainly come to misery. He will find that the whole universe, including his own inner nature, is against him in such a venture. Especially is it true that the man who despises God's grace and will not have his mercy will find that the omnipotence of the eternal God was wrapped up in the goodness of God that he refused and that it rebounds on him to his doom.

3. *The cross and blessedness*

A question arises here. How is this idea of sharing the cross related to the Christian's happiness or blessedness? Here we come on one of the great paradoxes of the Christian life. One finds his happiness (perhaps better, blessedness) by sharing the cross. Jesus expresses this paradox in the Beatitudes by saying that those who mourn are happy (or blessed) (Matt. 5:4). In the passages already cited, we learn that one saves his life by losing it; one dies to live. It is a matter of experience that they are the happiest Christians who give themselves most completely to God in the service of others. The Son of man came, not to be served, but to serve, and to give his life a ransom for many (Mark 10:45). Happiness is not found in this world by avoiding responsibility and giving oneself to a life of ease and luxury. Selfishness always leads to misery. Jesus for the joy that was set before him, endured the cross, despising the shame (Heb. 12:2). He found his joy by enduring the cross, not by evading it. So must we.

Theologians once held, perhaps some do yet, that God was impassible. They held that he could not suffer and be a blessed God, too. This was a strange position for people to hold, the symbol of whose religion was a cross. The cross stands for what it cost God to save us. He finds his blessedness in blessing others, even when blessing them means a cross. Any man will find that a religion without a cross at its center is a religion without genuine joy and peace. The cross helps us to understand God, to interpret the universe, to find the true meaning of life. All the fundamental tendencies of the moral universe meet in the cross of Christ.

We will not pursue further, at this time, the idea that the Christian shares and expresses the spirit of the cross. We think we have said enough to make this point clear. Much that is said in the following chapters will in reality be a further development of this idea.

BECOMING A CHRISTIAN,
OR
THE BEGINNING OF THE CHRISTIAN LIFE

I. Three Stages of Salvation

   1. Salvation as a definite act or transaction
   2. Salvation as a process
   3. Salvation as a consummation

II. The Nature of Salvation

   1. Deliverance from sin
   2. Development of a Christlike personality
   3. A new habitation

III. Union with Christ

   1. Set forth in the New Testament
   2. Faith the means of union with Christ
   3. Union with the living Christ
   4. Union with God
   5. Union with Christ through the Spirit

IV. God's Saving Act

   1. In Christ God forgives our sins
     (1) Scriptures setting forth the idea
     (2) The meaning of forgiveness
     (3) Objections to the doctrine of forgiveness
   2. In Christ we are justified
     (1) The doctrine defined
     (2) The doctrine perverted
     (3) The Roman Catholic doctrine of justification
     (4) Summary of the values of the doctrine
   3. In Christ we are reconciled to God
   4. In Christ we are adopted into the family of God
   5. In Christ we have new life
     (1) New Testament terms used for this idea
     (2) The need of regeneration
     (3) The nature of the change
       a. Mysterious
       b. Moral and spiritual renewal
       c. Wrought by the Spirit of God
       d. Reproduces the image of Christ in us
       e. Produced by the use of means
       f. Produced by faith
       g. Conscious transaction

6. In Christ we are sanctified
    (1) Meaning of the term
    (2) All Christians sanctified

V. The Conditions of Salvation
1. Repentance
    (1) Other terms used
    (2) What is repentance?
        a. Understanding of one's condition
        b. Death to love of sin
        c. Renunciation of sin
    (3) Repentance and reformation
    (4) Christian life a life of repentance
    (5) Repentance and conversion
2. Faith
    (1) The meaning of faith
        a. Christ the object of faith
        b. Two aspects of faith
            (a) We receive Christ as Saviour
            (b) We submit to him as Lord
    (2) An objection to Christian faith
    (3) Why salvation is by faith
    (4) Faith and a life of righteousness

VI. The Consciousness of Salvation
1. The normal Christian experience
    (1) Consciousness of sin
    (2) Conscious communion with God
2. The lack of assurance
3. What is necessary to assurance

CHAPTER IV.

BECOMING A CHRISTIAN, OR,
THE BEGINNING OF THE CHRISTIAN LIFE

In our last chapter we saw something of what Christ did on our behalf. We took there something of a view of his objective redemptive work. We come now to consider the meaning of this redemptive work as it works itself out in human experience.

What does it mean to become a Christian? What kind of a transaction is it? What do we mean by salvation? How is a person saved?

These are some of the questions involved when we study them from the standpoint of experience and life.

Is salvation something that takes place all at once or is it a continuous process?

I. Three Stages of Salvation

In approaching the matter, it will help us to keep in mind that salvation is an act, a process, and a consummation. We might put the matter in the form of a question. Is a Christian saved, is he being saved, or is he to be saved in the future? It is made abundantly clear in the New Testament that he is all three—saved, being saved, and going to be saved.

It is not our purpose here to discuss at length these three phases of the matter. But we do wish to set out clearly that these three phases are to be found in the New Testament. Most of what we have to say from here on will bear on one of these three aspects of the matter.

We take up now an examination of the use of the verb "to save" and the noun "salvation" in order to show that salvation is presented in these three ways in the New Testament and in our experience. The use of these words (to save and salvation) is not the only evidence, however. There are other terms used in the New Testament that bear out the matter. In fact, the whole presentation of the Christian life makes it clear that all three of these phases are fundamental in the Christian experience. We will examine briefly these terms (to save, salvation) with a look at some other facts, to show that salvation is regarded in these three ways in the New Testament.

1. *Salvation as a definite act or transaction*

In the first place, these terms denote a definite act or transaction. It is this transaction that initiates the Christian life. It makes one a Christian. In Luke 7:50 Jesus said to the sinful woman: "Thy faith hath saved thee." The verb here in Greek is in the perfect tense. This indicates that the saving was in some sense a transaction completed. Evidently it refers to the forgiveness of the woman's sins spoken of in verse 47. In Luke 19:9 Jesus says concerning Zaccheus: "To-day salvation came to this house." The verb here is in the aorist tense, which indicates that salvation came to Zaccheus as a definite event. In Ephesians 2:8 Paul says: "By grace have ye been saved through faith." This is a perfect tense again, denoting a transaction completed. In some sense the Christian has been saved. In writing to Titus, Paul said in 3:5 that according to his mercy, God saved us through the washing of regeneration. Here the apostle uses the aorist to denote salvation as a definite act. (Cf. also Luke 8:12; John 5:34; 10:9; 1 Cor. 1:21, et al.)

Besides these uses of the terms to save and salvation, there are many others that speak of the Christian as having been forgiven, justified, reconciled, adopted, sanctified, and so on. There is abundant evidence in the New Testament that the Christian life begins in a definite transaction and that this transaction is an act of salvation on God's part. We are entirely in accord with the New Testament in thought and language if we speak of the Christian as one who was saved at a definite time in the past or as one who has been saved at some past time.

2. *Salvation as a process*

We should not be in accord with the New Testament, however, if we thought of God's saving activity in the Christian's life as having been terminated with this initial transaction. Not only does the Christian life begin in a definite act of salvation on God's part, but he also sustains and continues this saving activity. The Christian life must be sustained. It must be sustained by God's mercy. The redeemed life is not a self-contained and self-sustained entity. This act of God in saving the sinner brings him into a new relation to God. But the sinner, after experiencing the grace of God, can no more keep himself in a saved state than he could bring himself into such a state at first. There is no stage of that life and no phase of it that is self-sustaining. Paul speaks in Romans 5:2 about Christ as the One through whom we have had access by faith into this grace in which we stand. If one should be disposed to emphasize the fact that *we stand* in this grace, and that it is thus our work, it would be in order to notice that it is in the grace of God that we stand, the same grace by which we were justified; and that we stand by faith, the same kind of faith by which we were justified; and that this faith is directed to the same Lord and Saviour in whom we were justified. Thus we see that the redeemed life of the Christian is not a self-contained or self-sustained life; it is sustained by faith in the grace of the same Saviour and Lord in whom we were justified. In Ephesians 2:8 Paul says that by faith ye have been saved—a perfect passive form of the verb. The perfect tense in Greek denotes something done in the past, but the force or effect of which continues to the present. So when Paul says that by grace ye have been saved, he means that ye were saved in the past and continue saved up to the present. And the continuance is as much God's work as the beginning was.

But the Christian life needs not only to be sustained; it needs to grow and increase. If it does so, it must be by the grace of the same God who saved us at the beginning of the Christian life. There are a few places in the New Testament where salvation is spoken of in this progressive sense. In 1 Corinthians 1:18 Paul says that to those who are perishing the word of the cross is foolishness, but to those who are being saved it is the power of God. Here the words "perishing" and "being saved" are present passive participles and seem to be used in a progressive sense. Those who are in the process of perishing are so blinded spiritually that they see nothing but foolishness in the word of the cross, but those who are in the process of being saved experience in this word of the cross God's power for their salvation. We have a similar use of both these expressions in 2 Corinthians 2:15. The apostle says that we are a sweet savor of Christ unto God, in them that are being saved, and in them that are perishing. Here, as in 1 Corinthians 1:18, he seems to be speaking of perishing and salvation in the progressive sense.

These terms (to save and salvation) are seldom used, however, in the New Testament in a distinctively progressive sense. Even the two given above could be questioned, though the evidence is largely in favor of that sense.

There is abundant other evidence, however, that the Christian life is meant to be normally a life of growth. The writers of the New Testament constantly used growing things to illustrate that life. Paul and the author of Hebrews manifested great concern that their spiritual children should show progress in the Christian life. They were distressed when this was not the case, as the third chapter of 1 Corinthians and Hebrews 5:11 ff. will show. In the passage from Paul, he rebukes the Corinthians because they are still carnal and babes in Christ. The

author of Hebrews reproves his readers because they are
still babes when they ought to be teachers. They ought
to be fullgrown (perfect) men.

Protestant theology has usually used the term sanctification to denote the development of the new life begotten in regeneration. The word does seem to be used
in that sense in places, though that is hardly its characteristic use in the New Testament. (See for this use of
the term Rom. 6:19, 22; 2 Cor. 7:1; 1 Thes. 4:3-4, 7, 13;
1 Tim. 2:13; Heb. 10:14; 12:14; 1 Peter 1:2.) Again,
some of these might be questioned, but hardly all of
them.

3. *Salvation as a consummation*

A third thing is still more strongly emphasized in the
New Testament than the fact that the Christian life is
normally a growing life: namely, that the Christian is
moving toward a glorious consummation in which his
salvation will be completed.

In the Synoptic Gospels, Jesus teaches that the kingdom of God is a present experience (Mark 1:15; Matt.
10:7; 10:9, 11, et al.), a growing reality (Mark 4:26-29,
30-32; Matt. 13:33), and something that is coming to a
consummation (Matt. 13:30, 49-50; 25:31, et al.). In
John's Gospel eternal life is mainly a present reality
(3:36; 5:24; 6:47, et al.); but here also we find that
there is a consummation to be expected (6:39-40, 44,
et al.). God will raise up his people at the last day.

Paul lays great stress on what the theologians call
eschatological salvation. He says that our salvation is
nearer than when we believed. The present is like a
dark night, but he encourages them to lift up their heads
and look for the day (Rom. 13:11-14). In 1 Corinthians
15, he dwells on the Christian's hope of the resurrection,
which will consummate his salvation. Death is the
last enemy which Christ will conquer. In Romans 8:24
he says that we are saved by hope. The Christian
looks forward with eager expectation to the day of

final deliverance (Rom. 8:23). Even the whole creation, which has been subjected to vanity on account of man's sin, longs to share in this glorious consummation that is coming to the children of God (Rom. 8:19 ff.). Man's assurance that he will be finally delivered from sin lies in the indwelling Spirit of God. God has put his Spirit in the heart of the believer. This indwelling Spirit is the firstfruits of the coming harvest (Rom. 8:23). The Spirit constitutes God's pledge money, the earnest of our inheritance, God's pledge that he will complete the transaction begun in regeneration (2 Cor. 1:22; Eph. 1:14). The Spirit is God's seal guaranteeing our final deliverance (2 Cor. 1:22; Eph. 1:13; 4:30).

In 1 Peter 1:5, we have an instructive statement on the eschatological phase of salvation. Peter says that we are kept by the power of God through faith unto a salvation ready to be revealed in the last time. Peter has just said that God begat us again to a living hope by the resurrection of Jesus Christ from the dead. He does not think of either end of our salvation as dissociated from the other. It takes both ends of it to make the complete transaction. Neither Jesus, Peter, Paul, nor any other New Testament writer thought of salvation as completed here. It begins here, but is completed in the future. It comes to its full completion "in the last time."

Salvation must be eschatological to be complete. It must be brought to finality. What God has begun he will complete unto the day of Jesus Christ (Phil. 1:6).

This is the reason our salvation is by hope (Rom. 8:24). God has done much for the believer. But what he has done is only the beginning. We look for better things. What he has done is the ground and basis of hope for what he will do; and what he will do is to grow out of and continue what he has done. It will be the consummation of what he has done and is doing for us here.

This is in line with the faith that he is a God of purpose and of grace. He does not do something for us and then quit. What he does for us at any particular time is a part of his larger plan for us. We do not see nor understand the complete plan. We do not know what we shall be when he shall have completed his work in us. But we know that, when he shall appear, we shall be like him (1 John 3:2). And that is sufficient.

Our plan is to discuss in this chapter the beginning of In the next chapter we will deal mainly with mat- our salvation or what it means to become a Christian. ters that concern the expression and development of the Christian life. In the final chapter we will discuss the consummation of our salvation.

II. The Nature of Salvation

In this section we do not propose to discuss in detail what takes place in salvation. We come to that a little later. What we wish to do here is rather to inquire into the general nature of salvation. Before taking up a more detailed discussion of God's saving activity, we wish to look into the nature of salvation, as well as the stages of it just discussed. It will be seen that these two things —the stages and the nature of salvation—are closely related and interlinked.

As to the general significance of salvation, three things might be pointed out:

1. *It is deliverance from sin*

The word translated to save has for its general meaning the idea of deliverance. It was used for deliverance from any kind of danger or peril.

In the Old Testament the mark of God's favor was found in deliverance from disease, death, captivity, and all kinds of temporal evil. This view was confined more to this life and to the visible and temporal world. In the New Testament the emphasis is changed. The main concern is with the spiritual and eternal world. We do not mean by this that New Testament Christianity is an "other worldly" religion. It concerns itself with this life and with the temporal world. But it is concerned with the temporal world for the sake of the eternal. The center of New Testament Christianity is in the coming of the eternal into time in the person of Christ. This does not diminish the significance of the temporal. It heightens its importance. But the seen and temporal world gets its significance from its relation to the spiritual and eternal. This world is not a self-contained system. It gets its meaning in relation to a world that transcends the visible and temporal order.

So in the New Testament salvation is primarily salvation from sin. We find that note in the Old Testament, especially in some of the psalms and the prophets. But it does not stand out in the clear and definite way that it does in the New Testament. Deliverance from temporal evils and deliverance from death have a much larger proportionate emphasis. But in the New Testament the big thing that stands out is God's grace that saves from sin. In the Old Testament Moses and Joshua were national heroes because they delivered Israel from her national enemies and oppressors. But Jesus came to deliver from sin.

This might be thought of as the negative aspect of salvation, since it speaks of deliverance from something. This would hardly be an accurate idea, however, because it is a positive something, only negative in form. Salvation from sin can take place only by the incoming of a greater power to take possession of man and displace sin in his life. A stronger one than the householder must come in if the householder is to be overcome. Paul graphically sets this out in the seventh chapter of Romans. The rule of the Spirit of life in Christ must displace the rule of sin and death (Rom. 8:2). If one looks at a great forest of trees in late winter, covered with dead leaves, he need not bother about how the trees will rid themselves of the dead leaves. The coming of new life with the arrival of spring will cause the dead leaves to shed and give place to fresh foliage. So man is delivered from the old life of sin and evil by the inflowing of a new life in Christ.

2. *Salvation is development of a Christlike personality*

If we were going to give a statement that would be all-comprehensive as to what salvation means, we perhaps could not do better than to say that it means to be made Christlike in character. This is our destiny as the author of First John gives it. We do not know what we shall be, but we do know that, when he shall be manifested, we shall be like him (1 John 3:2). This is God's purpose for us and the thing toward which he would direct all the factors that come into our lives (Rom. 8:28-29). Jesus sets before his disciples as the goal of their striving that they should be like God, which is to be like Christ (Matt. 5:48). This would include the idea of being freed from sin. To be like Christ is to exclude sin from the life.

One advantage that Christianity has over other systems, from an ethical point of view, is that Christianity has its ethical ideal set out in the form of a concrete historical person. If anybody wants to know what Christianity proposes to do for man, he can find out by looking at Jesus. He is the embodiment of what God proposes to make men. When unbelievers would criticize Christianity as a present-day force in the world, that criticism usually takes the form of saying that the professed followers of Christ are not like him. That is usually considered the most deadly criticism that can be directed against Christianity in our present-day world. That criticism at least pays Jesus the compliment of conceding that he is the highest ideal that the critic knows. In his teaching Jesus gives his ideal as to what a citizen of the kingdom of God should be. It is toward this ideal that the Christian should move by the grace of God. It it also noticeable that, when Jesus tells us what kind of a man a citizen of his kingdom should be, he is giving us in fact a picture of himself. The picture of Jesus as given in the Gospels and the kind of man that he says the citizen of the kingdom should be match each other. To be saved means to be on the road to becoming that kind of a man. To be saved means to enter the kingdom and to grow toward an ideal citizen of the kingdom.

A comparison of Mark 9:43 and 45 with 9:47 will show that entering into life and entering into the kingdom mean the same thing. Mark 10:23, 24, and 25 with 10:26 will show that entering the kingdom and being saved mean the same thing. To be saved one needs to enter the kingdom and to grow toward the ideal set by Jesus for kingdom citizenship.

It is significant that in places in the Gospels the verb usually translated "to save" in the American Standard Version is translated "to make whole." In Matthew 9:21 the woman with the issue of blood said that if she could but touch his garment she would be made whole (literally, "saved"). Jesus said the woman was made whole by her faith. In Mark 5:23 Jairus prays Jesus that he (Jesus) will lay his hands on the daughter of Jairus that she may be made whole. In Mark 6:56 as many as touched Jesus were made whole. To translate the word in these instances "to make whole" is not a literal translation, but it is a true one. To heal a man physically or mentally was to make him whole. To recover one from sin is to make him whole spiritually. To make one whole is to make him like Jesus. As someone has truly said: "Jesus was the only complete man the world has ever seen; all the rest of us are only fragments." To save us is to save us from being fragments into being whole.

3. *Saved man will have a new habitation*

A third thing to be considered in regard to the nature of salvation is that man renewed in the image of God will have a new environment.

This is what Paul refers to as the heavenly kingdom (2 Tim. 4:18). God's renewed people will inhabit the new heavens and the new earth. This is what people mean by heaven. It is pictured in the book of Revelation as the new Jerusalem coming down out of heaven to man.

Jesus indicates that he is going to prepare a place for his people (John 14:2).

With many people the idea of place is primary in thinking of man's destiny. This is evidently a mistaken idea. The main thing about any man is not where he is but what he is. Of course, place or environment is important, but it is not so important as character. Good surroundings do not make a man happy and contented. A bad man carries his own misery within himself. "Myself am hell." In one of his essays Emerson suggests that one reason some people are always on the go is that they are seeking to escape the misery of a bad self. But Emerson also indicates that such a person cannot find surcease from his misery because his misery is the result of his bad self, and a man cannot escape a bad self by going to another place. When he gets there, that same bad self will be there and the misery that inevitably inheres in it.

On the other hand, there is deep down in the human heart the conviction that the good man ought to be happy and that the bad man does not deserve to be, and will not be happy. And so it will prove to be in the end. Not only so, but in the end man's outer estate will correspond to his inner condition and character. This is not always true in this life. Sometimes the good have the least of "creature comforts" and worldly prosperity, and the wicked prosper and grow fat. This is recognized in both the Old and the New Testament. But it is also recognized in both that this should not be true, and will not be permanently. In some places it becomes a definite problem to the faith of the saints. The writer of some of the psalms shows that he is perplexed by such a paradoxical situation. It is dealt with at length in the book of Job. The disciples face the problem in John, chapter nine, when they meet the man born blind.

In the story of the rich man and Lazarus, Jesus indicates that the righteous may suffer here but will be blessed in the next life, while the wicked who prosper here will be punished after death (Luke 16:19 ff.).

One of the most instructive passages in this matter is what Paul gives us in Romans, chapter eight. Paul teaches that the Spirit of God abides in the Christian. This constitutes one a Christian and gives one a consciousness of the fact (Rom. 8:9, 12 ff.). The Spirit causes the Christian to yearn for complete deliverance and look to the time when he shall realize his glorious destiny (Rom. 8:23). Not only does the Christian yearn for deliverance, but the whole creation also longs to participate in the glorious destiny that awaits the children of God (Rom. 8:18 ff.). It would seem, then, that Paul expected a glorious environment for the glorified saints. Some people undertake to tell us rather definitely about where and what this environment is to be, but the Scriptures hardly seem to justify such a position.

III. Union with Christ

So far in this chapter we have considered something of the nature and stages of salvation. In the rest of the chapter we wish to consider more definitely the initiation of the Christian life. When God saves the sinner (initially), just what does he do for him? What takes place when one becomes a Christian? The rest of this chapter will be devoted to a consideration of this question.

Our salvation is in Christ Jesus. By this is meant, not only that our salvation comes from him, but also that it is due to the fact that we are brought into a vital relationship to him.

1. *Set forth in the New Testament*

This fact is set forth in many ways in the New Testament. Especially is it taught in John's Gospel, in the First Epistle of John, and in the writings of Paul. These writings are mystical in the sense that they set forth constantly and definitely this vital relation of the saved with Christ.

In John's Gospel, Jesus is the light of the world (9:5);
he is the bread of life (6:35); by eating his flesh and
drinking his blood we dwell in him and he in us (6:56);
he is the good shepherd in whose hands we find safety
(10:27-28); he is the vine, we are the branches (15:1
ff.); he is in us, we are in him (14:20). Paul also uses
a number of expressions that set forth this union with
Christ. Christ is the head, we are members of his body
(Rom. 12:4 ff.; 1 Cor. 12:12 ff.); he is the husband, the
church is the wife (Eph. 5:22 ff.); he is to us what the
foundation is to a building (1 Cor. 3:10 ff.; Eph. 2:20).
We are crucified with Christ (Gal. 2:20); we are risen
with him (Col. 3:1); we are buried with him in baptism
(Rom. 6:4); we suffer with him and we shall be glorified with him (Rom. 8:17). In union with him, Paul
says he can do all things (Phil. 4:13). Especially in
Ephesians and Colossians Paul constantly speaks of being in Christ and of Christ being in us. In one place he
goes so far as to say: "To me to live is Christ" (Phil.
1:21). By this he seems to mean that for Paul to live
in the world means that Christ lives again in and through
Paul. Here is the idea of the reincarnation of Christ in
his people, spoken of in the preceding chapter.

2. *Faith the means of union with Christ*

The means by which union with Christ is established
and maintained is faith. In John 6:56, Jesus says that
if we eat his flesh and drink his blood, we abide in him
and he in us. The parable of the vine in John 15 shows
that to abide in the Lord and live a life of faith mean
the same thing. In John 6 when Jesus speaks about eating his flesh and drinking his blood, he is speaking of the
act and attitude of soul in which we appropriate Christ
as our life and salvation. In Galations 2:20, Paul says
that the life which he now lives, which is Christ living
in him, is by faith in the Son of God. In Ephesians 3:17
Paul prays for the Ephesians that Christ may abide in
their hearts by faith.

It is a question as to whether this life in union with Christ should be spoken of as mystical. Some would call this Christian mysticism. Others object to calling mystical anything that is Christian. They do this on the ground that mysticism is nonrational—a matter of losing oneself in God or the All in an unconscious or superconscious state. If mysticism is to be identified with such an unconscious state or superconscious rapture, then this union with Christ should not be called mysticism. Paul and others may have had states of rapture of which they could give no very rational account. (See 2 Cor. 12:1 ff.). But it would be a mistake to identify the life in Christ with such experiences. Paul himself seems to regard them, along with speaking in tongues (1 Cor. 14), as superfluities and luxuries of the Christian life rather than being of its essence. But being united to Christ by faith is not a luxury or superfluity. It is of the essence of that life. It is that without which the Christian life cannot be.

This life is mystical in the sense that a Power outside of and beyond man lays hold of him, comes into his life and takes possession of him. It is superrational in the sense that it is beyond man's power thoroughly to comprehend. But so are many facts of life—one might say, all the facts of life.

The fact that this life in Christ is by faith is a guarantee that it will not be a life of blind unconscious or superconscious mysticism. The gospel of Christ is a gospel of truth. Nobody in the New Testament emphasizes this more than Paul. Paul argues, pleads, coaxes, persuades, labors day and night that his converts may be intelligent. He appeals to the mind of his hearers and readers. He does not think of a believer as one who blindly stumbles into the Christian life. He thinks rather of the Christian as one who hears and apprehends in an intelligent manner the truth as it is in Jesus, then grows in the Christian life by a constantly growing apprehension and appropriation of that truth.

With these writers (Paul and John), as everywhere else in the New Testament, faith is an intelligent act. It is first of all perception and appropriation of the truth. The life in union with Christ is a life of faith, and faith without the element of intelligent apprehension would not be faith.

3. *Union with the living Christ*

This conception of union with Christ by faith has no meaning apart from the New Testament teaching that Jesus is now the risen, reigning Lord. The faith that saves is not simply faith that looks back to the historic Jesus; it looks up to the living Christ. Christ is a living person with whom we must be vitally united by faith if he saves us from our sins. The cry "back to Christ," meaning back to the historic Jesus of the Synoptic Gospels and away from the transcendent Christ of Paul and John, is a motto that means to devitalize Christianity, for merely a historic Christ cannot save. He must be superhistoric. As a matter of fact, the Christ of the Synoptic Gospels is just as transcendent as the Christ of John and Paul. But some of the critics think they get in the Synoptic Gospels a Christ with no element in him that cannot be measured in terms of human life and history. The Christ who is presented in the New Testament as the object of saving faith is the Jesus who having been slain by wicked hands was raised from the dead by God (Acts 2:23-24; 5:30-31). He is the Christ who in the Spirit can be called Lord (1 Cor. 12:3). We do not merely reach back by a stretch of imagination over nineteen centuries to the Jesus of history; we reach up by faith to the Christ who lives and reigns at the right hand of God.

This Christ with whom we were united by faith is not only the one who rose from the dead and lives forevermore; he is the Eternal One. He is the One who said of himself: "Before Abraham was born, I am" (John 8:58). The fact that he was eternal made it possible for Abraham to see his day. Abraham saw him as the

One who transcends time. He is the One in whom all things consist and unto whom all things were created (Col. 1:16-17). He is the One who is the effulgence of God's glory, the very image or reproduction of his substance, and who upholds all things by the word of his power (Heb. 1:3).

4. *Union with God*

This union with the living Christ is union with God. The significance of this union with Christ is that in him we come to know God with all that that implies. To talk about union with Christ signifies nothing if he is nothing more than a historic character whom we know through the New Testament records. These records are essential, for the Christ we know in Christian experience is not another than the historic Christ, yet he is more than historic. He not only lived a life in time and space, but in his resurrection and ascension he transcended the historical order. And when we know him as the transcendent Christ we are conscious that in knowing him we know God. Our consciousness of union with Christ and with God are inseparable. No man knows the Father except the one to whom the Son wills to reveal him (Matt. 11: 27). For a knowledge of God we are absolutely dependent on Jesus Christ his only begotten Son. But in and through the Son we do know the Father. It is not a question between knowing God in Christ and knowing God outside of Christ. It is a choice between knowing God in Christ and not knowing him at all. The claims of Jesus in this respect are absolutely true to experience and have been vindicated in experience. Outside of an experiential knowledge of Jesus Christ as Saviour and Lord, men may speculate about God and come to hold certain opinions about him that are correct; but they never come to know God himself. But by faith in Jesus as Saviour and Lord men are vitally united to God in an experience that constitutes such a knowledge of God as means nothing less than salvation from sin.

The Gospel of John which puts so much stress on union with Christ also tells us that to know Christ is to know God. This Gospel tells us that there is no other way to know him. No man has seen God at any time; the only begotten Son who is in the bosom of the Father he has declared him (1:18). And Jesus said: "He that hath seen me hath seen the Father" (14:9).

5. *Union with Christ through the Spirit*

This union with Christ is something that takes place in the realm of spiritual experience. We have said that the Christ that we know in this experience is more than the Christ of history. He is not another Christ, but he is more than historical. And our knowledge of him is of a higher order than that in which we know the facts of history or of everyday life. Paul says that no man can call Jesus Lord save in the Holy Spirit (1 Cor. 12:3). The Christ we thus know is time-transcending in nature. He is eternal and spiritually omnipresent. He goes with his people to the last place and to the consummation of the age (Acts 1:8; Matt. 28:20).

This Christ cannot be known apart from the Spirit of God, and knowing him is a recreative experience. It gives a different tone and quality to one's whole experience and life.

Paul says that if any man is in Christ there is a new creation (2 Cor. 5:17). It is a transaction in which God's creative power through his Spirit is at work in the realm of character and producing a new result.

This union with Christ is not to be interpreted after the pantheistic fashion. Our union with Christ does not mean the losing of the finite self in the infinite All. The surrender of our wills to the will of God in Christ does not mean the losing of our wills. It does not mean to annul personality. It does not mean the throwing off of moral responsibility by merging oneself in the impersonal Absolute. It means rather the finding of oneself. The prodigal son went home to his father when he came to himself (Luke 15:17). One never comes to himself until he comes to Christ. When one comes to Christ he finds his will invigorated, his mind quickened, his moral nature renewed—he finds himself.

IV. God's Saving Act

Every blessing that we enjoy as Christians grows out of our union with Christ. A full discussion, therefore, of union with Christ would involve all that follows in regard to salvation. So we will take up next what God does for us in Christ.

Thus we see that by faith we are brought into union with Christ. As a result we are brought into a new relationship with God. God does something for us. The most general term used in theology, and perhaps in the New Testament, for what God does for us is salvation. But there are many ways in the New Testament to represent what God does for us in Christ. Some of these we will now consider.

1. *In Christ God forgives our sins*

When man sins against God two things result. Man is alienated from God, and God's displeasure comes on man. In saving us man's alienation is changed in his repentance and God's displeasure is removed.

(1) Scriptures setting forth the idea

As already stated, in Old Testament times emphasis was laid on other forms of deliverance, such as deliverance from enemies (Psalm 27:1 ff; Jer. 23:5 ff.), deliverance from disease (Psalm 103:3), and deliverance from death (Psalm 49:14-15). But even in the Old Testament salvation from sin was the chief blessing. We might look at several passages in which forgiveness of sins is set forth. In Psalm 32 David speaks of the blessedness of the man "whose transgression is forgiven, whose sin is covered." The Lord does not impute to him iniquity, and in his spirit there is no guile. So long as he kept silence and refused to confess his sin, God's hand was heavy upon him; he was scorched with the drought of summer. But when he confessed his sin, the Lord forgave the iniquity of his sin. We have a close parallel to this in Psalm 51. This psalm is even yet a classic, and will be to the end of time, in which a soul convicted of sin pours out its confession to a God of mercy and pleads for forgiveness and cleansing. The penitent in each of these cases has come to recognize that sin has broken his communion with God and that there is no possibility of peace and joy for him until his sin is forgiven and he is cleansed from its defilement. In Psalm 103, along with the blessing of being healed of disease, praise is ascribed to Jehovah because he forgives iniquities (v. 3). He does not deal with us after our sins, nor reward us according to our iniquities (v. 10). Because of his transcendent lovingkindness (v. 11) and fatherly pity (v. 13), he removes our transgressions as far from us as the east is from the west (v. 12).

In Jeremiah 31:31-35, the prophet tells about a new covenant that Jehovah will make with his people. This covenant will not be like the old covenant that he made with them in delivering them from Egypt. That covenant they did not keep. This covenant will be based on a greater deliverance than the deliverance from Egypt. It will be based on a deliverance from sin. He will forgive their iniquity, and their sin will he remember no more. This will give such an inner knowledge of God that they will keep this covenant. By this forgiveness the knowledge of God will be put in their hearts.

In the New Testament the forgiveness of sins is one of the fundamental blessings that men were to receive in the messianic salvation. John the Baptist was to "go before the face of the Lord to make ready his ways; to give knowledge of salvation in the remission of sins" (Luke 1:76-77). Forgiveness of sins was one of the elemental blessings that Jesus taught his disciples to pray for (Matt. 6:12; Luke 11:4). After the resurrection Jesus commissioned his disciples to preach, in his name, remission of sins, upon condition of repentance, to all the nations (Luke 24:47). Peter announced to the people at Pentecost that after repentance they should be baptized unto the remission of sins (Acts 2:38). He preached to Cornelius and the company assembled at his house that the prophets all bear witness that through the name of Jesus every one who believes on him shall receive remission of sins (Acts 10:43).

In Ephesians 1:7 Paul says: "In whom [Christ] we have our redemption through his blood, the forgiveness of our trespasses" (cf. Col. 1:14). This seems to identify redemption and forgiveness of sins; at least, it makes forgiveness the chief element in redemption. Without forgiveness there is no redemption.

This list of passages is by no means exhaustive, but it is representative of the teaching of the Bible on the subject. It shows that forgiveness of sins was the fundamental blessing of the gospel of Christ. That idea was not unknown to Old Testament saints, but the idea comes out in its clearness and fulness in the new dispensation. The book of Hebrews shows that the forgiveness of sins was an essential element in the new covenant. It was in the forgiveness of sins that men should know God (8:11-12). This was in accordance with the prophecy of Jeremiah (Jer. 31:31-34).

(2) The meaning of forgiveness

We might inquire a little more particularly as to what is meant by the forgiveness of sins. The term translated to forgive in the New Testament means to send away. It is exactly our term to remit, send back or away. To remit sins is to put them away. But still the question remains: To put them away in what sense? What does it mean to put away sins? It does not mean to put away in any mechanical or spatial sense. Sins cannot be put away thus. To remit sins is evidently a figure of speech. Sometimes the matter was thought of as analogous to the releasing of a debtor. Jesus thought of it thus when he taught the disciples to pray: "Forgive our debts as we forgive our debtors" (Matt. 6:12).

We have the impressive statements in the Old Testament that God puts our sins behind his back (Isa. 38:17) and remembers them no more (Jer. 31:34). He casts them in the depths of the sea (Micah 7:19). He washes us, and makes us whiter than the snow (Psalm 51:7).

It is not exactly true to say that to forgive sin is to make us as if we had not sinned. This is not true in the consciousness of the sinner. The consciousness of a forgiven sinner is not the same as the consciousness of one who has not sinned. "Once a sinner always a sinner—in this sense at least, that he who has but once sinned can never be as if he had never sinned. His very blessedness to all eternity is a different thing from the blessedness of the sinless. The man whose iniquity is not imputed is a very different being from the man whose iniquity was never committed."[1]

But forgiveness does mean that sin is removed as a barrier to our fellowship with God. Sin breaks man's fellowship with God. It is a personal offense against God. "Against thee, thee only have I sinned, and done that which is evil in thy sight" (Psalm 51:4). "Your iniquities have separated between you and your God, and your sins have hid his face from you, so that he will not hear" (Isa. 59:2). As the Holy One of Israel, Jehovah will not accept the offerings of a sinful and rebellious people, nor hear their prayers. They must repent of their sins and do the right (Isa. 1). But when sin is forgiven, the block to fellowship is removed. The cloud that shuts out the face of God is blotted out. In this sense sin is remitted, sent away. It is like the revival of human fellowship after friends or loved ones have been separated by a wrong done by one to another. Forgiveness sought and obtained renews the former intimacy of confidence and love. It is this that gives to one the uplifting sense of freedom, peace, and joy upon realizing that his sins are forgiven. He is released from the enslaving sense of guilt. A great burden is gone from

[1]Forsythe, *Christian Perfection*, pp. 5-6.

the soul. A new light comes in. Often the whole face of nature seems to be transformed. A joy unspeakable and full of glory comes into the soul. We realize that we are loosed from our sins (Rev. 1:5), which have bound and enslaved us.

Forgiveness is a personal act that law, physical, social, or moral, cannot explain. Law knows nothing of forgiveness. There are those today who insist that law reigns in the world, and that there can be no variation from the reign of law; law is supreme and invariable. It does not make any difference what form the law may take; it may be physical law or it may be moral; but if law speaks the last word, forgiveness is excluded. There can be forgiveness only where personality and personal relations are the ultimate reality. God is a person and God is more than law, physical or moral. If a man does not believe in a personal God, he cannot believe in forgiveness of sins. On the other hand, the experience of the forgiveness of sins gives one such an assurance of relationship with a personal God that one cannot lose the consciousness of God without also losing the sense of forgiven sin. This transcendent act of God is an act that not only carries with it the idea of God's personality; it is also an act of grace on his part. As such it transcends law. Grace does not nullify law, but it transcends law. Law cannot forgive, but God can. Law cannot forgive, because law knows nothing about grace. Grace is a personal quality. It is the highest conceivable quality of moral character. Law cannot have character. Character belongs only to a person. Forgiveness, therefore, is an act of grace on the part of a personal God; and in this act the God of grace rises above but does not violate or nullify law.

But while this transcendent personal act on the part of God removes sin as that which blocks our fellowship with him, it does not immediately remove all the consequences of our sin. It does not take us out of the physical, historical, social, and moral order of things with which we are connected. It does show man's superiority to this order. It reveals man as of more worth than the whole order of things to which he belongs and of which he is the climax and goal. It shows that man is not enslaved in that order. It makes man the master of the order of things. It shows that this order exists for man. Nothing shows the transcendent worth of man and his mastery of the world order like the grace of God that forgives sins.

The grace of God that forgives sins and thus restores the sinner to the fellowship of a holy God will finally deliver the forgiven sinner from all the evil consequences of his sin. This is true both with reference to the individual and to the redeemed race. Sin broke man's fellowship with God and brought spiritual death, followed by a horde of evils consequent upon sin and spiritual death. When sin is forgiven, man's fellowship with God is restored and as a consequence all the ills that followed upon sin will be removed, but this cannot be done at a bound. To do so would probably mean violently to dislocate man from his historical, social, and moral connections as a member of the race and as a part of the order of nature.

For instance, a body that is maimed by disease, caused by sin, is not usually at least, restored to perfect soundness upon the forgiveness of sin. If one wastes the strength of youth in prodigal living, God will gladly forgive the penitent prodigal when he returns home, but the substance of his physical and sometimes his mental manhood is not given back to him in this life. Again, the social results of our sins are not always at once counteracted when our sins are forgiven. God forgave David his awful sins in connection with Bath-sheba and Uriah, but the sword never departed from David's house until his death. Many a bitter tear he shed over the consequences of his sin, although he knew the sweetness of God's forgiving grace. We see this clearly in the matter of physical death. The heart of the penalty of sin is spiritual death. But physical death came in consequence of sin. When one is forgiven, spiritual death is removed and the sinner is restored to communion with God. This means that in the end death in its completeness and totality will be abolished, but not this side of the resurrection. There are intimations, also, that the whole natural order will be renewed in the final consummation of things.

But while we are not at once delivered from all the consequences of our sins, when we are forgiven, we are put in such a relation with God that all the ills of life may become redemptive forces in our lives working for the one supreme purpose of transforming us into the image of Christ (Rom. 8:28 ff.). This will be discussed later on in connection with the Christian doctrine of providence.

The experience of the forgiveness of sins as a gracious act on God's part, not only removes sin as a barrier to fellowship with God, but also gives one an insight into the character of God that otherwise would be impossible. In other words, the forgiven sinner understands God, and consequently has a fellowship with God, that would be impossible for a man who had never sinned. How could a man who had never sinned understand that element in God's character that we express by the term grace? The grace of God is the most glorious element in his character according to the Christian view. This grace we know only in its redeeming work in our lives. A sinless being can never know a God of grace. The conception would have no meaning to him. Sometimes the preacher says that God might have sent angels to announce the gospel to sinful men rather than send redeemed sinners. But to say the least of it, this is doubtful. What would an unfallen angel know about the grace of God that saves a sinner? The sinner who has experienced God's redeeming grace knows, and can make the other sinner know, something of that grace. He has an insight and a fellowship, and undying love for a God of grace that an unfallen sinner, man or angel, will be a stranger to for all eternity. Redemption in Christ, then, does not put man back in the place of an unfallen Adam. It puts him on a new basis, gives him an insight into God's character and fellowship with God that such an Adam could never have. It, therefore, gives him a type of holiness that would be impossible for such an unfallen man. For instance, the redeemed sinner will, as a result of an experience of God's grace in saving him, have reproduced in his life the quality of grace in relation to his fellows. This is seen in that the redeemed man has in him the spirit of grace as manifested in his evangelistic and missionary spirit. Such a spirit is not something incidental or accidental in the Christian life; it is of the essence of Christianity. An unfallen Adam might be a man of legalistic justice; he could hardly be a man of grace. Hence the redeemed sinner will be a better man than the unfallen Adam could ever have been. This does not mean to excuse or to condone sin but to glorify the grace of God.

We might say, then, that the forgiveness of sins is the fundamental blessing in salvation, and that the forgiveness of sins through the grace of God changes the whole of life into a redemptive order. The ills of life that before were of a fundamentally retributive aspect now become primarily remedial and redemptive in that they can, by God's grace, be made to contribute to the development of Christian character.

(3) Objections to the doctrine of forgiveness

We may now consider two objections to the doctrine of the forgiveness of sins through the grace of God. One is an objection to the doctrine from the standpoint of the divine nature; the other is with reference to the supposed effect of the doctrine upon the life of the forgiven sinner.

The first objection is that the doctrine of forgiveness is not consistent with the unchangeableness of the divine nature. God cannot change, we are told. So the change is not in God, it is in the sinner. It is like riding a bicycle against the wind. While one is riding against the wind, he feels the force of the wind resisting him and holding him back. But when he turns around and rides with the wind, he feels the wind bearing him on. So, while living in sin and resisting God, one is conscious of the divine resistance; but when one readjusts himself in his relation to sin and God, he feels the divine love and approval bearing him on toward the goal. But just as it was not the wind but the rider that changed, so we are told, it is not God that changes, but man. When man changes, he feels as if God had changed. This is sometimes carried to the extent of denying that God changes in his attitude toward the sinner. All the change, we are told, is in the sinner.

But while it is true that the sinner changes when he repents of his sin toward God, this only states one side of the matter. God does not change in his ultimate purposes concerning the individual or the race, in his attributes or his nature, but God does change in his attitude toward the sinner when the sinner changes. God is not the slave of his own immutability. Nor is God an impersonal force. He is a moral personality. As a person he can will. As moral his attitude is not the same toward the sinner and the righteous. This objection would not only make forgiveness impossible; it would make any new beginning on God's part impossible. There could be no miracle. The incarnation is logically ruled out on this ground. God could not have willed at a definite point in history to enter into an essentially new relation to the race in the person of Jesus Christ. Creation also would be impossible. So would recreation or regeneration. Revelation as an act of self-disclosure on God's part goes, too; on this view revelation is only man's feeling out after, and perhaps his discovery of, some truth about God. Everything distinctive in Christianity would disappear on this view. God becomes only an impersonal force and his immutability becomes the stagnation of death.

This objection falls in with the view that denies that God pronounces upon the sinner any condemnation. As guilt is interpreted to mean only a guilt consciousness, so forgiveness is interpreted to mean only a subjective feeling on the sinner's part, not involving any change on God's part. The change was in the sinner. But we must insist that forgiveness is more than a subjective feeling to which corresponds no objective reality. We must maintain this position if we would do justice either to the biblical teaching or to Christian experience. Forgiveness is God's act. He changes his attitude toward the penitent sinner. It is the apprehension of this changed attitude on God's part that brings peace and joy to the sinner's heart.

This is practically the same objection as the one considered a few paragraphs back in which forgiveness was denied on the ground of the inviolability of law. It makes no difference whether God is enslaved by his own immutability or the invariability of law; in either case his personal activity in forgiving sin is denied, and in either case salvation in the Christian sense of the term is impossible. The view of forgiveness implied in this objection answers to the view of sin that speaks of the guilt consciousness of the sinner but denies or ignores guilt as an objective reality in the sinner's relation to God. If there is no objective guilt, there is no need of an objective forgiveness. If God does not condemn sin, there is no need that he should forgive. If, on the other hand, God as a holy God condemns sin, the only hope for the sinner is in God's forgiving grace. If sin, as committed against God's holiness, breaks man's fellowship with God, then the only thing that can renew that fellowship is to have the guilt of sin removed in an act of remission that puts away the guilt of sin.

The other objection to the doctrine of forgiveness as an act of grace on God's part is that it will encourage the sinner to live in sin. Will God's gracious forgiveness of sin encourage the forgiven sinner to live in sin?

We answer, No; but on the other hand it will deliver from sin.

Briefly consider some reasons for this answer. First, because forgiveness is on the basis of the redeeming work of Jesus. Sin is not forgiven without an adequate expression of God's holy displeasure against sin. In the cross of Christ God condemned the world's sin. Let no one think that forgiveness is an easygoing thing, either for God or for man. If one thinks that forgiveness is an easy matter, let him remember how hard it is for man to forgive his fellow man; for society to forgive those who violate its conventions and proprieties; for the state to forgive the criminal. Forgiveness cost God much. It cost him his best, even his only begotten Son. It is in the blood of Jesus that we have redemption, even the forgiveness of our trespasses (Eph. 1:7; Col. 1:14). It is in the blood of Jesus that we are loosed from our sins (Rev. 1:5).

Secondly, because our forgiveness is conditioned upon our repentance. In repentance we repudiate sin. We condemn sin with something of the same hatred and horror of it that God had for it in condemning it in Christ's cross. This is a revolutionary, a regenerative experience. One can never think, feel, or act toward sin as he did before repenting.

This is brought out in what Jesus says about our forgiveness as being conditioned on our forgiving our fellow man. Jesus says that if we forgive not, neither will the Heavenly Father forgive us (Matt. 6:15). How searching that statement! How exacting of petty, vengeful human nature! Forgiveness is such a revolutionary experience that one cannot claim it unless he finds reproduced in his own attitude toward his fellow man something of God's gracious attitude toward him. Only as God's grace reproduces itself in us can we claim that grace has nullified sin in us. Unless our fellowship with the God of grace is so real that we find ourselves in a very practical and searching way manifesting a genuine communion of that grace, we cannot claim that our sins are put away by his grace. "There is forgiveness with thee that thou mayest be feared" (Psalm 130:4). What a sense of reverence, of awe, of holy horror for sin and righteous fear of God did we find in our hearts when first we found that by faith in the crucified One our sins had been remitted; and with every passing day the wonder grows, our horror of sin deepens, and our reverential fear of God, the God of all grace, increases.

We see, then, that forgiveness is not just the remission of penalty. If that is all that forgiveness meant, it would not be salvation from sin; it would only cancel the evil consequences of sin and leave man in sin. What men need to see, what they will see if they really repent, is that the great evil is not punishment for sin, but sin itself. When God forgives, sin itself is undone. In other words, it is a transaction that changes a sinner into a saint.

2. *In Christ we are justified*

Justification in the New Testament is a Pauline doctrine. No other New Testament writer uses this term to any appreciable extent to express salvation. In one of his parables, Jesus spoke of the publican as going down to his house justified rather than the Pharisee (Luke 18:14). For Paul this is the main term for expressing what God does for the believing sinner.

(1) The doctrine defined

Notice that it is something that God does for the sinner. There is such a thing as the justification of the righteous. This means that the righteous is vindicated as being righteous and on the ground that he is righteous. It is in this sense that the word is used when it is said that wisdom is justified of her children (Luke 7:35); that is, the children of wisdom act in such a way as to vindicate the ways of wisdom. Again, Jesus tells us that the publicans and all the people "justified God," on hearing the message of John the Baptist, by responding to the message and acting on it, while the Pharisees and lawyers rejected for themselves the counsel of God (Luke 7:29). The people justified God by responding in such a way as to say that God was right. They endorsed God's message as given by his messenger. Paul incorporates the meaning of Psalm 51:4, "that thou mightest be justified when thou speakest," in Romans 3:4 when he says, "That thou [God] mightest be justified in thy words," thus showing God to be in the right.

We have no difficulty in understanding this use of the term. It means that one who is seen to be in the right is endorsed as being so. The righteous man or cause is vindicated as being righteous. The difficulty comes when we are told that God justifies the ungodly (Rom. 4:5).

Paul's doctrine is that the sinner, who has been under God's condemnation on account of his sin, upon condition of faith in Christ, is forgiven and received into God's favor. The difficulty lies in the fact that the doctrine is paradoxical. Paul states and defends the doctrine at length in his epistles to the Galatians and to the Romans. In these epistles Paul sets out this doctrine of justification by faith over against the idea of justification by works. He affirms that the latter is impossible. No flesh shall be justified in God's sight by works of law (Rom. 3:20). That kind of justification would be a justification of the righteous. It would simply be a recognition of man's goodness. In that case, God would only give man credit for what he had earned; he would pay him what was his (man's) due. Whatever God did for man would be in payment of a debt (Rom. 4:4).

The paradox of Paul's doctrine is that God does not justify the righteous but justifies the sinner. He justifies the unrighteous rather than the righteous. God's justifying act here is something more than a recognition of man's attainment; it is more than a declaration of the status quo. Justification by works would simply be God's recognition of man's achievement. In Paul's doctrine he emphasizes that justification is by grace on

God's side and by faith on man's. It is not something that man achieves; it is something that he receives. Man receives what God gives. Paul emphasizes that it is a gift on God's side, a gift of grace.

The theme of the book of Romans is found in the phrase "the righteousness of God." Paul uses this phrase in two senses. He uses it to designate a quality in God's character. It denotes an attribute of the divine Being. It is used in this sense in Romans 3:25-26 when the apostle tells us about the work of Christ as showing the righteousness of God. Here the author evidently means that God's character is shown to be righteous in the and our sins in Christ in such a way as to show that he is a righteous God and so that his character is not compromised in saving us.

But Paul uses this expression, the righteousness of way that he saves sinners in Christ. God deals with us God, in a different sense, even in this same paragraph. In Romans 3:21-22, he speaks of "the righteousness of God" as something that God bestows on men in Christ upon condition of faith. He has just concluded a lengthy argument to show that all men are sinners and that no one can be justified by works of law. Justification or righteousness[2] is something that God gives, not something that man earns.

In Romans 1:17, Paul says that in the gospel "is revealed a righteousness of God from faith unto faith." He bases this on an Old Testament text: "The righteous shall live by faith" (Hab. 2:4). He thus connects this righteousness of faith received as a gift from God with the Old Testament. He says that this righteousness of God revealed in the gospel is witnessed by the law and the prophets (Rom. 3:21). In chapter four of this book he cites David (Psalm 32) and Abraham (Gen. 15:6) as examples of justification by faith, thus making the prin-

---

[2]It is important to keep in mind that these two words in our New Testament are the translation of the same Greek word.

ciple of justification by faith the unifying principle of the Old and New Testaments.

In summing up the meaning of this doctrine, we might emphasize three things:

One is that it is the justification of the sinful. God must justify the righteous if men are to be judged on the basis of their own attainments. But there are none righteous before God. All have sinned and fall short of the glory of God (Rom. 3:23). Jew and Gentile —all men—rest under the judgment of God. Men could be justified by the deeds of the law if they could keep the law; but no man does this. The failure is not in the law, but in the weakness of the flesh (Rom. 7:12; 8:3). The justification of the sinner means that, when the sinner believes in Christ, he is delivered from the condemnation resting on him because of his sin, and is received into God's favor. He is accepted of God on account of his faith in Christ rather than condemned on account of his sin.

The second thing is that men are justified on condition of faith. Faith is set over against works of law. We do not earn our acceptance with God by deeds of law; we receive it as God's free gift. It is by faith on our part, because it is by grace on God's part (Rom. 4:16). God gives, we receive. Our faith appropriates what God offers in mercy.

Sometimes the argument is made that, since our salvation is conditioned on faith, then after all it depends on something that we do. Then it is said that it could depend on baptism or any other prescribed condition as well as on faith. But this misunderstands the nature of faith. Faith cannot be put in the category of works that man does. Paul sets it over against works of law by way of contrast. Justification by faith is the antithesis of justification by works. Justification by works is a plan by which man seeks to put God under obligation to him by performing certain things required by God. Justification by faith is a plan in which man gives up all

claim on God, recognizing that he can do nothing to
merit God's blessing. Instead of claiming something
from God, he receives something as a gracious gift. Faith
then is not a work. It is rather the sinner's recognition
that he can do nothing and that whatever is done for
him must be done by a God of mercy. Faith gives up all
effort to do for oneself and gives way for God to do.
It is not doing something, it is getting self out of the
way so that God can do something.

The third thing is that justification by faith is based
on Christ's work for us. The faith that justifies is not
a dependence on something that the sinner does for himself; it looks rather to Christ and what he has done for
us. Justification by faith is grounded in the work of
Christ on our behalf. It is through the redemption that
is in Christ Jesus that we are justified (Rom. 3:24). We
are justified in his blood (Rom. 5:9).

(2) The doctrine perverted

The doctrine has been badly perverted in Protestant
theology. We do not refer now to the objection, always
urged by some to the doctrine of salvation by grace, that
this doctrine would encourage people to live in sin. That
objection is raised to the idea of God's gracious forgiveness of sin, as we have seen. There have always been
those who objected to the Christian doctrine of salvation
on the ground that it was too easy and who held that
the only way to produce moral living was on the basis
of law without mercy. But that method will not produce the highest type of living; it will lead to despair
on the part of a sensitive conscience.

The perversion of the doctrine that we refer to is its
perversion by Christian interpreters—orthodox and liberal. Protestant theologians in general have defined
justification as a judicial or forensic act on God's part.
We are told that the word translated to justify was a legal
term; that it meant to declare just; that it was equivalent to pronouncing one accused of crime not guilty.
Furthermore, we were often told that to acquit a crimi-

nal did not mean that he had not committed the crime, but that it means that he was not legally bound after that to answer for the crime before the law. He was released from responsbility to the law for the crime of which he had been accused. This, we are told, was done on the basis that Christ had paid the penalty for the sinner's sin.

This way of interpreting the matter often set justification as a "judicial" act over against regeneration or the new life in Christ. These were distinguished as the legal and vital aspects of salvation. The more orthodox writers usually were careful to tell us that God did not stop with justifying the sinner, but that he also regenerated him as well; that in justification the sinner was given a new standing with God, while in regeneration he was given a new life, this to be followed with sanctification in which the new life would be developed to its fulness. Some writers of a more radical type used this method of interpreting Paul to discredit his whole interpretation of Christianity, including his doctrine of the person of Christ, the atonement and salvation by grace. Oftentimes the question was discussed as to which was the dominant factor in Paul's teaching—the legal or the vital. Also liberal theologians took advantage of such an interpretation of Paul to set him over against Jesus. Jesus was set out as having taught a religion in which God was regarded as the Father of all men; all men were encouraged to come to him in penitence for their misdeeds; God stood ready to forgive without atonement or mediation of any kind. Over against this Paul was set out as the originator of dogmatic and supernatural Christianity, thus perverting the beautiful and ethical Christianity taught by Jesus.

This interpretation of Paul's doctrine of justification as forensic has been the dominant one in Protestant theology. A good example of this interpretation is to be found in Sanday and Headlam's Commentary on Romans in the International Critical Series. This work on

Romans is one of great scholarship. These writers set out that justification is a "forensic" act, that it has reference to a "judicial verdict, and to nothing beyond."[3] They insist that this construction be put on the matter, although this should reduce the state effected by justification to a "fiction." This method of interpreting Romans says that the apostle gives in chapters 1-5 his doctrine of justification and in chapters 6-8 his doctrine of the new life, or sanctification.

The same interpretation of justification as a forensic act is found in Beyschlag's *New Testament Theology*.[4] He says that the attempt to deduce the new life from justification on exegetical grounds has failed. The expressions "justification of life" in Romans 5:18, and to "reign in life" in 5:17, 21 he refers to the "future blessed life, the hope of which is disclosed to him (the sinner) by justification."

These two are selected as samples of this method of interpreting Paul's doctrine of justification as forensic. Many others could be cited. Our position is that the whole discussion of Paul's doctrine of justification as legal or forensic misses the point. He used a legal term (justification, the same is true of adoption), but he did not use it in a legal sense. Paul had no legal doctrine of justification. He put a new meaning into the term. In this and in a number of other instances, Paul and other New Testament writers adopted a current term but put new life and content into it. To insist that, because this was a legal term, Paul used it to describe a legal transaction is to confuse the form with the substance in interpreting the New Testament, and to deny that Paul had any originality in his use of language. It is not a safe method to consult a lexicon to discover in what sense the Greek language of Paul's days used this term and then say with finality that Paul used it only in that sense. Before coming to a final conclusion as to what Paul

---

[3] Page 36, Elworth Edition, 1906.
[4] See *New Testament Theology*, by W. Beyschlag (English Translation), Vol. II, pp. 183 ff.

meant by this term, we need to give close attention to
Paul's whole discussion of this doctrine. His whole discussion will give us what he means, not the lexical definition of one term that he uses. Our contention is that
Paul's whole discussion shows that he uses this term to
describe a vital experience, not a forensic transaction.

Paul's doctrine of justification as set out in Romans,
chapters 1-5, is not a forensic transaction but a vital
one. In these chapters, and elsewhere in his writings,
Paul passes from forensic terms to terms expressing union
with Christ and life without the slightest jar or hesita-
tion. These terms are so interwoven as to show that in
Paul's mind they express phases of a unitary view of
the Christian life, not a patchwork representation of
different (and almost discordant) views. Now if Paul
has a unitary view, it must be considered vital and not
forensic. His forensic terms can be viewed in a vital
sense and as expressing phases of a vital interpretation of
salvation; but his vital terms cannot be regarded as
phases of a forensic interpretation. Beyschlag is clearly
wrong when he refers such expressions as "justification of
life" and "reign in life" and the blessings of the justified
life (in Rom. 5:1-11) to the future world. Paul is thinking about the justified man as enjoying peace with God,
as rejoicing in hope, as having the love of God shed
abroad in his heart, and as enjoying life, eternal life, here
and now. He is thinking of these blessings as coming to
the justified man as a direct result of his justification.
And when we say as a direct result of his justification,
we do not mean a result beyond justification and distinct
from it, but rather as something involved in justification
itself.

Moreover, Paul is setting out in Romans, chapters 6-8,
not something in addition to justification, but what is
involved in justification. Paul's thought on two sides
seems after this order: sin, condemnation, death; faith,
justification, life. We contend that in Romans 6:1 ff.
Paul is not saying that, in an experience to be distin-

guished from justification, the believer dies to sin and rises to walk in newness of life; but he is saying that justification itself is such an experience. He is setting out what justification itself means, not something in addition to justification.

This is also true of what he says in chapter 8. In this chapter he discusses life in the Spirit. This life in the Spirit he does not think of as something in addition to justification but as a privilege belonging to the justified. This chapter begins with language that describes the justified. There is no condemnation for those who are in Christ Jesus. Justification is the opposite of condemnation; it is deliverance from condemnation. To be justified, then, is to be in Christ Jesus; and to be in Christ Jesus is to have "the law of the Spirit of life in Christ Jesus" set us free from "the law of sin and of death." It is to have a new life; it is to be delivered from the bondage that belongs to a servant of sin under the law. All the blessedness of life in the Spirit belongs by right to the justified man.

Dr. James Denny is right, then, when he says that justification is a regenerative transaction. He says that justification by faith is not a part of Paul's gospel; it is all of it. According to Dr. Denny, Paul teaches that justification regenerates, and that nothing else does.[5]

Justification is God's judgment on behalf of those who believe in Christ. It means that God takes their part, that he undertakes their deliverance. He is for them rather than against them. He is against those who set themselves against him. But when a man changes his attitude and gives himself up to God in Christ, then God undertakes for this man, and puts himself against all this man's enemies. God sets the whole course of the universe to working on behalf of such a man.

It has been a baseless charge, therefore, when men have tried to discredit Paul's gospel by saying that his

[5] See *Expositor's Greek Testament*. Vol. Two, p. 575.

doctrine of justification was a legal fiction; that is, that
it represented God as pronouncing a man righteous,
when, as a matter of fact, he was not righteous. It is
simply an act in which God forgives the sinner and receives him into his favor. It is no more a legal fiction
than is forgiveness. Nor is it true to say that it is a
forensic transaction in which a man is declared righteous
without being made so. He is made righteous in relation
to God. He is forgiven as a matter of mercy. God's
displeasure is removed. Such a change in relation to God
revolutionizes one in the deepest recesses of his being.
Such a one is made new. There is in his case a new
creation. All things become new.

The nearest thing in form in the New Testament to
Paul's doctrine of justification is what we find in John's
Gospel about Christ's power to judge and to give life.
This is well brought out in John 5:19 ff. Here Jesus
says that the Father has given him power to judge and
to give life. A careful reading of this passage shows that
the power to judge and to give life are two aspects of the
same thing. The believer passes out of death into life.
This is also described as passing out of judgment or condemnation. To be delivered from judgment (condemnation) is to have life. Paul describes this as justification.
To be justified is to have a favorable judgment from
God. It is to be delivered from condemnation. (Paul
uses a form of the same word that John uses for judgment.) The idea in both Paul and John is that a favorable judgment from God means life; an unfavorable
judgment means death. When we say, then, that Paul's
doctrine of justification is not forensic, we mean that it
is not forensic in the sense in which that term has been
used in Protestant theology; that is, a judgment favorable to the sinner but a judgment that did not change
the sinner's character nor bestow spiritual life. The
biblical idea of judgment is different from this in both
Old Testament and New. God's judgment meant life or
death. The biblical writers knew nothing of a judgment

of God that did not mean life or death. The idea of a forensic transaction in which God gave a judgment favorable to the sinner, delivered him from condemnation, but did not thereby bestow life on the sinner—such a conception is out of harmony with the ethical monotheism of both Testaments and with Paul's theology. It did not come from Paul except by a process of abstract thought that misinterpreted Paul. It is a fundamental fact of Old Testament religion that man lives by the favor of God. That idea is at the bottom of Paul's doctrine of justification. When God justifies a man he makes him right; that is, he makes him right with God. And in monotheistic religion to make a man right with God means everything. With the prophets of the Old Testament, that was the foundation of all religion and of all ethics. So was it with Paul and all New Testament writers. With Paul it was also the sum of all blessings. Paul indicates in Romans 8:31 ff. that, if God justifies us and is for us, we need not worry about anything else. If God is for us, nobody else can condemn us and nothing can separate us from the love of God. Who can be against us if God is for us?

Conservative theologians have tried to prevent the inevitable ill results of a forensic doctrine of justification by hastening to assert that Paul teaches regeneration or the new life in addition to justification. Nevertheless, those evil results have followed. The preaching of such a forensic doctrine—sometimes in popular and one-sided forms—has led to a superficial spiritual life. It has led people to feel that salvation was a transaction in which they might be delivered from the penalty of sin—be declared just—whether they were ever made righteous or not. Paul's doctrine of justification is something more radical than that and should not be blamed for such superficial results.

(3) The Roman Catholic doctrine of justification

One reason why Protestant theology has made such a sharp distinction between justification and regeneration was that it was trying to avoid the mistake of Roman Catholicism which identifies justification and sanctification[6] and says in substance that one is accepted of God only to the extent that he becomes actually righteous. So it holds that justification is not something complete once for all at the beginning of the Christian life, but something gradual and progressive. This idea Protestantism rightly rejected, saying that it makes the ground of our acceptance a goodness to be cultivated in the sinner and hence denies in principle the doctrine of salvation by grace. As a result of its position on this point, Romanism has no doctrine of assurance but rather holds that for one to claim assurance of acceptance with God is dangerous and presumptuous.

Over against the Roman doctrine Protestanism developed its doctrine of justification in which it held that the ground of justification was nothing in the sinner himself. Justification, it held, was the imputation to the sinner of the righteousness of Christ. And perhaps moved by the desire to make it perfectly clear that the ground of the sinner's justification was Christ rather than any goodness in himself, it emphasized the distinction between justification and regeneration. Protestant theology was so afraid that the sinner's change of heart or his own goodness might be made the ground of his justification that it thought that justification and regeneration must be kept distinct if not disjoined.

That justification and regeneration are not separate transactions is testified to by Christian experience. One is not conscious, in becoming a Christian, of two transactions, one in which he is acquitted of guilt or justified, and another in which he is renewed in his moral nature or regenerated. But he is conscious that in being justified from sin he is made a new creature in Christ Jesus.

This is far from the Romanist position that one is justified only to the extent that he is sanctified. In Paul's

---

[6]That is, sanctification in the sense of the progressive attainment of righteousness.

doctrine there is no danger of making one's own right-eousness the ground of one's acceptance with God. On the other hand, it is the fact that our justification is conditioned upon faith in Christ that makes it a re-generative transaction. When one comes to see that his salvation is dependent on Christ and what Christ has done for him and then puts his trust in Christ for sal-vation, it takes any spirit of self-righteousness or legal-ism out of one. It takes one entirely up out of himself and makes him altruistic in spirit. The fact that justi-fication is by faith guarantees, then, that this doctrine is the only basis upon which a righteous life can be built.

(4) Summary of the values of the doctrine

We may sum the matter up, then, by saying that the doctrine of justification by faith has the following values in the religious life:

a. It gives one assurance of acceptance once for all with a holy God. This it does because it recognizes that the sinner's acceptance with God is on the ground of Christ's redemptive work. The sinner puts his trust in Christ and his redemptive work for acceptance with God. Since Christ's offering was complete, made once for all, the sinner has assurance of a permanent, once-for-all acceptance with a God of righteousness.

b. Since it gives this assurance of acceptance with God on the basis of the redeeming work of Christ, it brings spiritual peace, joy, and freedom (Rom. 5:1 ff.). It is, therefore, the only doctrine that can meet legalism. It gives freedom from the law method of salvation and sets the spirit free to serve God in love and joy. Christ is the end of the law for righteousness to everyone that believeth (Rom. 10:4). That is, Christ puts an end to the law method of obtaining righteousness and brings in the method of faith. Therefore slavish fear is supplanted by filial trust. The old Jewish method of trying to earn righteousness with God is nullified, put out of business, by Jesus Christ, and, therefore, the bondage of the letter is supplanted by the freedom of the spirit. If the Son shall make you free, ye shall be free indeed.

c. The doctrine of justification by faith is the only basis upon which righteous men and women can be developed. So long as men try to earn salvation, their lives will be slavish and self-centered. But faith in Christ with reference to our acceptance with God takes us up out of our selfishness and faces us out to serve God and men.

3. *In Christ we are reconciled to God*

This is another term used by Paul to denote God's act of saving the sinner. This term means practically the same as justification. It views sin as causing an alienation or estrangement between God and man. When this alienation is removed the sinner is said to be reconciled to God.

That reconciliation is synonymous with justification is seen in Romans 5:9-10. In verse 9 Paul speaks of being justified in the blood of Jesus; in verse 10 he speaks of being reconciled to God through the death of his Son. It is clear that these two expressions refer to the same experience. Paul's statement in 2 Corinthians 5:19 shows the same thing, for he defines reconciliation as being the nonimputation of trespasses.

A question that arises in regard to reconciliation is whether man's reconciliation to God consists in the removal of man's enmity toward God, or whether it is the removal of God's displeasure toward man, or whether it is both. It has been argued that since the reconciliation is always spoken of as man's reconciliation to God and never as God's reconciliation to man, it means the removal of man's enmity toward God and not the removal of God's displeasure toward man. But the two passages just referred to as showing that reconciliation and justification are synonymous would show that this interpretation of the matter is wrong. If reconciliation is synonymous with justification, the nonimputation of sin,

then it involves a change in God's attitude toward
man. The same thing can be shown in another way. In
Romans 5:10 Paul speaks of our being reconciled to God
as enemies. What is meant by our being enemies? If
we can find the answer to that question, it will help us
to answer the question as to what takes place when we
are reconciled to God. Does Paul mean by our being
enemies to God that we are at enmity with God, or does
he mean also that God condemns us? Fortunately we
have another use of this term in the same letter that
will answer that question. It is in 11:28. Speaking of
Israel he says: "As touching the gospel, they are enemies
for your sake; but as touching election, they are beloved
for the fathers' sake." Here their being enemies is set
over against their being beloved. And since their being
beloved clearly describes God's attitude toward Israel,
the former term could not be limited to Israel's attitude
toward God. In Romans 5:10, when Paul speaks of the
enemies of God being reconciled, he does not mean by
enemies merely those who have enmity toward God, but
he means those who are condemned of God. For these
enemies to be reconciled to God, then, means the removal
of God's displeasure as well as the removal of man's
enmity toward God. There is a statement from Jesus
that shows the same thing. It is found in Matthew 5:23-
24. Jesus says that if one brings his gift to the altar,
and there remembers that his brother has aught against
him, he shall leave his gift before the altar, go and be
reconciled to his brother. Note that his brother has
something against him, but Jesus says he is to be reconciled to his brother. For him to be reconciled to his
brother means to remove his brother's enmity, not simply to dismiss his own. So for the sinner to be reconciled
to God means that the sinner shall receive the pardoning
grace of God. Doubtless it is meant to describe a mutual
transaction, but the emphasis seems to be on the removal
of God's displeasure in the nonimputation of sin.

4. *In Christ we are adopted into the family of God*

The term adoption seems to be used in three senses, or rather with reference to three different applications. In Romans 9:4 Paul uses it with reference to Israel as a nation in her peculiar relation to Jehovah. In Romans 8:23 he used it with reference to the redemption of the body in the resurrection for which the Christian anxiously waits. But the usual application of the term is with reference to our being made God's children spiritually when we become Christians. The term is a forensic term, as justification is, and denotes the act by which one not naturally a child is made legally the child and heir of the one who adopts him. The term, however, is not to be taken as describing merely a legalistic transaction. Paul in Romans 8:15 and Galatians 4:5 emphasizes the conscious possession of the Spirit in connection with our adoption or as a consequence of it, and shows that by this conscious possession of the Spirit we are delivered from the bondage of fear and of legalism. He also points out the fact that as a consequence of our adoption, we not only are made sons of God but also heirs, and, therefore, inherit with Christ all the spiritual riches of God.

It is evident that this term is, on one side, synonymous with justification, and, on the other, with regeneration. It is a legal term like justification used to describe what God does for us in saving us. Justification emphasizes the removal of the condemnation of sin; adoption emphasizes our new standing as sons in relation to God. Like regeneration, it puts our salvation in terms of sonship—adoption being the legal term, regeneration the experimental or biological term. The two ideas are so closely related that we will not dwell on adoption here but will pass on to discuss regeneration.

5. *In Christ we have new life*

(1) Some New Testament terms used for this idea.

One of the most common terms used in theology and in preaching to describe God's saving act is the term

regeneration. The term means to beget or generate
again. Our term new birth means practically the same.
The term regeneration has passed into religious termi-
nology mainly from the influence of the expression of
Jesus in John 3:3, 7, where he speaks of being begotten
or born again or more properly from above. Peter uses
the same word (compounded with a preposition) in 1
Peter 1:3, 23. There are other terms in the New Testament used to describe this experience of being renewed
in the grace of God. One is Paul's figure of a new creation. In 2 Corinthians 5:17, he says: "If any man is in
Christ, he is a new creature" (literally, "there is a new
creation"). Here the apostle describes this saving act
on God's part as being a creative act in which he so renews one that "the old things are passed away; behold,
they are become new." He says in Galatians 6:15: "For
neither is circumcision anything, nor uncircumcision, but
a new creature" (literally, creation). In Ephesians 2:10,
15; 4:24, and in Colossians 3:10, he uses the same figure.
In Romans 2:29 Paul says that true circumcision is that
of the heart, in the spirit, not in the letter. This evidently refers to regeneration as that which makes one a member of the true spiritual Israel. Another figure found in
Paul's writings and in some other places is that of death
and resurrection. In Romans 6:1 ff., Paul sets forth the
idea that the Christian is one who has died to sin and
risen to walk in newness of life. This death to sin might
be set forth in experimental terms as meaning repentance. To die to sin is to repent if we look at it as a
human act; if we look at it from the point of view of
the divine efficiency, it is equivalent to regeneration. In
Galatians 2:20 Paul says: "I have been crucified with
Christ; and it is no longer I that live, but Christ liveth
in me." In Galatians 6:14, he glories in the cross
through which the world has been crucified to him and he
to the world. (See also Gal. 5:24 and Col. 2:20.) This
reminds us of the saying of Jesus that if any man would
come after him, he must deny himself and take up his

cross. One shall lose his life by saving it and save it by losing it (Matt. 16:24-26). "Except a grain of wheat fall into the earth and die, it abideth alone; but if it die, it beareth much fruit" (John 12:24). "The hour cometh, and now is, when the dead shall hear the voice of the Son of God; and they that hear shall live" (John 5:25).

(2) The need of regeneration

The necessity of regeneration has been shown in a general way in our discussion of the doctrine of sin. In studying the doctrine of sin, we saw that sin was universal and that man was helpless in its power. In this sense man is totally depraved. He is entirely helpless in the power of sin unless and until delivered by the grace of God. If we look at the ethical and religious standard set up for men by Jesus, we see at once the necessity for regeneration. His standard was a high standard. If men get into the kingdom of heaven, they must have a righteousness exceeding that of the scribes and Pharisees (Matt. 5:20). The righteousness of the scribes and Pharisees was external and legalistic. Jesus demanded a righteousness that was inner—a righteousness of motive, purity of heart as well as of outward life (Matt. 5:21 ff.). The regenerating grace of God is the only thing that can give men the graces of character demanded in the Sermon on the Mount of those who are to be citizens of his kingdom. Jesus said that we should be perfect as the Father in heaven is perfect (Matt. 5:48). He recognized the law as demanding love for God with all the powers of one's being and love for one's neighbor as one loves himself (Luke 10:25 ff.). Such a standard brings only despair unless one is given some spiritual dynamic other than is to be found in the natural man.

The necessity of regeneration comes out clearly in Paul's discussion of the power of sin in human life. This is shown in the sixth and seventh chapters of Romans, especially the seventh, in which he gives a chapter out of his own spiritual experience. He describes his state of

unconsciousness of condemnation (v. 9a), his awakening
to a knowledge of the demands of the law and his sense
of condemnation and death that followed (vv. 9b-11), his
efforts to break the power of sin (vv. 15 ff.), and finally
his despairing cry for help (v. 24). Then comes his tri-
umphant victory in Christ Jesus (v. 25). In the eighth
chapter he says that the law (rule or dominion) of the
Spirit of life in Christ Jesus freed him from the law (rule
or dominion) of sin and death (v. 2). The thing that
the law could not do has now been done; sin has been
condemned in the flesh; that is, its power has been broken by the incoming of a power superior to the power of
sin, namely, the power of a new life in Christ Jesus (v.
3). Nothing short of the incoming of this new life would
do. The old man could not be cultivated into submission to the will of God, "for they that are after the flesh
mind the things of the flesh" (v. 5). "The mind of the
flesh is death" (v. 6) "The mind of the flesh is enmity
against God: for it is not subject to the law of God,
neither indeed can it be: and they that are in the flesh
cannot please God" (vv. 7-8). Some have thought that
Paul's statements here are unduly dark and pessimistic.
They have charged it up to his Pharisaism and have
tried to leave out this dark picture of the sinfulness and
helplessness of the natural man as not belonging to
Paul's best Christian thought. But this account shows
that this doctrine is not simply the remains of Paul's
Pharisaic dogmatism but grew up out of his own experience under the law and under grace. When he states
how the carnal mind is set against God and can bring
only condemnation and death, he is only telling us
what he knows from his own experience.

(3) The nature of the change

What kind of a change is regeneration? Just what
is it that takes place when a man is born again?

a. Someone might say that there is no use to discuss
that question, for the change is a mysterious one and

therefore, cannot be understood. So, it may be said, what is the use to try to understand it?

Can regeneration be understood? No, not entirely. It is a mystery, but so is most everything else we deal with. Jesus told Nicodemus that it was like the wind —as much as to say that the blowing of the wind was as much a mystery as regeneration; yet we know that it blows. So it is with the commonest facts and experiences of life. Matter is mysterious, mind is mysterious, will is mysterious, love is mysterious. Yet we know something about all of these. But we do not know all about any of them. Regeneration is a fact of experience, and we know something about it as a fact of experience, just as we know any of the other realities mentioned.

In seeking to understand what kind of a change regeneration is, there are two sources of information open to us, each of which is essential to the end in view. One is the New Testament teaching in regard to the matter; the other is experience, our own and that of others whose testimony is available for us. We have seen that the New Testament uses a variety of expressions to describe this transaction—most or all of them analogies drawn from other realms of life and experience to try to set forth the nature of this transaction. The very fact that so many different terms are used is evidence that we are dealing with an experience whose fundamental significance it is difficult to set forth. Yet by a study of these, especially in the light of our own experiences of the regenerating power of God's grace, we can know something of the nature and significance of this experience.

Certainly one would not be justified in assuming either of two attitudes in regard to the matter. One is to say that, since it is mysterious, there is no use to try to find out anything about it. That would be equivalent to saying that, because we cannot know all about it, there is no use to try to find out anything about it. To affirm that it is mysterious is to say that we know something about it. To know that there are limits to what we know is worth something. The other attitude we should not assume is the attitude of rejecting the idea because we cannot fully understand it. If we are going to accept only that which we understand fully, how much will we accept? Our creed would be brief indeed on that kind of a basis. We would not believe in our own existence, for that is manifestly a very mysterious thing. Yet we accept the fact whether we can fathom the depths of its significance or not.

b. This change is primarily of the nature of a moral and spiritual renewal. It is a change the main significance of which is to be found in the realm of character. In this change the fundamental moral disposition is changed. The affections and activities of life no longer center in self, but in God. Love for God and for one's fellows becomes the controlling factor in life. One dies to sin and rises to walk in newness of life (Rom. 6:1 ff.).

It is difficult for some to keep from thinking of regeneration as the addition of some kind of substance, or some new faculty to one's being. The "new creation," (2 Cor. 5:17), the "new life" that never perishes (John 5:21, et al.), the "divine nature" of which we are partakers (2 Peter 1:4),—all of these, they think, must signify the addition of a new metaphysical element or substance to one's being, and not a "mere" change in moral disposition. Dr. Strong seems almost to think of the matter thus, when he speaks of our sharing in a new humanity, of which Christ is head.[7] But let it be said that there is nothing that could happen to any man of more fundamental and far-reaching significance than a change in moral disposition. This is truly a new creation. It is of such tremendous significance that Paul can say because of it that old things are passed away; they are become new (2 Cor. 5:17).

A true philosophy is coming to see that the fundamental concept in regard to reality is not "substance," but personality. And the most meaningful thing about per-

[7] See *Systematic Theology*, Vol. III, section on regeneration.

sonality is the moral quality of the person, the question of character. A certain type of nonevangelical theology has taken for its slogan in recent years "Salvation by character," meaning by this the development of character within and of oneself rather than dependence on the "merits" or "imputed righteousness" of another. This "new theology" is right in its insistence on the idea that there can be no salvation apart from character.   There can be no salvation for man other than actually making him righteous.   And to the extent that a one-sided orthodox Protestantism has talked about being saved by an "imputed righteousness" apart from any righteousness of our own, as if we did not need to be made righteous, but could go to heaven on a righteousness transferred to our credit by a mere trick of bookkeeping—to the extent that it has meant that or made the impression that it meant that, to that extent has it deserved the scorn of all minds of any ethical perception or seriousness.   A justification that meant no more than that would indeed give one only a "fictitious righteousness."   But to save one is to make him righteous, and one is not saved except as, and to the extent that, he is made righteous.   But there can be no genuine and permanent righteousness apart from the grace of God manifested in Jesus Christ. The grace of God embodied and made available for us in Jesus Christ is the fact of fundamental significance for us.   So long as one fails to find and appropriate God savingly revealed in Christ, he misses the way of righteousness and truth.   Now regeneration is a transaction in which the moral nature is so changed that one can never again rest in a life of sin.   Righteousness becomes the passion of the soul.   This does not mean that all evil or sinful propensities are at a stroke eliminated from one's being; but it does mean that such a revolutionary transaction has taken place in the soul that it can never rest until it is free from sin.   The dominant passion of the soul becomes love for righteousness and hatred for sin. In principle the soul is made sinless.   This is why the man that is begotten of God cannot sin. He cannot live in sin as his natural and native element as formerly he did; he cannot habitually sin, cannot continually sin; he cannot live a life of sin (1 John 3:6-9).

c. This change is one that is wrought in the moral nature of man by the Spirit of God. Nothing but divine power could produce the change. Both experience and Scripture bear testimony to this. It is a new creation in which old things pass away and all things are made new (2 Cor. 5:17). It is a birth from above in which one is cleansed (born of water) and given a spiritual disposition (born of the Spirit) (John 3:3 ff.). It is a change that is not of blood (natural descent), nor of the will of man (human nature on its higher, spiritual side), nor of the will of the flesh (human nature on the lower side), but of God (John 1:12). God's power works this change. The gospel is the power of God unto salvation (Rom. 1:16). God draws men to Christ (John 6:44). The Spirit convicts of sin (John 16:8-11). This was manifested on the day of Pentecost. It was after the Spirit came that men hearing the gospel were pricked in their hearts and cried out, saying, "What shall we do?" (Acts 2:37.) All through the Acts and Epistles we find that it was the Lord who wrought with the disciples to save. No man can call Jesus Lord except in the Holy Spirit (1 Cor. 12:3). Paul may plant and Apollos water, but God must give the increase (1 Cor. 3:6). It is unto God that salvation is ascribed in the book of Revelation (12:10, et al.).

Christian experience bears witness to the same truth. The man who experiences regeneration knows as well as he knows daylight from darkness that he himself did not work the change. He submitted to God, and God changed him. He knows the power that deals with him as something new in his experience. He knows it as some power different and higher in nature than the social forces that influence his life. It is the spontaneous impulse of the Christian heart to thank God for one's own salvation or for the salvation of another.

d. The divine Spirit regenerates us by reproducing in us the moral and spiritual image of Jesus Christ. The thing that God had in mind for us in predestinating us to salvation is that we shall be made like Jesus Christ (Rom. 8:29). It is in Christ that we were chosen before the foundation of the world (Eph. 1:4). We do not know yet what our eternal destiny is to be, but we do know that, when Christ shall appear, we shall be like him, for we shall see him as he is (1 John 3:2). In regeneration one is crucified with Christ. The old man dies and Christ comes to live in us. By faith we are so united to him that he becomes the inner motive power and dominant passion of our lives. (See Gal. 2:20.) This was so true of Paul that he could say of himself, "To me to live is Christ" (Phil. 1:21). We are sometimes tempted to think of the saving work of the Spirit as being detached and unrelated to the person and work of Christ. This is a mistake. The Spirit came to bear witness to Christ (John 15:26; Acts 5:32). He regenerates us by making Christ to dwell in us the hope of glory (Col. 1:27).

e. This shows that, while it is the Spirit that regenerates us, ordinarily at least the Spirit uses means in renewing us. It is by the word of God that we are begotten again (1 Peter 1:23). Perhaps it would be going too far to say that God could not regenerate a man without the use of ordinary gospel agencies; yet we certainly are safe in saying that this is his usual way. We need not be dogmatic in limiting God to the use of such means. We can allow the infinite One some liberty to work in ways that we do not comprehend or know of. Yet when that is said, perhaps we are still warranted in saying that God regenerates, at least as a distinct experience such as brings one into conscious fellowship with God, only by using gospel agencies that give one a knowledge of Jesus as Saviour. This is necessary because man is a rational being. He is not saved in some magical way that has no relation to his rational and moral nature, but by coming into conscious fellowship with Christ. This is the point of what one might call Paul's philosophy of missions in Romans 10:12 ff.

f. This carries with it the idea that man is regenerated by faith. Through faith are we sons of God (Gal. 3:26). To as many as received him gave he the right to become the children of God (John 1:12). Faith is a regenerative act, because it brings one into union with God as revealed in Christ.

There has been an age-long debate between Calvinism and Arminianism as to which precedes, faith or regeneration. Calvinism has said that regeneration as God's quickening act must be first, because a dead man cannot act. An unholy man cannot perform a holy act. Then, it is said, to hold that man exercises faith before being quickened into life would be to hold that man within and of himself does something that brings the favor of God, and that cannot be allowed. On the other hand, those who hold the other position say that, if one is regenerated before he exercises faith, then man is saved without his own consent and God deals with him as a thing and not as a person.

We are sometimes told that we are not to think of either of these as coming ahead of the other in point of time, but that one precedes the other logically. The Calvinist says that logically regeneration must precede, since God's power is the cause of man's act; so God's quickening activity causes man's response in an act of faith. The Arminian, however, says that faith logically precedes, since faith is the condition of salvation. It is barely possible that each is right. Looked at in one way, faith may logically precede; looked at in another, the quickening power of God may precede. A more accurate way of expressing it is to say that faith and regeneration imply each other; they are inseparable; they are two aspects of one spiritual experience.

We must remember that we cannot have one without the other. You could not have a believer who was unregenerate, nor a regenerated man who was not a believer. The Calvinist is right in insisting that the power of God must regenerate and that man cannot within and of himself believe. God must produce faith in his heart. On the other hand, it is true that men are regenerated by faith. By faith we become the children of God. God regenerates. But he does not regenerate irrespective of man's faith. He regenerates by producing faith in man's heart. And regeneration is not complete until man exercises faith. In the act of faith on man's part regeneration is completed. So the question as to which precedes, regeneration or faith, becomes a meaningless question.

g. What has been said in the last few paragraphs will help to answer another question; namely, whether regeneration takes place in the conscious or the subconscious region of man's personality. Some hold that regeneration takes place in the subconscious mind. The discussions of William James[8] on the question of religion favor this view. Dr. Strong[9] states it very definitely in his theology. He says that regeneration takes place in the subconscious region of personality and is known only in its results. This falls in with the Calvinistic position that regeneration precedes repentance and faith, and is open to the same objections. If regeneration takes place in the subconscious region of personality and is known only by its results, then regeneration would hardly be a transaction on the moral plane, but would be a submoral transaction. In favor of the view is the suddenness of some conversions and the mysteriousness of the change. But while conversion is sometimes sudden, it is doubtful if there can be found a case in which there were not definite influences leading up to it. It is true that there is an element of mystery, a depth to the experience that we cannot fathom; yet it is not a magical, irrational,

[8] See *Varieties of Religious Experience.*
[9] See *Systematic Theology,* as above.

nonmoral transaction. It is a transaction in which man is in possession of his faculties, and it is never complete at least until one consciously and freely surrenders to Christ as Saviour and Lord. This is a conscious transaction.

6. *In Christ we are sanctified*

(1) Meaning of the term

It is customary at this point in treatises on theology to discuss the doctrine of "sanctification." This term, we are told, is used in the Bible in a twofold sense. It means, first of all, consecration or dedication to God. This use is frequent in the Old Testament and is not unknown in the New. Used in this sense it included things as well as persons and did not possess moral significance. The Temple, the altar, the city of Jerusalem—anything connected in a special way with Jehovah and his service—were spoken of as holy. We speak today of the Holy Land, the Holy City, holy days, and so on. But the words holy and holiness did come to have ethical significance in the Old Testament. So do the terms sanctify and sanctification in the New Testament. Things are sanctified as they are consecrated to God, as they are regarded and treated as sacred or dedicated to divine service. But since the character of God was regarded as ethically righteous, it was recognized that men who are acceptable for his service must be also righteous in character. This thought is given great emphasis in places in the Old Testament, especially in the psalms and the prophets. And when applied to persons in the New Testament, the idea is fundamentally ethical. The thing that makes sanctification necessary is man's lack of righteousness or his sin. The term is used in the New Testament both for the initiation of the Christian life and for its development. The New Testament speaks of all Christians as "saints" or "sanctified ones" (Acts 9:13; Rom. 1:7; 1 Cor. 1:2; 2 Cor. 1:1; Eph. 1:1; Phil. 1:1; Col. 1:2). In this sense the term is synonymous with justification or regeneration. This is sometimes called positional sanctification, as distinguished from progressive sanctification. Then it is used with reference to the progressive cleansing or purification of the soul (1 Thess. 5:23; Heb. 12:14). It is in this sense that the term is usually used in discussions in systems of theology. But there are very few places in the New Testament where the term is unquestionably used in the sense of a progressive work. The preponderating use of the term is in its application to a definite act at the beginning of the Christian life.

(2) All Christians sanctified

Every Christian, then, however imperfect he may be, is sanctified in the sense that he is dedicated or consecrated to God by the power of the Spirit and by his own act of faith. One element in faith is surrender to Christ as Lord. Faith is thus an act of dedication. One dedicates himself to God and separates himself from all that opposes his consecration to God. There should be—normally there will be—a deepening consecration to God and his service, and a more complete separation of oneself from all the forces and factors of life that hinder this consecration; but this is only the carrying out of what was involved in that first act of consecration.

Every Christian is sanctified also in the sense of an inner purification or transformation of character. In this sense sanctification means about the same as regeneration. One who is dedicated to a God of love and righteousness will necessarily become like him in character. The thing that renews one in heart and character is the fact that he is dedicated by an act of self-surrender to a righteous God. Fellowship with a holy God produces holiness in man. Here again there should be progressive sanctification; but the prevailing use of the term in the New Testament is in the sense of the initial dedication or cleansing from sin.

All these terms that we have discussed are different ways of describing what God does for us at the beginning of the Christian life. What God does is represented as forgiveness, as justification, as reconciliation, as adoption, as being born again, as sanctification. There were other terms used, but these are the main ones. Being brought into fellowship with God in Christ is such a wonderful transaction that the writers of the New Testament have used a rich variety of expressions to give us some conception of the glories of what it means. They have held it up before us and turned it round and round like a great diamond flashing its beauty back to us from many angles. We have lost some of the beauty and richness of their description by reducing their expressions to rigidly technical terms and dealing with them as logical abstractions. All these terms are different ways of representing what God does for a soul at the beginning of the Christian life, when that soul is brought by the power of God's grace out of a life of sin into fellowship with God in Christ.

V. The Conditions of Salvation

We will consider now what are usually called the conditions of salvation. By this we mean the spiritual attitude one must assume in receiving the grace of God that saves from sin. In other words, what must one do to become a Christian?

There are many terms used in the New Testament to describe the experience of becoming a Christian. Perhaps the essential elements can all be summed up in the two terms repentance and faith. It is no accident that the experience of becoming a Christian has two fundamental aspects, for in this experience man is concerned with two fundamental relations of life. One is his relation to sin; the other, his relation to God as a God of grace, revealed in Christ as Saviour. The inward turning from sin is repentance; turning to Christ as Saviour is faith. Each implies the other. Neither is possible without the other. At the same time and in the same act that one turns from sin he turns to Christ. Sin and Christ are the opposite poles of the moral universe and one cannot turn from one without turning to the other.

Repentance and faith are not two acts or moral attitudes; they are two aspects of one act or attitude.

1. *Repentance*

(1) Other terms used to describe repentance

Repentance is not the only term used in the New Testament to describe the act or attitude denoted by that word. Jesus says: "If any man will come after me, let him deny himself, and take up his cross, and follow me" (Matt. 16:24). To deny oneself means to renounce self as sinful and selfish; to renounce the old self as unworthy. To take up the cross is to die; to die to the old self and give oneself to a new Master, Jesus Christ. Jesus says also: "Whosoever will save his life shall lose it" (Matt. 16:25). To lose one's life here is to give it away to another, to give it to Christ and one's fellows in service. He put this over against saving one's life in such a way as to lose it. To save it (so as to lose it) means to keep it for one's self, to live the self-centered life. To lose it (so as to save it) is to renounce the self-centered life. Paul speaks about Christians as those being crucified with Christ (Gal. 2:20), and about those who have crucified the flesh with the affections and the lusts thereof (Gal. 5:24). He glories in the cross through which the world has been crucified to him and he to the world (Gal. 6:14). All these are different ways of expressing the idea of repentance.

(2) What is repentance?

The term that is translated repentance in the New Testament means a change of mind. This involves at least three things.

a. Either as an element in repentance or as a precedent condition, it involves the understanding of one's condition as a sinner. One must come to realize something of the guilt and condemnation of his sin. This is ordinarily spoken of as conviction of sin. Some theologians speak of it as the intellectual element in repentance. It comes as a result of hearing gospel truth and the enlightening work of the Holy Spirit. One cannot repent until he comes to see something of the nature of his sin. This does not mean that the consciousness of sin must be present in the same form and to the same extent in every case. In some cases the consciousness of sin may take the form of a sense of guilt and condemnation. In others it may be the sense of moral failure. But in every case the hearing of the gospel intensifies this consciousness of sin. In some cases at first it is nothing more than a vague uneasiness, a consciousness that somehow things are not right with us. The hearing of the gospel intensifies and clarifies this, so that it becomes a definite consciousness of sin. Sin comes to be seen as sin. This means that it comes to be seen as against God. As seen in relation to a God of holy love it comes to be seen in its true character.

b. A second thing involved in repentance is that the love of sin shall die in one's heart. This is usually spoken of as the emotional element in repentance. One may see himself ever so clearly as a sinner and even understand the ruin involved in sin, but unless the love of sin dies in his heart, it will make no difference in his life. He has not repented.

This is not to be identified with fear of punishment. One may have fear of punishment without gospel repentance. This fear of punishment may produce what has been termed "hell-scared religion." But unless there is something more in one's religion than the fear of punishment he will not escape punishment. This fear of punishment may be intensified into remorse of conscience, so that one has no rest day nor night. But remorse of conscience is not repentance. That is to say, repentance is a gospel grace, not simply a state of mind produced by a knowledge of the law which brings a message of condemnation for sin, but no message of salvation from sin.

One may often have great emotion because of sin and yet not repent. He may freely weep, but when the emotion passes he goes back to his old sins.

The emotional element in true repentance may be described as "godly sorrow that worketh repentance" (2 Cor. 7:10). It is a sorrow that grows out of a true understanding of our sin as it is related to a God of grace. It is contrition. "A broken and a contrite heart, O God, thou wilt not despise" (Psalm 51:17). When one has this contrition on account of sin, it will lead on to the third and final element in repentance.

c. The third element is in the renunciation of sin. It is the repudiation of sin by an act of will. Because the love of sin died in one's heart, there is a revulsion of one's whole moral nature against it. Sin is repudiated, not so much because one sees that he will be punished for sin, as because one sees sin in its true nature and comes to hate it. This leads to a changed life in regard to sin. "How can we that are dead to sin live any longer therein?" (Rom. 6:2). Such a thing is a moral impossibility. Repentance is never complete until the will thus repudiates sin. This repudiation of sin and a contrite heart on account of sin always go together. They are two aspects of one state of mind.

This shows that the change of mind here spoken of is not simply an intellectual change. The mind includes the whole moral nature of man. To make up one's mind is not simply an act of the intellect. To repent is to think back over one's course, to see the wrongness of it, and make up one's mind to change. It is no superficial matter; it goes down to the depths of the moral life. This change is an inner change. It is such a change as revolutionizes one's life in relation to sin.

(3) Repentance and reformation

There may be a marked change in the outer life following repentance, or there may not be. Sometimes evil habits have so fastened themselves on to the life that such an inner revolution is the only thing that will change them. Sometimes there may be a marked change in the habits of life without such an inner revolution. In that case you have reformation without repentance.

Sometimes the outward life may have been so correct, judged by the standards of social morality, that no special outward reformation was needed. So you may have reformation following repentance, or you may have reformation without repentance, or you may have repentance where reformation is not needed.

We are not to conclude, however, that because reformation is not needed in some cases repentance is not needed. Reformation as ordinarily spoken of means a change in which vicious moral habits are left off. A man may have no vicious moral habits, but yet need to repent of sin toward God. Not all men are grossly immoral, but all men are sinners. Sin is against God. Repentance is the repudiation of sin against God. Repentance, therefore, is a religious act or attitude of mind. It is not simply the repudiation of sin; it is the repudiation of self as evil and sinful. It is to deny oneself and take up the cross (Matt. 16:24). It means death to the sinful self.

(4) The Christian life a life of repentance

We should not think of repentance as being an act performed at the beginning of the Christian life, not needing to be repeated. It is an attitude that belongs to the Christian life as a whole. The initial act of repentance is the beginning of a life of repentance. Jesus says we should take up the cross daily (Luke 9:23). Paul says that Christians have died to sin (Rom. 6:2), but he also exhorts them to reckon themselves to be dead to sin (Rom. 6:11). The sinful self has to be crucified daily. The old man, as Paul calls him (Col. 3:9), has more lives than the proverbial cat. He will not stay dead when killed. Oftentimes the deepest repentance does not come at the beginning of the Christian life. When one first emerges from the darkness of sin, his eyes are not yet accustomed enough to the new light of the gospel to see sin in all its heinousness. The more one lives in fellowship with a holy God, the more one see himself as sinful and corrupt. It is not a sign of special piety to hear one boasting of his own goodness. The term good is one that Jesus says men should use with a good deal of caution (Mark 10:18).

(5) Repentance and conversion

It is sometimes said that conversion is the outer change corresponding to repentance, or repentance and faith, as an inner change.[10] Sometimes it is said that conversion is made up of repentance and faith—repentance and faith being the elements in conversion.[11] Neither of these statements is objectionable. Conversion means a turning. It is that change in which one turns from sin to God. It is such a change as is evident, or becomes evident, to men. In that sense, it is an outward change. Yet when Jesus speaks of conversion, he lays emphasis on the inner qualities of mind and heart. He says that one must turn and become as a little child in order to get into the kingdom of God. (See Matt. 18:3.)

2. *Faith*

(1) The meaning of faith

Faith is the aspect of conversion in which the soul turns to Christ for salvation. As shown above, it is inseparably connected with repentance. Since repentance is a believing response to the truth of the gospel concerning us as sinners, it might be included in faith. In some places in the New Testament we find faith alone stated as the condition of salvation; in others we find repentance alone; in still others we find both; while in others yet we find other terms carrying the same meaning as these terms.

Faith is a term of such rich content and deep significance that it is difficult to define it in a simple statement. Christian faith, however, might be defined as trust in Jesus Christ as Saviour and surrender to him as Lord.

a. Christ the object of faith. This implies that faith is something more than belief of a doctrine or the accept-

---

[10]See *The Christian Religion in its Doctrinal Expression*, by E. Y. Mullins, pp. 377 ff.

[11]See *Systematic Theology*, by A. H. Strong, Vol. III, pp. 829 ff.

ance of a dogma. No doctrine, however important, can be the object of faith in the full sense of the term. One can believe a doctrine with his intellect. He can trust a person with his heart or will. Nor is the church the object of faith. The Roman Catholic Church makes faith implicit surrender to the church, so that one is pledged to believe in the realm of doctrine what the church prescribes to be believed and practice in the realm of morals what the church prescribes to be practiced. One believes in Christ only on the authority of the church. But this falls far short of Christian faith. It is indeed a fatal perversion of faith. It puts the church in important respects where Christ belongs and calls for submission to the church such as a Christian can yield only to Christ. It enslaves the mind and conscience to the church and its hierarchy.

The place of doctrine in relation to faith is to present Christ to us as the object of faith and then to help explain the meaning of Christ as we know him in experience. Doctrine, then, has an important place in the life of faith, but no doctrine as such can be the object of faith.

Christ is the object of faith by virtue of the fact that he is the incarnation of God and is, therefore, the revelation of God's saving grace. He is the object of saving faith because he is the one who atones for sin and is thereby the one who achieves redemption for us.

Faith in Christ and faith in God are indistinguishable. We can say that we trust in Christ for salvation or that we trust in God through Christ. In the New Testament and in Christian experience, faith in Christ is faith in God.

b. Perhaps the meaning of faith can be made a little clearer if we remind ourselves of two aspects of the act of saving faith.

(a) One is that in saving faith we receive Christ as Saviour. There are many ways of expressing this in the New Testament. It is called coming to Christ. "Him that cometh to me I will in no wise cast out" (John 6: 37). "Come unto me, all ye that labour and are heavy laden" (Matt. 11:28). It is called receiving him. To as many as received him, to them gave he authority (or power) to become the sons of God (John 1:12). It is called eating his flesh and drinking his blood. Christ says that unless we eat his flesh and drink his blood, we have no life in us; but, if we eat his flesh and drink his blood, he abides in us and we in him (John 6:52-59). This statement of Jesus has no reference to partaking of the Lord's Supper, but it does refer to that which our partaking of the supper symbolizes. In the Old Testament this act of faith is called a looking. "Look unto me, and be ye saved, all the ends of the earth" (Isa. 45:22). It is called a hearing. "Incline your ear, and come unto me; hear, and your soul shall live" (Isa. 55:3). Men are said to call upon the Lord. "It shall come to pass, that whosoever shall call on the name of the Lord shall be saved" (Acts 2:21; Rom. 10:13). But the most common term is the one translated as a verb "believe," and as a noun "faith." The passages are too numerous to quote or even refer to. The meaning of the word carries with it the idea of trust, confidence, repose in one. (See John 3:14-16, 18, 36; Acts 10:43; 13:38-39; 16:31; Rom. 1:16; Gal. 3:26; Eph. 2:8, and many others.)

(b) The other aspect of faith that needs emphasizing is that in faith one submits to Christ as Lord. In the same act in which we receive him as Saviour, we give ourselves to him as Lord. We become his servants by virtue of the fact that he saves us from sin. Jesus emphasizes this in relation to his disciples. The very term disciple implies that we become learners in his school. We come under his authority as teacher. We must have the teachable spirit, the spirit of humility and submission. This is why Jesus says we must become as little children and have the spirit of humility (Matt. 18:1-4). Jesus emphasized this childlike humility in contrast to the spirit of pride and selfishness that desired the greatest place for self in the kingdom. The same thought is brought out clearly in Matthew 11:25-30. Here Jesus thanks the Father that the truth has been concealed from the wise and prudent, the proud and self-sufficient in spirit, but that he has revealed it unto babes, those who are humble and teachable. Jesus says that none can know the Father except those to whom the Son wills to reveal him. Therefore, if a man would know God, he must enter the school of Christ, take his yoke, submit to his authority, have the spirit of meekness after the supreme example of Jesus himself. The demand for supreme authority in our lives comes out in those passages where he says that he must come ahead of father, mother, brother, sister, wife, house, or lands, even of life itself (Matt. 10:34 ff.; Luke 14:26); also in the passage where he says that one cannot be his disciple unless he forsakes all (Luke 14:33); where he demands of the rich young ruler that he sell all and follow him (Mark 10:21); where he refuses to allow one to go back to bury the dead or bid farewell to his loved ones (Luke 9:57-62); where he makes the acknowledgment of one before the Father to depend on the confession of him by that one before men (Matt. 10:32-33); where he teaches that obedience to his teaching is the only solid foundation for character and destiny (Matt. 7:24-27); where he claims that he as judge will be the arbiter of the final destinies of men (Matt. 25:31 ff.). So we see that even in the Synoptic Gospels Christ presents himself as absolute Lord of conscience and of life, calling for self-surrender on our part.

In John's Gospel, we find the same truth. Jesus is one with the Father (10:30), the way, the truth, and the life (14:6), the bread of life (6:35), the light of the world (8:12; 9:5), the true vine of which his disciples are branches (15:1 ff.), the good shepherd who gives his life for the sheep (10:11), the mediator of creation (1:3), the life of the world (1:4), the eternal Son of God

(1:18). In short, all the finalities of the soul are found in him. To believe on him is not to be condemned (3: 18), to have eternal life (3:36); not to believe on him is to be condemned, to have God's wrath abide on us.

Paul speaks of the obedience of faith (Rom. 1:5). This may mean the obedience that grows out of faith, or it may mean the obedience that is identical with faith. Whichever construction is put upon it, it is sure that Christian faith has at its heart submission to Christ as Lord. Paul delighted to call himself the slave of Jesus Christ. In Romans, chapter six, he shows that a Christian is one who has become the servant of righteousness (v. 18). Paul and Peter speak of obeying the gospel (2 Thess. 1:8; 1 Peter 4:17). This is not submission to baptism, but submission to the Christ who is presented in the gospel as Saviour and Lord.

(2) An objection to Christian faith

Here is the point where the modern objection to Christianity becomes sharpest. This objection, however, does not usually assume the guise of an objection. It usually appears in the form of an explanation that devitalizes the gospel by removing the objectionable feature. It claims the name of Christ and lauds him as the great religious leader and hero, but objects to making him Lord of the conscience and of life. In the name of freedom and the autonomy of personal life, objection is made to what the objector considers an abject surrender of one's conscience and will to another. Such a surrender, it is claimed, would destroy our freedom and degrade our personality.

But, as a matter of fact, those who assume this attitude of surrender toward Christ do not find their personalities degraded, their wills weakened, or their freedom lost. They find, on the other hand, that their wills are set free and that they are given a power over themselves and their environment and especially over moral evil that they never knew before and in many cases that they never dreamed possible. It is this freedom in the gospel that Paul urges the Galatians that they should not surrender but contend for (Gal. 5:1). The point to remember here, however, is that this freedom comes only by a faith that makes one the willing slave of Jesus Christ. This is one of the paradoxes of the gospel for which logic furnishes no explanation; it is understood only when experienced. As a matter of experience, however, it is as clear and definite as the experience of vision or hearing.

Man thinks that his first need is freedom. His first need is a master. Freedom comes only by submission to Jesus Christ as rightful Lord. Anything short of this attitude of trust and worship toward Jesus Christ falls short of Christian faith. In Ephesians, chapter five, Paul uses the illustration of husband and wife to set forth the relation between Christ and the church. Sometimes a woman objects in the name of freedom to being subject to a husband. But it is only in subjection to the lordship of love that the true woman finds the fulfilment of her womanly nature and the realization of her normal aspirations. Of course, the domination of the wife by brute force on the part of the husband is a degradation of her personality. But this is not the kind of subjection that Paul talks about as the divine ideal for the marriage relation. Nor is the lordship of Christ in the Christian's life the domination of force; it is the mastery of the soul by the love of God embodied in Christ and realized by faith in him. It is a mastery that sets one free from the dominion of sin—sets him free, however, not to be a law unto himself, not to throw off all moral restraint and authority and be a spiritual anarchist in the kingdom of God, but sets him free to serve God.

There is a certain type of mind, delighting to call itself "modern," that is infatuated with the idea of autonomy in the moral and spiritual life. This type of mind thinks that for the soul to be free, all external authority must be rejected. But the choice here is not a choice between the authority of Christ and freedom;

it is a choice between the authority of Christ that brings freedom and the dominion of sin. The power of Christ is the only power that can set the soul free from the dominion of sin. This he does by subduing the soul by the power of his redeeming grace. But this grace becomes operative in the soul only as the soul is mastered by it. The dominion of sin from which the soul needs to be delivered does not necessarily take the form of sensuality; it may be the type of self-centered life just spoken of that denies in principle its dependence for the truth on any power or person outside itself, particularly any Person above the realm to which it belongs. But the self-centered life is a sinful life, whether it manifests itself in the form of sensuality or in the form of intellectual and moral pride that denies one's dependence on rightful authority. It was this kind of spirit that Jesus rebuked in the cities of his day and that called out his great saying in Matthew 11:25 ff., in which he commends the childlike spirit and shows the necessity of possessing that spirit if one would know the truth and have spiritual rest. It was this same spirit that makes the cross of Christ and his spiritual authority over the soul of man both a stumbling block and foolishness to some "modern" minds. It was this spirit that, while proudly parading its submission to the authority of the law, desired to make a show of the flesh and win its own salvation by keeping the law rather than accept the gospel of the grace of God.

(3) Why salvation is conditioned upon faith

Paul says that justification is by faith that it might be according to grace. Faith and grace are correlative ideas (Rom. 4:16). Each implies the other. If salvation is to be of grace on God's part, it must be by faith on man's part. Salvation by grace means salvation as a free gift on God's part. But God cannot give except as man receives. Receiving salvation as an unmerited gift on God's part is faith. God gives salvation, man receives.

Opposed to Paul's idea of salvation by grace through faith was the doctrine of salvation by works; that is, that man by his obedience to the law was to deserve salvation. Paul strenuously opposed this on the ground that it would utterly pervert the gospel. When the Judaizers insisted that Gentiles who accepted the gospel should also be circumcised and keep the law, Paul objected, holding that faith in Christ was sufficient to save. He said that this would make salvation a matter of debt on God's part rather than a matter of grace (Rom. 4:4).

There are, then, no conditions of salvation that have been prescribed in any arbitrary way. The only conditions are the conditions that are necessarily involved in the relations of a God of mercy who would, as a matter of grace, save an undeserving sinner to the sinner that he would save. The moral relations in the case make it impossible for God to save the sinner who does not recognize and acknowledge his sinful condition and cast himself in his helplessness upon a God of grace. That is to say, God cannot save a sinner without making the sinner willing to be saved. In this sense, repentance and faith are not conditions of salvation; they rather constitute salvation; that is, saving a sinner means to bring him to that state of mind in which he renounces sin and trusts himself to a God of grace. As the necessary moral relations involved in the case, repentance and faith are the universal and invariable conditions of salvation. Or using faith as including repentance, we may say that faith and faith alone is the condition of salvation. God himself could not save the sinner without faith on the sinner's part. To say that he could would be to say that God saved a man without saving him.

It follows, then, that the conditions of salvation have never changed. To say that some men were saved in one age of the world on one set of conditions, and other men in another age of the world on other conditions is to make God an arbitrary God. It is nonsense to say that men were saved in Old Testament times by the law and in New Testament times by the gospel. Not one man was ever saved by the law, because no man could keep its requirements. (See Acts 13:39; Rom. 7:10 ff.) To say that men were saved by the law would make void the gospel of the grace of God. Men were saved in Old Testament times just as they are in New Testament times, by faith in God and his promises of grace. (See Rom. 4.)

It will be readily seen that this excludes baptism or any other ceremony or rite, as a condition of salvation. Paul says that the gospel is the power of God unto salvation (Rom. 1:16). He clearly distinguishes between preaching the gospel and baptizing, in a way that would have been impossible, if he had thought of baptism as a prerequisite to the enjoyment of salvation through the gospel (1 Cor. 1:14-17).

On the other hand, Paul regards baptism as symbolical of a salvation procured by faith (Rom. 6:1-4). The expression of Peter about being baptized into remission of sins (Acts 2:38) can be explained in the same way; that is, that baptism symbolizes our entrance into a state of remission of sins. John 3:5 probably does not refer to baptism at all, but to the cleansing from sin in the new birth, of which baptism is the symbol. In Acts 22:16, Ananias told Paul to rise and be baptized and wash away his sins. This can be taken either literally, after the manner of the Roman Catholic Church, or symbolically, as Baptists do. Between these two positions there is no standing ground either in logic or in Scripture. The Catholic position utterly perverts the whole gospel order and denies the doctrine of salvation by grace. So does any other position that makes man's salvation from sin to depend on baptism or anything else than faith in the crucified and risen Redeemer.

But someone may say that, since faith is the sinner's act and since faith is the condition of salvation, after all the sinner's salvation depends on something that the sinner himself does. And since the sinner's salvation is to depend on something that the sinner does, why should it not depend on baptism as well as on faith? Why could not God make baptism a condition of salvation as well as faith? The answer is, that in the sense that this question implies, God did not make faith a condition of salvation. As already pointed out, faith is not an arbitrarily appointed condition of salvation. Faith is the condition of salvation, because the moral relations of the case demand faith. The grace of God that gives salvation must be appropriated by man's faith. Otherwise grace is in vain. But any act not necessarily involved in the moral relations of the case, if made a condition of salvation, would be an arbitrary prescription on God's part.

Moreover, faith as a condition of salvation is not an act by which man merits or earns anything. It is the act by which the bankrupt sinner receives the grace of God. It is an act in which the sinner puts all his trust for salvation in Another and in what that other has done for him. It is not an act in which the sinner makes any claims for himself; it is rather an act in which he acknowledges that he cannot help himself and in which he signs away his life to Another. So there is involved in the act of faith the very opposite of any claim to doing anything by which one wins the favor of God; it is an act in which one acknowledges the utter impossibility of doing this and by which one casts himself on Christ and what he has done for his acceptance with God.

(4) The relation of faith to a life of righteousness

The objection is sometimes made to the doctrine of salvation by grace through faith that it would encourage one to live a life of spiritual ease and sin rather than one of good works and righteousness. This has been a standing objection since the days of Paul. He anticipated this objection in his letter to the Romans. Doubtless he had come across it many times in his contest with the Judaizers. Paul shows that a Christian is one who has died to sin and been made alive to righteousness by faith in Christ (Rom. 6:1-4). This constitutes a moral guarantee (the only kind of guarantee that will apply in the case) that the Christian will live a life of righteousness. It is morally impossible for him to do anything else.

It is sometimes thought that James and Paul do not agree on this question. Paul says that one is justified by faith apart from works of law (Rom. 3:28). James says that a man is justified by works and not only by faith (James 2:24). But we must remember two differences in point of view between Paul and James. One is that they are using the term works in somewhat different senses. Paul is talking about legalistic works—works as a basis for meriting the favor of God. And Paul's view was that as a basis for a sinner's acceptance with God, works of law were utterly useless. James is talking about works as the outgrowth and expression of a living faith. Again, Paul's question was: Upon what condition is a sinner justified before God? His answer is: Upon condition of faith, not on condition of works as a meritorious basis. James's question was: What kind of faith is it that justifies? Is it faith that produces good works, or faith that repeats only a formal creed? His answer is that faith that produces no works is a dead faith, and he contends that this kind of faith will not save (James 2:14). No doubt Paul would have endorsed James's contention, and James would have agreed with Paul. There is no contradiction unless one insists on taking the author's words apart from their connection and without reference to the author's intention. In that case language has no meaning whatever.

It is not true that salvation by faith encourages one to a life of sin and discourages a life of righteousness. On the other hand, faith in Christ as Saviour from sin is the only thing that will lift one out of a self-centered life and produce a life of righteousness. True righteousness is not possible so long as one lives a self-centered life. The doctrine of salvation by works leads to a self-centered life. But in the act of faith one looks beyond self; he trusts in another. He gives himself up to another. Moreover, faith unites to Christ and his Spirit becomes the controlling power of the Christian's life. As Christ gave himself for us, so those who follow him will give themselves to him and to the service of their fellows. Gratitude to God for a salvation received as the gift of his grace will not let one live for self while the world is dying for what he can give.

VI. The Consciousness of Salvation

One of the outstanding things about salvation in the Christian sense of the term is that it is a conscious transaction. This was presupposed in all that has been said about salvation, but it is well now to give special consideration to it.

1. *The normal Christian experience*

The normal Christian experience is one in which the Christian has conscious acceptance with God. The whole religious atmosphere seems to change with the coming of Jesus. Old Testament saints had conscious communion with God, but they did not have that full note of joy and confidence in their relation with God that we find in the New Testament. Especially is it true from Pentecost on that men had this full assurance of acceptance with God. Forgiveness of sins was no merely external transaction that the forgiven sinner might happen to hear about or not.

(1) In the first place, there was the consciousness of sin

This was produced by the preaching of the gospel. The man who had no consciousness of sin and in whom it could not be produced by the word of God was hopeless. The bigger sinner is not always more conscious of his sins, but the more one is conscious of sin, the more is he likely to rejoice in salvation and love the God who forgives in mercy (Luke 7:14 ff.).

(2) Salvation from sin was a transaction in which one was brought into conscious communion with God

In this transaction one finds God. He comes to know God (John 17:3). God comes to possess man and man to possess God. He shall be their God and they shall be his people (Heb. 8:10). In a real sense a man has no God until he comes to possess him in this great revolutionary crisis of life. In this crisis a covenant is sealed by which the soul becomes consciously given over to him. When sin was removed and the soul came into fellowship with God, the soul was often flooded with joy. (See Acts 8:8; 13:52, et al.) The justified man had a heritage of peace to which he was entitled by virtue of his new relation with God (Rom. 5:1). Another element that comes as a result of this fellowship with God in Christ was hope. New Testament Christians were forward looking (Rom. 8:24).

This does not mean that Christian experiences were alike then any more than they are now. Some were more emotional and cataclysmic than others. Lydia did not seem to have the agitation of soul that the jailer had (Acts 16). Nor does it mean that one must be able to go back in memory to the exact time when he had an experience of salvation. There are varieties of Christian experience, just as there are differences among men in every other respect. But every normal Christian experience is an experience of conscious acceptance with God in the forgiveness of sins, an experience that brings love, joy, peace, and hope to the soul.

2. *The lack of assurance*

Yet it must be recognized that there are cases of those who have been regenerated who do not have clear and definite consciousness of acceptance with God. This is recognized in the New Testament and is verified in Christian experience. John says that he wrote his Gospel that men might have life by believing in Jesus as the Christ (20:31). He says that he wrote the First

Epistle in order that those who believe may know that they have eternal life (5:13). This clearly implies two things. One is that it is the privilege of a saved man to know that he is saved. The other is that a man may be saved and not have this assurance. If salvation and assurance were inseparable, then John's writing of the Epistle was in vain; he was in that case writing to bring to Christians something that they could not be Christians and not have.

Sometimes assurance is lacking in the beginning of the Christian life; sometimes one may have it and lose it. Sometimes the lack of assurance is caused by sin and disobedience in the life; sometimes it is due to a lack of understanding of some of the fundamental and elemental things in the Christian life, such as the ground of our forgiveness in the redeeming work of Christ, of faith as the essential and all-inclusive condition of salvation. In some cases, the lack of assurance is caused by the fact that one did not get just the kind of experience he was looking for. Some people want the kind of religious experience Paul had, and, therefore, are constantly dissatisfied with the one God has given them. In still other cases, lack of assurance is due to intellectual perplexities. One may be disturbed because he cannot work out to his own satisfaction all the problems concerning God and his dealings with man.

3. *What is necessary to assurance*

A word might be said now as to how assurance is produced or what is necessary to assurance.

In the first place, one needs a clear understanding and a firm grasp of the elemental things in salvation. This is not to say that he needs to be an expert theologian. He does not. Nor is it to say with the Catholic creeds that, if he does not believe certain dogmas, he shall be anathema. But he does need a firm grasp on the fact that Christ has made full provision for our sins and that we are saved by faith in him. There can be no definite assurance of salvation where one does not definitely grasp this fact. Sometimes one may know that he has been changed without having a clear consciousness of salvation, but this clear consciousness of salvation will come when one firmly grasps the fact that it is faith in the crucified and risen Redeemer that saves. Along with this there must be definite surrender to Christ as Lord. The will must be surrendered to him. There must be no conscious and wilful disobedience to Christ.

Putting together what has been said, it will be seen that the sum of it is that one must have clear and definite faith to have assurance of acceptance with God. Faith brings its own assurance; and nothing but faith is necessary.

Dr. Strong says: "The ground of faith [meaning saving faith] is the external word of promise. The ground of assurance, on the other hand, is the inward witness of the Spirit that we fulfil the conditions of the promise."[12] This statement is somewhat misleading. It makes the impression that the ground of saving faith is one thing, and that the ground of the faith that brings assurance is another thing. But this is a mistake. The faith that saves is the faith that assures. Saving faith carries its own assurance, and, if it does not, it is because the faith is not clear and definite. So, if one needs assurance, he will not get it by having developed in him a new kind of faith or faith in a different object. Assurance will come when faith is clarified, strengthened, and aware of what it is about. Christ is always the object of faith, and the Holy Spirit always is the power that produces faith in Christ. This is true both in salvation and assurance. In other words, Christ and the Holy Spirit both bear the same relation to saving faith that they do to assuring faith, for these are one faith, not two.

There are pointed out in the New Testament certain ethical and spiritual qualities that mark the regenerated

---

[12] *Systematic Theology*, Vol. III, p. 844.

man. Some of these are the possession of the Spirit (Rom. 8:9, 14; 1 John 3:24), obedience to Christ or God (John 14:15, 21; 1 John 2:34), a life of righteousness and of victory over sin (1 John 3:6-9), love of the brotherhood (1 John 3:10 ff.), the power to discern the truth (1 John 2:27). These are all the result of our faith in Christ. When we are asked to look at these as evidences of regeneration, we are simply asked to let our faith become clear and self-conscious and know what it is about. We are not asked to take something outside of or beyond saving faith as evidence of our salvation.

THE CHRISTIAN LIFE

I. The Christian's Mission and Work

1. Development of the new life
2. To bring others to know and serve Christ
3. To apply Christian principles to all of life

II. Providence

1. The doctrine stated
2. Objections to the doctrine
   (1) Based on a mechanical view of the universe
   (2) Based on the exaltation of man
   (3) Based on the fact of evil
3. Providence and redemption
4. Providence and faith

III. Prayer

1. The nature and factors in prayer
2. The purpose and scope of prayer
3. Objections and difficulties in prayer
   (1) In relation to God's will
   (2) In relation to God's foreknowledge
   (3) In relation to the order of nature
   (4) Answer to difficulties practical
4. Conditions of answer to prayer

IV. The Perseverance of the Saints

1. Meaning of the doctrine
2. Support for the doctrine
   (1) Relation of the human and the divine
   (2) The nature of the new life
   (3) Christ's intercession for his people
   (4) The sealing of the Spirit
   (5) Direct statements in the New Testament
3. Objections to the doctrine
   (1) That it is inconsistent with man's freedom
   (2) That it encourages to a life of sin
   (3) That the Bible teaches the opposite
      a. Some passages teach that perseverance is necessary
      b. Some passages show that perseverance is evidence of regeneration
      c. Some passages show a lack of development
      d. Some passages stress the danger of rejecting gospel truth

V. The Development of the Christian Life

1. The need of growth
2. Foes of growth
3. The means of growth
4. The condition of growth
5. The perfection theory of growth
6. The goal of development

VI. The Church and the Christian Life

1. The use of the term in the New Testament
    (1) With reference to a local assembly
    (2) In an institutional sense
    (3) In a general or universal sense
2. The nature of the church
    (1) Christianity fundamentally ethical, personal, and spiritual
    (2) The nature of Christianity determines the nature of the church
        a. As a spiritual body
        b. Church membership as voluntary
        c. The church as a democracy
3. The functions of the church
    (1) The church the body of Christ
    (2) The church and the Spirit of Christ
    (3) The primary function of the church
    (4) Results of worship

CHAPTER V

THE CHRISTIAN LIFE

Having seen something of how the Christian life begins in an act of faith on man's part and an act of forgiveness and regeneration on God's part, in which the sinner is brought into conscious fellowship with God and renewed in the moral image of Jesus Christ, let us turn our attention now to the life that the Christian lives in pursuance of this act of faith and in fulfilment and completion of God's saving act. It is our purpose in this chapter to consider only some of the outstanding and important phases of this life.

I. The Christian's Mission and Work

To discuss in full the Christian's mission and work would necessitate the treatment of several of the phases of practical theology. This would manifestly be out of order here. What we are concerned with is simply to consider briefly some of the fundamental principles of that life, especially when it is viewed as a life of redemption.

1. *The development of the new life*

The first thing that we mention is that the Christian's mission is to work out and exemplify in his daily activities the life implanted in his heart when he becomes a Christian. This life seeks embodiment and expression. This is expressed in many ways in the New Testament. The Christian is said to follow Christ (Mark 1:16 ff.; 2:14). He is a disciple; that is, a learner in the school of Christ (Matt. 28:19). The Spirit of Christ is in him and he is led by the Spirit (Rom. 8:9 ff., 14). The Spirit of Christ lives in him (Gal. 2:20) and he strives to bring every thought into subjection to Christ (2 Cor. 10:5). He is to work out his salvation, because it is God that works in him both to will and to do (Phil. 2:12-

13). We are not meaning to say here that the Christian life is simply the embodiment of some principle of divine life implanted at the time of regeneration which lives on independently of further reinforcement from the divine presence. God continues to work in us, as these references show. He continues to energize in us and through us, and our mission is to work down and out to the limit what God works in us in the way of willing and doing.

That is a comprehensive statement that Paul makes when he says to the Philippians that they should work out their own salvation with fear and trembling (Phil. 2:12). The word translated "work out" means to work out to finality, to bring to completion. Paul does not mean, however, that one can work out his salvation without God. He does not mean to say that God began the process and now turns it over to man to finish. The thought is quite different from that. Paul gives as the reason for his exhortation that it is God that works in us, both to will and to do. The emphasis is on the fact that God works in us.

God works; he works in us; he works both to initiate (to will) and to complete (to do). It is not a co-operative effort in the sense that God carries one end of the load and man the other, working as equals. The apostle never would have exhorted his readers to work with fear and trembling if he had thought of the matter in that fashion. Paul does not speak here in the spirit of a modern, self-sufficient man, standing erect, with expanded chest, defying the universe and boasting that he is the captain of his own soul. He speaks as a Jew reverently bowing in the presence of the Lord of the universe, conscious of his own creatureliness and sinfulness. But he is conscious that the Lord of the universe as holy and gracious is dealing with him for his salvation. He is the same Paul who has insisted that man receives salvation by faith and that he does not achieve it by works. God initiates and God energizes to complete the task. But the faith by which man receives salvation is a faith that obeys. Paul had just exhorted them to obey. He has just held up Christ as the great example of obedience and as the great example of exaltation as the result of obedience. Now he urges them to have the same actively obedient faith. If they have, they will work out to expression in their lives what God works in them by the power of his Spirit. Impression must come to expression. Faith must crystallize in character and life. Divinely implanted impulses must be brought to fruition in fixity of character and Christian service. Otherwise the divine intention fails of complete realization. In this working out of our salvation, we find encouragement in the fact that God not only works to will, but also to do. He energizes in all our aspirations and our strivings. But his purpose is not realized except as we yield to him and work out to expression in life what he works in us.

What we have been saying means that the Christian is to live his life on a redemptive basis. He is to remember that he is a man redeemed. He is also to remember that his fellow man is one for whom Christ died. This was uppermost in Paul's mind when he thought of his fellow man. Paul would not willingly put a stumbling block in the way of the weakest brother. The thing that made him so careful was the recognition that the weak brother was one for whom Christ died. To sin against him was to sin against Christ (1 Cor. 8:11-13).

2. *To bring others to know and serve Christ*

The Christian's mission, in another phase of it, is to bring others into saving relations with Christ and develop the Christ life in them. Every Christian should be an evangelist, a herald of good news. In this sense every Christian should be a preacher. This is the spontaneous impulse of the new life in us—to bring somebody else to know Christ and enjoy the great blessing that he gives. Our mission is to bear witness to Christ

from Jerusalem to the uttermost part of the earth. Any
form of Christianity that does not have throbbing through
it a mighty missionary and evangelistic impulse is a de-
generate form. And the Christian's mission is to do all
he can to develop the Christ life in others after they
have been brought into saving relations with him.

There are those who look on such evangelistic and
missionary effort as an impertinence. They evidently
consider Christianity as being on the same basis as
other systems that men have evolved or discovered and
regard it as having about as much claim on the lives of
men as these other systems. If that is all there is to
Christianity, they are correct. If Christ is to be brack-
eted with the other great philosophers and religious
leaders of mankind, then it is an impertinence for his
followers to ask and expect that all men everywhere
shall acknowledge him as Saviour and Lord to the exclusion of all other masters. On the other hand, if he is
what we have claimed for him, what we believe he
claimed for himself, and what he has proved himself to
be by what he has done for men: in that case no man
can really know him without having a burning passion
that all other men should know him. In that case, the
message about him and his saving power is truly *the*
gospel—the only gospel for lost and ruined men. For one
who knows him to refuse to make him known is treason
to him and treachery to those who are dependent on us
for a knowledge of that gospel. Missions and evangelism, therefore, are not incidental or secondary in the
Christian life; they are of the very essence of Christianity. And any form of so-called Christianity that does
not practice the spread of the gospel among men thereby
proves itself false in its claim.

3. *To apply Christianity to all of life*

The Christian's mission is to do all the good he can
in every realm of life, in every possible way. He is to
seek to make regnant the will of God in the whole ex-

tent of human life and society. There are those today who set over against each other evangelistic effort and social service. They would disparage one in favor of the other. Those who emphasize evangelism and decry social service seem to think that anything except direct religious work is irreligious. Every good work is religious if done with a motive to glorify God. There is no conflict between serving God and helping men. Surely the Christ who healed the bodies of men and performed a miracle to feed the hungry multitude does not represent a God who is displeased with anything that makes this world a better place in which to live. The type of piety that thinks that the only function of religion is to cause a man to withdraw into some monastery and save his own soul and let the world go to the devil—that type of piety belongs to the middle ages, if it belongs anywhere. Nor is it the only function of Christianity to save the souls of men from hell in the next life; they need to be made righteous in every relation of life. The regeneration of the individual and the regenration of society should never be put over against each other as antithetical things; it is not a question of one to the exclusion of the other. They are rather two things that are mutually dependent. The only way to regenerate society is through the regeneration of the individual units of society. And the only power that can regenerate the individual is the gospel of Christ. Nor has the gospel done its full work in the life of the individual unless he is made right in every relation of life. The gospel makes a man live right in the world, not withdraw from the world. Jesus taught his disciples to pray that God's kingdom might come and God's will be done on earth as it is in heaven (Matt. 6:10).

There are those who protest that it is useless to try to make this world a good place in which to live. This world, they say, is a fallen world and cannot be redeemed. It is useless to try.

On the other hand, there has been a certain type of American religious thought that has been unduly optimistic in its thought about human society. It seemed to think that essentially human nature was good, and that with a little effort a condition of society could soon be attained that would be almost ideal. At least some religious leaders put the emphasis at the wrong place. They emphasize changing social conditions rather than changing men. They said our first task is to change conditions; good conditions will make good men.

This emphasis was wrong. This is a fallen world. There is some truth in the idea that good conditions make good men. But fundamentally it is the other way around. Good men make good conditions rather than good conditions making good men. Men are influenced by their environment. But the worst trouble with men does not lie in their environment; it lies in them. They are self-centered and sinful. They must be changed on the inside, and only the power of God can do that.

But this does not justify any Christian in assuming the attitude of saying that the world is so bad that nothing can be done about it; that Christianity was never intended to save the world but only a few from the mass of the fallen race; and that we should seek to save these and let the world go on its way to perdition.

But the objection is made that evil cannot be eradicated from our world and that there is no use to try. That is probably true. In fact, this writer would affirm that it is true. The New Testament seems everywhere to assume that evil will persist to the end. Only at the final consummation will there be a complete separation of the good from the bad and complete victory over evil. Jesus seems to imply this in the parable of the tares (Matt. 13:24 ff.) and in the parable of the dragnet (Matt. 13:47 ff.).

To one raising this objection there is a very clear and definite answer: namely, that there is a great deal of difference between hoping to make the world perfect and working to make it better. Orthodox Protestant theology has held that no human individual could obtain perfection in this life; but it has also held that there was the possibility of indefinite improvement for any Christian in this life. Jesus himself taught that the perfect character of God was to be our ideal (Matt. 5:48). Toward that ideal we are to strive. But Jesus no doubt knows that no one of us could entirely obtain that ideal in this life. But he evidently meant for us to take the ideal seriously and strive toward it as long as we live in this world.

Neither the human individual nor human society is perfectible; but both can be made better by the grace of God. And he is a poor Christian who does not advocate doing something about the evils of life and actually try to do something about them. Even the man who objects most strenuously to what is called the "social gospel" will work vigorously to limit the power of a concrete evil like the liquor traffic.

Jesus called his disciples the salt of the earth and the light of the world (Matt. 5:13-14). They can be used for the spiritual salvation and definite transformation of some men. But it is also true that Christian men and women can be a leavening influence in human society and raise the moral standards of a community and even of a nation. What can be done in one community or nation can be done for the whole world. Jesus himself speaks of the kingdom of heaven as a leavening power in the world (Matt. 13:33). He is also represented as telling his followers to make disciples of *all* nations. We are to go as far as we can toward Christianizing all the world.

II. Providence

1. *The doctrine stated*

It is an essential factor in the Christian view, that the world be considered as a providential order. By providence we mean that God is working out a purpose in the life of man.

Faith in the world as a providential order is involved in the Christian belief in the personality of God, in the doctrine of creation and in the relation of God to the world and to man. Especially is it involved in the Christian doctrine of redemption and in the Christian's experience of salvation and fellowship with God in Christ. One will likely believe in providence if he believes in a personal God who is good and at the same time omniscient and omnipotent, and who created and sustains all things. If, furthermore, one believes that this God is not only the Creater and Sustainer of all things, but is also the Redeemer God revealed in Christ, who by the power of his grace seeks sinful men and draws them into fellowship with himself, then belief in providence becomes a certainty. One cannot believe in such a God as is revealed to us in the Old and New Testament Scriptures and in the redemptive work of Jesus Christ and not also believe that this God is working out some great and good purpose in the life of the human race.

It is certain that Jesus and the writers of the New Testament believed in such providential care over the lives of God's children.

2. *Objections to the doctrine*

Many people, however, would deny that the world is a providential order. They hold that there are certain things in life that make it impossible to believe in any divine purpose that we can discern or know. There are many others who are skeptical regarding the matter, and many others, while believing in some general way in divine providence, are greatly perplexed and often distressed about the matter.

The reasons for this skepticism and denial might be summed up in general as three. These are interwoven and closely related.

(1) There is the objection based on what we may call the mechanical view of the universe.

This view holds that the world in all its phases is governed by law; that natural law is fixed and invariable; and that there is to be found no deeper meaning in life than such law expresses; that is, no *meaning* at all in the true sense of that term. Man himself is only the product of mechanical and biological forces and is only the highest manifestation of such forces.

This view has been greatly advanced and reinforced by the phenomenal advance of science and the scientific view of things in our modern world. By the application of the knowledge obtained in scientific investigation, we have brought in the machine age. We have been so successful in inventing and producing machinery that in the minds of many the machine looms larger than the man that made it. Man made the machine, and now the machine threatens to devour the man that made it.

In answer to this view, we might consider the matter, first, as to its bearing on our thought of man, and next as to our thought of God.

As to man, we must remember that man is greater than any science. Nature never gave us a science of anything. If invariable law spoke the last word, we would have no science. Science is the product of the mind of man, and man is greater than any science that he has produced. Man produces the different sciences by his free, purposeful investigation of natural phenomena. Man investigates the facts of nature, discovers the relations of these facts among themselves, and states these relations in what we term natural law. But the mind of man that discovers these facts and traces their relations is greater than the facts discovered. Moreover, man is purposeful and free in his studies of nature and her wonders.

As to the machine, man is greater than the machine that he makes and uses. Machines really do no work. Man does the work, using the machine as a tool. When a farmer harvests a crop of grain with a modern harvester, it is really the farmer who harvests the crop as truly as when the ancient farmer harvested his with his bare hands or with a reap hook or scythe. No modern machine or ancient scythe ever harvested a field of grain. When an adding machine gives you the sum of a long line of figures, it was the mind of man that did all the thinking in the case; the machine did none.

The progress of science and invention, the vast amount of work done by our modern machinery—all this is a testimony, not that we live in a world of mechanical necessity, but rather that we live in a world in which mind is superior to things and in which purpose controls the vast machinery that intelligence has produced. Man is superior to things and to law.

So far as God is concerned, law is God's method of working. The world is not governed by law; it is governed according to law. Natural law is not a force. Natural law is the statement of a method according to which some power works. A statement of the law does not define the nature of the power at work; it only states the method according to which it operates. God rules the world; natural law is his method of working.

Nor is natural law necessarily invariable. If the power back of the world and working in and through the world is in its ultimate nature personal, then there is no inherent reason why it might not vary from the regular method and transcend at times the method of natural law.

Nor is there any reason for denying that this power is purposive or benevolent simply because it works in regular ways. As a matter of fact, this very regularity may itself be evidence of a benevolent purpose. Neither God nor man could carry out a benevolent purpose in a world that operated by chance. If the sun rose in the east one day and in the west the next; if one year it was warm in the summer and cold in the winter and another year the matter was reversed; if one day lying degraded a man's character and the next day ennobled it: in such a topsy-turvy world it is difficult to see how any good purposes could be worked out. The regularities of nature and of the moral world do not militate against the idea that God is at work in the world. To a man who believes in God these things rather speak of the constancy of God's purpose; the regularities of the world's operation speak of the faithfulness of God in carrying out his purposes in the world.

(2) Then there is the objection to the doctrine of divine providence based on the exaltation of man.

Some men would agree with what we have been saying about man's superiority over nature and machinery, but would not recognize him as subordinate to God and his purposes. We are not speaking now of the type of thought that exalts man but makes him subservient to God. This kind of humanism recognizes God and would insist that belief in God exalts man. But there is a kind of nontheistic humanism that insists that man is the sole master of the world, that he is the architect of his own fortune, the captain of his own soul.

Such thought is receiving a rather severe jolt right now (1945). It must be confessed that if the human race is the architect of its own fortune, it does not seem to be making a very great success in working out its own fortune. It would seem that the race is failing so miserably in working out its destiny that it needs some help and guidance from a Higher Power. This failure of man is one reason, in the minds of Christians, for looking to such a Power for help in the crises of life, as well as at other times. According to the Christian view, the great failure of the human race lies just at this point. It has tried to get along without God. This effort to get along without God is close to the heart of man's sin and is largely responsible for man's failure and misery.

This humanistic effort to exalt man by dethroning God will not succeed in exalting man; it will only succeed in degrading him. Man is never dignified by denying God or refusing him the supreme place in human life. This has been tried in many lives individually and on a larger scale in communities. It has been tried on a large scale on bolshevist Russia now for some years. But it can never succeed. God alone is the guarantee of man's exaltation and success. Some men have even proposed religion without God. Such a suggestion is about as sensible as it would be for a man to invite his friends to a feast and make no provision for food to serve them.

(3) A third objection to divine providence is based on the fact of evil in the world.

There are two phases of this. One is the fact of sin; the other is the fact of suffering.

This objection goes back deep into the history of philosophy. It has been stated in summary fashion somewhat as follows. The fact of evil shows that God cannot be both good and almighty. If he is almighty and does not prevent evil, then he is not good. If he is good and does not prevent evil, then he is not almighty. If he were both good and almighty, he would prevent evil.

We had as well admit, to begin with, that this problem cannot be given an entirely rational solution. Clear-cut and summary solutions to such questions are usually false. For one thing, we need to remember that we cannot see things entirely as the Almighty does. It is entirely possible that there are factors entering into God's government of the world that we do not apprehend. There are others that we may see into somewhat but do not at all adequately comprehend. We will have to allow that there are some things that God knows that we do not. So far as the history of the world is concerned, the facts are not all in. We will have to wait on some of these. This is true of every individual and much more true of the race as a whole. It is also true that the life history of every individual is intertwined with that of the race and can be ultimately judged only as a part of that history.

So far as sin is concerned, God is not responsible for sin. He is responsible for creating the kind of world that made sin possible. But sin is chargeable to man's choice. Man is not an automaton. He chooses evil; and when he chooses evil he must bear the consequences. It would not be a moral world if man could not choose evil; nor would it be a moral world if he did not suffer the consequences of his evil choice. To say, then, that the world is a moral order is to affirm the possibility of sin and to affirm that man must bear the consequences of his sin. The only way that God could have guaranteed the exclusion of sin and its evil consequences would have been to make a nonmoral world. That means a world governed by mechanical necessity rather than by moral law. That kind of a world could not in any respect reflect the goodness of God. If God was to create a world through which he could manifest his goodness and which would include creatures capable of recognizing and appreciating moral goodness, then he must create a moral world with the risk of allowing sin in it with all sin's evil entail. As to God's almightiness, this does not mean that God can do anything that man can conceive. Some things that we conceive are morally absurd and contradictory. Such a conception is the idea of a moral world with sin forcibly excluded from it. As a matter of fact, it takes a greater God to create a moral order in which sin is a possibility than it does to create a mechanical world in which sin would be impossible.

Moreover, the Christian doctrine of redemption means that sin costs God more than it does man. We are safe in saying, then, that the values of redemption in God's mind and purpose were such that he was willing to create a moral universe, with all the evils attendant upon the entrance of sin and moral disorder, that he might bring man and the moral universe to the glorious consummation involved in this redemption. So far as there is any rational justification for allowing sin to enter our world, it must be found in the Christian doctrine of the moral order of the world, including the doctrine of redemption.

If God is justified in creating a moral order, with man as a free being as its climax, then the problem of suffering is somewhat relieved inasmuch as a large portion of the suffering of the world is due directly to man's sin. If we could take out of the world's history the suffering due to man's selfishness and his brutality toward his fellow man, the world's history would make different reading from what it does now.

As to the suffering that cannot be traced directly to man's sin, we need to remember the following facts: Man has found much of his mental, moral, and social development in life by striving to overcome the inconveniences, hardships, and sufferings of life. Man has found much of life's discipline by striving to wring from mother earth his sustenance and by fighting the apparently hostile forces of nature. These forces have often seemed utterly regardless of man's highest values and have ruthlessly swept away his most highly prized possessions. But man has risen by overcoming these forces. As an airplane must take off against the breeze, so man has been enabled to rise above the limitations of life by facing and overcoming difficulties.

On a somewhat higher level than this, the New Testament and Christian experience show us that God uses hardships and suffering for redemptive ends.

3. Providence and redemption

To understand the question of providence, we must see the world as more than a welter of conflicting powers; we must see it as more than a moral order. To get an intelligent grasp of this question, nothing will help us so much as to see the life of man from the standpoint of God's fundamental purpose concerning man. That purpose is clearly revealed in the Bible. It runs like a golden thread through the Bible. The Bible is not a book of history as such. The central interest of the Bible is God's redemptive purpose. History undertakes to record what has taken place in man's life and to relate these events in a causal sequence; it tries to trace the course of events in their causal connections. The Bible tells something of what has taken place in human life as the events of man's life reveal God's redemptive purpose. It is concerned with these events only from this point of view. Biblical history, therefore, leads toward, and centers in, one person, Jesus Christ the Redeemer of men.

Providence has too often been interpreted as if it meant, especially as related to individuals, that God had his favorites for whose benefit he directed the course of the world, and that he cared mainly or only for these, disregarding the interests of the rest of his intelligent creation and perhaps violating the order of the world to make things comfortable for these favorites. Thus providence has been interpreted as if God's main concern was to make man comfortable rather than to make him holy. This way of looking at the matter has put undue emphasis on the idea of the fatherhood of God regarded as indulgent kindness and on the idea of man's comfort and ease.

The centrality of redemption in God's providential dealing with his people is seen in Romans 8:28-29. In verse 28 Paul says that all things work together for good to those who love God, to those who are called according to his purpose. In verse 29 he gives a reason for this statement. He says: "For whom he did foreknow, he also did predestinate to be conformed to the image of his Son." He grounds providence in predestination. He believes in a providential ordering of the world, because he believes in a certain kind of God. He believes in a God of purpose and of grace. He, therefore, has confidence that God is working out a purpose of grace in the lives of his people.

Frequently, when people read the statement that all things work together for good to those that love God, they take it that the apostle means that all things work for the ease or the comfort or the pleasure of God's people. Then when they see good people suffering they decide that the apostle did not get the matter right. But the apostle does not say that all things work for the pleasure or ease of God's people but for their good. And he does not leave us in doubt as to what he meant by the good. He defines it in the next verse by saying that God designed that they should be conformed to the image of his Son. God designed everything that comes into the lives of his people to work toward their transformation into the spiritual image of Jesus Christ. The good that the apostle thinks of is not the good of worldly possessions or a comfortable existence, but the good of spiritual character. The highest treasures are the treasures of character. These are the treasures that Jesus tells his disciples to strive for, not the treasures that men lay up on earth and that soon pass away (Matt. 6:19). The treasures of character abide. The best thing that can happen to any man is that he be made like Jesus Christ in character. Doubtless God could have made a better world than this for the purpose of giving us ease and pleasure; but it is difficult to conceive of any concrete respect in which this world might be changed and made a better world than it is for the development of Christian character. Certainly to take temptation or suffering out of it would not do so. That does not mean that we are to be satisfied with the world as it is. God no doubt meant that we should find spiritual development by working to improve the world. From the standpoint of God's redemptive purpose, then, we arrive at the paradox that the best world is not a perfect world, but one where we should need to work to make it better.

In thinking of the idea of providence we should consider it in relation to the development of the kingdom of God in the world as well as in relation to the redemption of the individual. The coming of the kingdom and the redemption of the individual are vitally interlinked. The salvation of every individual is a factor in the coming of the kingdom. The kingdom comes through the saving of individuals. In studying God's purpose of redemption, we saw that it was not to be interpreted to mean that God purposed to save the individual as an isolated unit, without reference to his connections in the social and historical order to which he belongs. So we are not to take the idea of providence to mean that God works for the good of the individual without reference to his place in society or the kingdom of God. The good of the individual is a phase of the common good. The whole of biblical history shows that God is working toward an end that includes more than the good of individuals selected out of the mass; he is working toward a universal kingdom of good as the goal of history. Paul indicates in Ephesians 1:10 that God is moving toward the goal of heading up all things in Christ, the things in the heavens and the things on the earth.

This goal will perhaps not be attained until we pass beyond history. The goal of history is an end that transcends history. Time finds its meaning in relation to eternity.

Providence, then, is both general and particular. The idea of a general providence that did not include the minutest affairs and cares of life does not agree with Jesus' view of God. He says that not a sparrow falls to the ground without his notice. He clothes and feeds his people (Matt. 6:26 ff.; 10:29 ff.). We can cast all of our anxiety upon him, realizing that he cares for us (1 Peter 5:7). By keeping in constant communion with the Lord we can live above anxiety and have the peace of God to guard our hearts and our thoughts (Phil. 4:6-7).

One evidence for the idea of a particular providence is the testimony of those who seek thus to live in fellowship with God and under his control and guidance. Many who have given themselves in service to God and man have testified that their lives were lived under the sense of a divine mission and with a consciousness of divine leading. They have testified that it was this sense of such a divine mission and divine leading that gave meaning and motive to their lives. And their lives of sacrifice and toil with the results in blessing to mankind justify their claim that God called and directed them in his service. If anybody is qualified to speak on this subject, surely they are. They have a right to be regarded as experts in this field.

4. *Providence and faith*

What has been said will show that God's providence is not something that works in a mechanical or necessary manner. Since the good that God is working out for us is the good of redemption, our obtaining that good is conditioned upon our faith. Redemption is not something that comes to man automatically or mechanically. Redemption is a moral and spiritual matter and is morally and spiritually conditioned. The idea of providence has been too often presented as if it meant that everything that came into our lives was within itself a good independently of our attitude toward God and his providential dealings with us. This is not true. Whether or not the things that come into our lives are a blessing to us depends on how they are received. If received in the spirit of submission and trust in God, all things work together for good. Otherwise, what was intended for our good may even prove to be a curse. It is to those that love God that all things work for good, and we might safely say that all things work for good to the extent that we love God or are led to love him by the things that come to us.

The matter might be put thus: The reason that all things work together for good to the Christian is that the Christian is one in whom the dominant motive and passion in life is love to God. Since this is the dominant force in life, everything in life causes it to grow. When one is properly related to God, everything in life draws one closer to him and makes one more like him in character. Love to God is the alchemy that has the power of transmuting all the baser metals of life into the pure gold of Christian character.

This shows that the New Testament does not consider all things as good within themselves. Nor does Paul say that all these things within and of themselves work for good. His statement implies that it is because of God that all things work for good. It might be translated that God works all things for good; but whether it should be translated that way or not, that was clearly Paul's thought. The New Testament doctrine was that every detail of life, even the smallest, was under his control and he directs it all for our good.

It is God that makes all things work together for our good; and their being good to us is conditioned upon our faith and love toward him. In other words, all else becomes good to us. To the extent that one comes into fellowship with God does he overcome evil and transmute it into a means of good.

III. Prayer

The ideas of providence and of prayer are closely related in religion. One is not likely to believe in one if he does not believe in the other. If one believes that God exercises a providential care over the lives of men, then he will almost certainly believe that God responds to the prayers of his people.

Prayer in some form is practically universal among men. It is the expression of man's sense of dependence and helplessness. William James expresses it by saying that men pray because they cannot keep from it.[1] Man spontaneously calls for help in moments of peril, and in moments of exaltation he ascribes praise to the power or powers that control his destiny.

---

[1]*Principles of Psychology*, Vol. 1, p. 316.

1. *The nature and factors in prayer*

There are certain elements or factors that enter into prayer—one might call them varieties of prayer. In the broadest sense of the term, prayer is communion of the soul with God; that is, it is the conscious outgoing of the soul in spiritual fellowship with God. The soul reaches out in thought and aspiration after God and usually in spoken word expresses itself to him. There is also in this communion the side of waiting in an attentive and receptive attitude on God for spiritual light, strength, and guidance. It is the recognition of the unseen Companion. It is taking definite and conscious recognition of God.

As such a direct and conscious recognition of God, prayer is perhaps the most directly and specifically religious act of which man is capable. It is an act in which the soul seeks to establish personal relations with God as the Determiner of man's destiny.

One of the specific elements in prayer as communion with God is adoration. It is the recognition of the worth and worthiness of his character and gives expression to this recognition. It is the proper response of the soul in worshipful recognition of the character of God as holy love.

There enters into prayer also the element of thanksgiving. Thanksgiving is the expression of our recognition of God as the source of our blessings and an acknowledgment of the fact that God's gifts to us put us under obligations to the Giver. In adoration we are recognizing the worth of God's character; in thanksgiving we are recognizing our indebtedness to him for his blessings to us which are an expression of his goodness of character.

A large element in prayer also is confession. Confession has a large place in any religion that is ethical in character. As man comes to recognize God as holy, he comes also to recognize his own sinfulness and unworthiness in relation to God. Over and over again we find in the Old and New Testament Scriptures this factor of confession in prayer. In fact, it is one of the most prominent factors in prayer as recorded in the Bible. It naturally goes along with adoration of God as holy and righteous and thanksgiving to him as good and gracious. When man sees God as holy, he sees himself as sinful and unworthy.

Petition is a prominent element in prayer. It is to be feared that with many people it is about the only factor. For some people it seems to be about all there is in prayer. It certainly should not be the only thing in prayer, but it is very naturally a prominent one. Intercession is a special form of petition. It is asking God for a blessing on someone else rather than on self. This is an outstanding feature of prayer as we have it presented in the Bible, both by precept and example. Abraham pleading for Sodom (Gen. 18:22 ff.), Moses for Israel (Ex. 32:31 ff.; Deut. 9:25 ff.), Paul for the Jews (Rom. 9:1 ff; 10:1) are outstanding examples.

2. *The purpose and scope of prayer*

It has been stated that prayer is communion with God. We might ask: What is the purpose of prayer? We might say in accordance with this idea that the main purpose of prayer is the right adjustment of man's relations with God. Prayer is a matter of personal relations and adjustments. It is man as a person dealing directly with God as a person. In dealing with God man is dealing with an unseen and spiritual reality. Prayer is a recognition of the fact that this reality is a person, not simply an impersonal force or an abstract principle. Mrs. Eddy says that God is principle.[2] God is more than principle. He is a person. And prayer is direct dealing on man's part with this supreme spiritual power.

Where there is no recognition of the personality of God, there can be no prayer in the true sense of the word. There may be meditation, reflection, but these are not

---

[2]*Science and Health*, pp. 107, 111, 112, 113, 115, etc. Edition of 1913.

prayer. There can be no adoration, thanksgiving, petition, no personal communion of any kind. The supreme
thing that man needs is God himself rather than something that God can give. God is himself the supreme
blessing. He is man's chief need. When God gives himself he gives all else; without God nothing else meets his
need.

About what should man pray? What constitutes a
proper subject of prayer? The answer is: Anything that
concerns man is a proper subject of prayer. This means
that anything that is of concern to man is also of concern to God. The God and Father of our Lord Jesus
Christ is interested in anything and everything that
touches the lives of his human children. This does not
mean that we can ask God for anything we want and
get it. Far from it. But it does mean that in any situation, perplexed by any problem, we may bring ourselves with our problem to God, and when we find the
right personal adjustment with God, he will solve or help
us to solve our problem.

Prayer is not an effort on the part of man to persuade
an unwilling God to bestow some good on man. Rather
it is such an adjustment of man's personal relations with
God as makes it possible for God to bestow a blessing
he desires to bestow. It is not bringing a reluctant God
into harmony with man's will; it is rather bringing man
into harmony with God's will, so that God can do his
highest will concerning man. This is shown in the fact
that the Holy Spirit makes intercession for us. The
reason for this is that we do not know how to pray as
we ought (Rom. 8:26-27). The Spirit makes intercession for us with groanings that cannot be uttered. This
intercession is not intercession apart from ours, but it
is intercession in and through us. The groanings unutterable are the groanings of the human spirit possessed
and moved by the divine Spirit. The Spirit moves us to
pray in accordance with the divine will and, therefore,
God answers our petitions. Man cannot pray in accord-

ance with the divine will except as he prays under the tuition and guidance of the divine Spirit. When man desires any good, seeks any good, accomplishes any good, he finds that God desired, sought, and accomplished that good with him, in him, and through him. God takes the initiative in all good, and prayer is no exception to the rule. In every desire of good, in every heart yearning and longing, "unuttered or expressed," God is seeking to bring to pass his will for good to men. In prayer, then, man is not striving against God, but striving with God to bring to pass that which God wills should be brought to pass.

We might sum up, then, by saying that the purpose of prayer is that man may keep himself in fellowship with God and thus God can work in and through man to carry out his purpose of grace in the world. Its scope is universal in that anything that concerns us is a proper subject for prayer.

3. *Objections and difficulties in regard to prayer*

(1) In relation to the will of God

One question often asked is: Does prayer change the will of God? In many different ways and on many different grounds it is often maintained that prayer does not in any way change God. but that it only changes man.

In the first place, to answer this question correctly we would have to define what is meant by changing the will of God. If we mean by the will of God, God's ultimate purpose or plan for the universe and man, then we must say that prayer does not change his will. In this sense we must say that God's will (or his plan for man) includes prayer and its answer. In other words, prayer is grounded in the will of God. God included prayer and its answer in his plan for the world. We can pray in confidence, knowing that God intended that we should pray. But if we mean by the will of God an executive volition on his part, then prayer does change the will of

God. That is, God wills some things in response to man's prayer that otherwise he would not will. Dr. Forsythe is right, then, when he says that it is God's will that man by prayer should change God's will.[3] God does something in answer to prayer that he would not do if man did not pray. The only ground upon which this can be denied is to deny the personality of God. If God is a person and has regard in his dealings with man to personal relations and moral distinctions, then he must respond to man's direct approaches to him as a person. This is the same objection that we considered in relation to forgiveness of sins. As there pointed out, to hold that God changes in response to man's spiritual approach is not a denial of God's immutability. It is simply saying that God is a person and is not the slave of his own immutability; it is saying that God's immutability is the unchangeableness of his character and wisdom and that he is not an immobile, impersonal force.

Sometimes it is objected that to say that God changes his will in answer to prayer would make God the puppet of man. It is said that it is man's business to do God's will rather than God's business to do man's will. In reply, it may be said that prayer is doing God's will. It is God's will that man should pray. God adjusts himself to man as a person. He moves by his Spirit on man's heart to pray in the direction of his will. All praying that does not go in the direction of God's will is in vain.

(2) In relation to God's foreknowledge

Another phase of this same difficulty is with reference to God's foreknowledge. It is sometimes said that, in case God foreknows all things, then prayer cannot change anything and, therefore, prayer is useless. What is the use to pray, if things are already fixed and God knows beforehand what the outcome will be?

---

[3] See the volume on *Prayer* in the series, "Little Books on Religion."

In reply, it may be pointed out, in the first place, that this is no more a difficulty in regard to prayer than it is in regard to God's relation to man's personal activity in any other respect. It is simply a phase of man's relation as free and personal to God as sovereign and absolute. So far as prayer is concerned in relation to God's perfect knowledge, the same thing holds that was pointed out in regard to prayer in relation to the will of God, that is, God's foreknowledge includes prayer as an element or factor in it. If prayer is an element in reality and God foreknows all events, then God foreknows prayer and its answer in relation to all other events in the historical order. But God's foreknowledge is not within itself causative and does not render necessary the event that is foreknown; that is, the element of freedom or contingency is not taken out of the event in its being foreknown. Prayer and its answer are known of God as factors to be taken account of as to what God himself will do.

Jesus uses God's perfect knowledge as an encouragement to men to pray rather than as a discouragement. He says that, because God knows beforehand what our needs are, is a reason why we should ask for them to be supplied (Matt. 6:8). Sometimes men say that, because God knows beforehand what our needs are, therefore, there is no need to tell him. But he does know our needs and he knows that to keep in touch with God and to recognize and acknowledge our dependence on him is our chief need. Consequently he has made it so that our very need should draw us to him. All our minor needs should remind us of our one chief need. And many times, all unconsciously to ourselves, we are brought to recognize our need of God through some other need that we bring to him.

(3) In relation to the order of nature

Another difficulty often raised with reference to prayer is in regard to the order of nature. It is said that prayer cannot be answered in the physical realm because this would destroy the causal connections of the phenomena of the world. This objection is made on the ground that no force outside the physical realm can operate in that realm; otherwise we would have events occuring in the physical realm for which there were no physical antecedents or causes, and this would make science impossible. Unless events can be determined by their physical antecedents only, then science cannot trace the causal connections among phenomena, and, therefore, science is impossible.

We have met this objection at other points in our discussion; so it is not necessary to dwell on it here at length. All that needs to be said is that we know in experience the physical and the spiritual as mutually influencing and conditioning each other. Otherwise we must negate one or the other realm or have dualism. And, as a matter of experience, we do know the personal realm as being vitally linked with the sub-personal and as influencing that realm and being influenced by it. More especially, if we believe in a personal God of supreme power, we will see no difficulty in allowing that he controls and directs events in the physical as well as in the spiritual realm. In our own dealings with the physical we know that spirit or personality controls matter for its own ends and does so without violating the constitution of the physical or upsetting the order of the world. Much more can we believe that the same thing can be done by the God in whose will the whole world order has its existence and support.

The Christian will not, of course, expect God to do anything that will violate his fundamental purpose for the world.

Because of the difficulty here under consideration, some hold that prayer is answered only subjectively, not in the outer world. That is, they hold that prayer is answered only in its effect upon the one who prays. With some, prayer is reduced to a form of meditation only, a matter of reflection and aspiration. There is nothing of petition to a personal God. This is practically the pantheistic attitude. Others go further and recognize petition to a personal God, but would deny that it is answered except in the spiritual realm. They hold that God responds to our petitions in power to transform our characters and perhaps even to transform the characters of others, but deny that he changes the order of events in the outer world in answer to prayer. But biblical teaching and example, as well as experience, justify us in holding that God does bring things to pass in the physical as well as the spiritual realm in response to the prayers of his people. Dr. Karl Heim has indicated that, in answer to prayer, God may lift the fundamental laws of the physical universe off their hinges.[4]

(4) The answer to difficulties practical

In general, it may be said that the best answer to difficulties concerning answers to prayer is not the theoretical answer, but the practical answer of experience.

The great question is not, Can God answer prayer? but, Does he answer prayer? And the best way to find out concerning that is to pray. This does not mean that one can pray just to find out whether God answers prayer and by that means find out. If he prays just to find the answer to that question, he will not find it. To find out whether prayer is answered or not, one must pray in the spirit of religion, not simply in the spirit of scientific investigation or philosophical speculation. And so long as men find in experience that God does answer prayer, there is no use to set up speculative difficulties saying that he cannot. There is no objection to our seeking in so far as possible the limits within which God answers prayer, the principles governing his answering, and the method by which he works. But it is vain for us on a priori grounds to conclude beforehand that God cannot answer prayer. Men have often decided that things could not take place when, as a matter of fact,

---

[4]*The Church of Christ and the Problems of Today*, p. 139.

they were taking place all around them. The prayer instinct is one of the deepest in the nature of man; and millions have found that God has answered their cry with ready help. So long as man is what he is in nature and constitution, he will pray. When man ceases to pray, he will be something other than man.

4. Conditions of answer to prayer

In one sense, there is no such thing as unanswered prayer. Taking prayer in the sense of communion with God, one does not commune with God and fail to get a response from God. The very idea of communion carries with it a mutual activity on the part of God and man; so that, if God should not respond to man's approach, there would not be communion; there would be only an unsuccessful effort on man's part to establish communion. What man seeks, or should seek, in prayer is not, first of all, some *thing* that God may give, but God himself. So that, if there is prayer in the sense of communion with God, this carries with it the idea of a response on God's part, and this response is God's answer to man's approach. In this sense there is no prayer that is not answered. Sometimes, however, there is an effort on man's part to approach God without the proper spiritual adjustment on man's part. In this case, communion with God is not established. In that sense prayer may be unanswered.

Usually, however, when men speak of unanswered prayer, they have reference to petitionary prayer. That is, they mean that man asks for something and does not get what he asks for. In this sense also there may be unanswered prayers. Men ask God for things they do not get. This may be due to the fact that they ask God for things that God in his wisdom sees best that they should not have. He will not give the things that would injure his children. He gives good things (Matt. 7:7-11), and we must always in asking submit to his wisdom as to whether it is best that we should have what we ask for.

There are certain spiritual conditions, however, that are necessary to our obtaining and maintaining communion with God. Without these there can be no conscious fellowship with God. They are conditions of obtaining our petitions of God, because they are conditions of communion with God. A number of these conditions are named in the New Testament. One of them is faith (Matt. 21:22; James 1:6). If one prays in faith, God grants his petition. This does not mean that one can ask for just anything and believe, and then get what he asks for. One cannot have faith except as one is drawn into spiritual unity with God. This guarantees two things. One is that one will not ask contrary to God's will; man's will will be submitted to God's. The other is that one will be under the guidance of the Spirit and the Spirit does not lead us to trust God for something that it is not his will for us to have. Faith as a condition of successful prayer, therefore, carries with it two other conditions—praying in accordance with the will of God (1 John 5:14), and praying under the guidance of the Spirit (Rom. 8:26-27). It is stated in another way in John 14:13. We are to pray in the name of Jesus; that is, as those who live for him, those who seek to do his work in the world, those who represent him. We can only pray in his name as we live in spiritual unity with him. In John 15:7 this thought is presented in another way: We are to abide in Christ and have his word abiding in us. In other places men are urged to be persistent in prayer (Luke 11:5 ff.; 18:1 ff.). But persistence is simply one evidence of faith. It is faith holding on in spite of delay and discouragement.

Whatever term is used, then, in naming the condition of successful prayer, it is always in essence the same, namely, spiritual harmony or unity with God, surrender to his will. There must be no conscious holding back of ourselves from God. If we expect him to give himself to us, there must be the completest giving of ourselves to him.

IV. The Perseverance of the Saints

There is wide divergence of view within the ranks of those who discuss Christian theology on the question of what has been called the perseverance of the saints.

1. *Meaning of the doctrine*

To begin with, it needs to be made clear what the issue is.

Those who hold this doctrine mean by it that one who is truly regenerated will continue in faith and will be finally delivered from sin. We have already pointed out that there are three stages in the salvation of the individual: salvation in its beginning in justification and regeneration; salvation its its continuation and development; and salvation in its consummation in the final and complete deliverance of the whole personality from sin. The question here involves the relation of salvation in its beginning with salvation in its consummation. If a person is regenerated, is it certain that he will be brought to the consummation of salvation? Is there anything in the nature of the initial experience to guarantee its consummation? What do the Scriptures teach and what do observation and experience justify us in expecting?

What do those who hold this doctrine (the perseverance of the saints) mean by it?[5] They do not mean, as sometimes stated, that a justified person is saved in the end, no matter what happens after his justification. It rather means that justification or regeneration is a transaction of such a nature that it is the assurance that some things cannot take place. To say that this doctrine means that a justified man is saved even if he lives a life of sin or becomes an iniquitous character would be like saying that a white man will always be a white man even if he should turn to a Negro. The reason for affirming that a white man will always be a white man

---

[5]It should always be kept in mind that no doctrine is correctly stated unless it is so stated that the advocates of the doctrine will accept the statement. Otherwise the statement is a caricature or perversion of the doctrine. This is one place where many of our religious discussions fail.

is that there is assurance in the nature of things that he never will become anything else. This doctrine does not mean that a regenerated man will be saved whether he continues in faith or not; it means rather that a regenerated man will persevere in faith. The doctrine has sometimes been presented so as to make the impression that it mattered little whether the Christian continued in faith so far as salvation was concerned. Such a presentation of the doctrine said that God held to us; so we did not need to hold to him. Such an interpretation is "Hardshell" in its nature. It looks on God's purpose of grace as something that is carried out independently of all means and spiritual conditions. "Hardshellism" is no better as applied to the consummation of the Christian life than it is as applied to the beginning. Salvation is by faith in its beginning, continuance, and consummation. A man can no more be saved without faith in the middle or at the end of the Christian life than he can at the beginning. It is by faith all the way through.

Nor does this doctrine mean that a man after justification (or regeneration) by faith is then transferred to a basis of works and that from there on he must earn his way. It means that he must persevere in that in which he began, namely, faith. It does not mean that anything other than faith is necessary to salvation; but it does mean that perseverance is a quality in saving faith. The faith that does not have the quality of persistence in it is not a saving faith.

In 1 Peter 1:4-5 we have the matter set out quite definitely. The author states that we are being kept for a salvation that is to be revealed in the last day. But he not only says that we are being kept for this salvation, he tells how we are being kept, namely, by faith. We are not kept irrespective of faith; we are kept through faith. We do not keep ourselves; God keeps us. But he does not keep us in any mechanical, nonmoral or magical way. The same God who by his Spirit begot faith in our hearts at the beginning of the Christian life keeps that faith alive in our hearts. Thus we can have the confidence with Paul that he who began a good work in us will perfect it until the day of Jesus Christ (Phil. 1:6).

This statement of the matter makes it clear that the doctrine rightly conceived means that man is free in his persevering faith. It is a perversion of this doctrine to state it as if it meant that man was kept against his will. Man is no more saved in the end contrary to his will than he is at the beginning. He begins in a faith that is free and continues so. If one believes that faith can be produced by the Spirit in man's heart at the beginning of the Christian life without interferring with man's freedom, then there is no inherent reason why one should not believe that the same Spirit will keep faith alive without doing violence to man's will. If God can beget faith in the unregenerated sinner without doing violence to his freedom, why cannot God keep faith alive in the heart of the regenerate without interferring with his freedom?

2. *Support for the doctrine*

It is evident, from our discussion so far, that what one believes about this doctrine will likely be determined by what he believes about other fundamental Christian doctrines, particularly about the nature of sin and salvation. We are discussing it on the assumption that man is a sinner against God needing salvation by the grace of God. If one considers Christianity as only a good ethical system for improving one's moral condition, then there is scarcely common ground enough for a discussion of this question. But even where there is agreement on man's need of salvation from sin, there are wide divergences as to the ruin caused by sin and how man is saved from sin. A brief review of some of these elemental factors will help in support of this doctrine of the perseverance of the saints.

(1) This doctrine is supported by the right idea with reference to the relation of the human and divine activities in salvation.

The New Testament teaching is that the initiative in salvation belongs to God. This is in line with the idea that the Christian perseveres because God preserves.

The life of faith in man is a creative activity on God's part all the way through. Salvation is not a co-operative work on the part of God and man. It is God that works in us both to will and to do in bringing to pass his good pleasure in our salvation (Phil. 2:13). Synergism here is a false doctrine. Salvation is not partly, but wholly, of God. It is not true to say that God does the larger part of the saving; he does it all. Man's faith is a receiving faith. To be sure, it is active. It appropriates; it takes. But it takes as one who is wholly helpless. It seizes the grace of God as a hungry animal seizes food. But the sinner can do no more to save himself than an empty stomach can satisfy its own hunger.

(2) This doctrine is also supported by the suggestions in the New Testament as to the nature of the new life begotten in regeneration.

Especially in John's Gospel this life is represented as eternal and imperishable. We recognize the term eternal in this case as carrying a qualitative rather than a quantitative idea. It describes a kind of life rather than one that is unending in extent. It is a life of fellowship with God.

In regeneration one's moral nature is so revolutionized that he persists in faith in God, and, therefore, in a life of righteousness. This is John's view in 1 John 3:6-9. He says that the one who is begotten (or born) of God does not commit sin; that is, he does not live a life of sin. Not that there is any external constraint laid on him. His freedom is not interferred with. But he is given a new life by faith in Christ that cannot compromise with sin and that sin can never overcome. In regeneration there is something put within a man that will never let him rest in sin; he must fight sin until it is vanquished. This is not enslavement; it is freedom.

Nor does this mean that one never commits an act of sin after he becomes a Christian; it means rather that the general course of life is changed. John uses the present tense that denotes a habit of life, a constant attitude. It is this new life within that is imperishable in its nature that guarantees persistence in the fight on sin until sin is conquered.

The fact that we are by faith brought into vital union with Christ is a guarantee that the new life will persist. He becomes our life, our all. Because he lives, we shall live also (John 14:19). Christ dwells in us and we in him. And he that is in us is greater than he that is in the world (1 John 4:4). The living Christ, to whom we are united by faith, having justified us in his blood, will deliver us in the end from the wrath of God.

In 1 John 3:9 the expression, "his seed abideth in him," might be translated "his offspring abides in him"[6] (that is, God). In this case, it would mean that the new birth brings us into a life of fellowship with God; and our life of fellowship with God constitutes a moral guarantee that we will not live in sin. It is rather the guarantee that we will conquer sin.

(3) This doctine is also supported by the fact of Christ's intercession for the Christian.

Just before Peter's denial of Jesus, the Master said to him: "Simon, Simon, behold, Satan asked to have you [the apostles], that he might sift you as wheat: but I made supplication for thee [the one individual], that thy faith fail not" (Luke 22:31-32). Here we see that Jesus made intercession for Simon individually, and his request for him was that his faith should not fail. Jesus says that, while he was in the world, he kept those that the Father gave him. He so guarded them that not one of them was lost, save the son of perdition (Judas Iscariot, who was never saved). Now, since he is going away, he prays the Father to keep them (John 17:11-15).

[6]See Moffatt's translation.

These two examples of prayer for his disciples may give us some idea of the kind of intercession which Christ is making now on behalf of his people. The ground of our safety is the fact that Jesus is now living on our behalf. This is specifically expressed in the book of Hebrews: "Wherefore also he is able to save to the uttermost them that draw near unto God through him, seeing he ever liveth to make intercession for them" (Heb. 7: 25). The thought here is that he saves completely, to the end, because of his living to make intercession for those who come to God through him. His intercessory work guarantees the completeness of their salvation.

(4) Paul expresses the thought of the believer's security in a somewhat different way under the idea of the sealing of the Spirit.

Upon hearing and believing the gospel, we are sealed with the Holy Spirit of promise (Eph. 1:13). This sealing of the Spirit means that the Holy Spirit dwelling within us is God's promise or pledge that our redemption will be completed in the resurrection of the body. In the Holy Spirit we are sealed unto the day of redemption (Eph. 4:30). This is the meaning of Paul's expression that God has given us the earnest of the Spirit (2 Cor. 1:22; 5:5; Eph. 1:14). The word translated "earnest" here means pledge money that one put up as a forfeit to guarantee that he would not go back on a contract or trade entered into, but would carry out his part of the contract. The Holy Spirit of promise is the Spirit dwelling in us as God's guarantee that we shall enter into the full possession of our inheritance in the redemption of our bodies. God pledges himself to complete our redemption. The Spirit not only bears witness to the fact that we are sons of God, but also the fact that we are heirs of God and joint heirs with Christ (Rom. 8:17). As heirs of God we look forward to the time when we shall enter into possession of our full inheritance. We have the first fruits of the Spirit; that is, the Spirit dwelling within us is a beginning, a sample, of the fuller possession that we are to have later on. This gives us that groaning within ourselves, that eternal dissatisfaction with ourselves as we are, and that eager longing for the adoption, to wit, the redemption of our bodies that will consummate our salvation. We hope for fuller blessings than we now enjoy, and the Spirit within is God's guarantee that we shall enter upon that fuller possession. (See Rom. 8:23-25.)

(5) We have certain definite statements in the New Testament that cannot be explained on any other hypothesis.

We can consider only a few of the outstanding ones. Jesus says that he gives to his sheep eternal life and they shall never perish, and no one shall snatch them out of his hand. Nor is anyone able to snatch them out of his Father's hand (John 10:28-29). Here the unequivocal declaration of Jesus that those to whom he gives eternal life shall never perish would be difficult to harmonize with any view that allowed a Christian to fall away and perish. Jesus says again that the one who hears his word and believes on the one who sent him has eternal life and comes not into condemnation (John 5: 24). In Romans 8:35-39, after Paul enumerates the things that might be thought able to separate one from the love of God, he concludes by saying that none of these shall be able to separate us from the love of God which is in Christ Jesus our Lord. Peter says that we are kept by the power of God through faith unto a salvation ready to be revealed in the last day (1 Peter 1:5).

These passages seem clearly to affirm that God keeps those that believe in Christ and that there is no possibility of their perishing.

3. Objections to the doctrine

(1) Objection is sometimes made to this doctrine on the ground that it would be inconsistent with man's freedom.

The objection is based on an untenable idea of freedom. It is based on the idea that freedom means that character never becomes so fixed that it is certain that one will never change fundamentally from right to wrong or from wrong to right. It holds that for one to be free there must always be the possibility of such a change. One never becomes so fixed in evil that he may not choose the right, nor so confirmed in righteousness that he cannot choose the wrong. According to this conception of freedom there could not be irreversible fixity of character even in the next life. As a matter of fact a character fixed in righteousness is the thing that constitutes spiritual freedom. To have real freedom two things are necessary: one is an undying passion for righteousness and hatred for sin; the other is a sufficient moral dynamic to enable one to overcome sin. Regeneration gives both. Regeneration guarantees ultimate triumph over sin. There may be temporary reverses and setbacks. Ideally considered and seen from the point of view of the ultimate outcome, John's description of the regenerate man as one who does not sin is true to fact. And this is true of him, not because he is enslaved and his will destroyed, but because he is given a new moral dynamic and he is set free from the tyranny of sin. He is liberated from the thraldom that Paul describes in Romans 7, and enjoys the spiritual freedom described in Romans 8.

(2) Another objection is that this doctrine encourages one to a life of sin.

It is said that, if one has the assurance of final salvation, then he is at liberty to live as he pleases.

But it must be remembered that this doctrine is predicated on the presupposition that one is regenerated, and that regeneration means that one's moral nature is so renewed in the image of Christ that he can never again rest in sin. If the deepest longing of one's heart is for a life of sin, then, of course, he will live a life of sin. That is inevitable. But the fact that he longs for a life of sin is evidence that he has not been regenerated. There

can be no external constraint nor fear of punishment
that will keep an unrenewed man from living in sin. On
the other hand, the regenerated man will conquer sin
because the deepest passion of his soul is love to God and
hatred of sin. This doctrine does not mean that we will
conquer sin whether we fight it or not; rather does it
mean that we have the promise of such help as to assure
victory. Therefore we fight sin with courage and hope.

(3) Another objection is that the Bible teaches the
opposite doctrine popularly called "falling from grace";
that is, that one may be saved and then fall away and
be lost.

Sometimes the opposing doctrine is stated as being
that one must "hold out faithful" or he will be lost. But
theologians of all schools grant that one must "hold out
faithful"; that is, if one should cease to have faith, he
would be lost. The point at issue is whether or not a
truly regenerated man will cease to have faith. It is not a
question as to whether persistence in faith is necessary
or not; it is rather the question as to whether there is
anything in God's relation to the Christian and in the
nature of the new life begotten in regeneration that
guarantees the persistence of the believer in faith. To
cite passages in the New Testament that teach the necessity of perseverance in faith or that such perseverance is
necessary to final salvation is altogether a different thing
from showing that the New Testament teaches that one
may be a Christian and then fall away and be lost. With
this in mind we maintain that the passages claimed to
teach apostasy would come rather under one of the following heads:

a. Passages that teach that persevering faith is necessary to final deliverance from sin.

Under this head we would put such passages as Matthew 24:13; Mark 13:13; 1 Corinthians 15:2; Revela-
tions 2:7, 11, 17, 26; 3:5, 12, 21. Other passages of like
import could be found. These show that it takes a faith
of persevering, conquering power to save.

Here we must remember that a thing may be certain from the standpoint of God's purpose and yet humanly conditioned and from that point of view contingent. A good illustration of this is found in Paul's experience in the storm on his way to Rome as a prisoner (Acts 27: 14 ff.). In the midst of the storm Paul told the company on the ship that God had assured him that they would all, without the loss of a man, be saved (vv. 22-25). Yet later on when the sailors were about to escape in the boat, Paul told the soldiers that, if the sailors got out in the boat, they (the soldiers) could not be saved (vv. 30-32).

The salvation of a man elected to salvation is from all eternity certain in the mind and purpose of God, yet it is conditioned upon faith; and it is conditioned upon a faith that perseveres and conquers. A man may be elected to salvation and yet his salvation conditioned upon the fact that somebody shall preach to him the gospel. One might ask: "Suppose God should elect a man to salvation and then the proper conditions not arise." One might as well suppose any other absurdity. That assumption assumes that a set of conditions might arise that God did not know about and had not provided for. Such is the assumption that a regenerated man should not persevere in faith.

b. There are other passages where the thought probably is that perseverance in faith is evidence of regeneration and godly character. Perhaps this is the significance of John 8:31; Hebrews 3:6, 14; 4:14; 2 John 9. Possibly this is one of the thoughts underlying John 15:1 ff. (especially vv. 6-7).

This thought stated in another way means that those who have faith only in name and profession fall away and thereby manifest the superficial character of their faith. (See Matt. 13:20-21; Mark 4:16-17; 2 Peter 2: 20-22; 1 John 2:19.)

There are places where a superficial and temporary faith is recognized. In John's Gospel, such a faith is that based only on observation of miracles. In the parable of the sower Jesus describes such a faith mainly in emotional terms. Such a faith has not crystallized in character. No faith will save that does not involve the committal of the whole person to God and hence crystallize in character.

c. There are other passages where the writer is emphasizing the lack of development in Christian character or the loss of reward for faithful service. (See 1 Cor. 3:14-15; Heb. 5:12 to 6:8; 2 Peter 1:8-11.)

d. Still other passages seem to be emphasizing the danger of rejecting gospel truth on the part of the unregenerate when one knows it, especially where there has been spiritual enlightenment to understand the truth. (See Matt. 12:43-45; Luke 11:24-26; Heb. 10:26-31; 2 Peter 2:20-22; 1 John 5:16.)

There might be question about the two passages in Hebrews referred to here. The one found in 5:12 to 6:8 clearly describes regenerated people (6:1 ff.) and seems to contemplate the possibility of their falling away from faith. This may be, however, a purely *ad hominem* argument in which the author appeals to his readers on the ground that their contemplated turning away from Christianity does not offer anything better but only complete loss of everything. It is not quite so clear in the second passage (10:26 ff.) that he refers to regenerated people. But in either case the language following rather indicates that, so far as his readers are concerned, he expects them to continue in faith. One thing is certain from these passages, namely, that the author did not believe a man could switch back and forth between a saved and a lost condition. So far as this author is concerned, he makes it clear that if one should fall away, he is gone forever. There would be in his case no turning back, and the author holds this on grounds exactly contrary to those who teach the possibility of falling from a saved state. Those who teach the possibility of apostasy do so on the ground that the will does not be-

come so fixed that it may not change to the opposite.[7]
The author of the book of Hebrews argues for the impossibility of renewing the apostate to repentance on the
ground that he would have become so fixed in character
and will that it would be impossible for him to change.
Sin tends to fixity of character in evil, especially wilful
sin against the grace of God manifested in Christ.

V. The Development of the Christian Life

It is customary to discuss the development of the
Christian life under the term sanctification. But, as already stated, the prevailing use of this term in the New
Testament is to denote the initiation of the Christian
life, not its development. Besides the term sanctify (or
sanctification) is only one of a number of terms used to
denote the development of the Christian life. For these
reasons, we prefer to use the expression growth or development of the Christian life.

1. *The need of growth*

That the new life begun in regeneration needs development would hardly seem to need proof. That this life is
susceptible of growth and needs to grow is everywhere
assumed in the New Testament. This is shown by some
of the terms used for Christians. One of the earliest and
most common designations for them was disciples. A
disciple is a learner, a pupil in the school of Christ. Becoming a Christian is enrolling in the school. One must
start in the elementary things and advance grade by
grade. Then the Christian is sometimes called a soldier.
When one enlists in the army, he must go through a
course of drilling and discipline before he can become
an effective soldier. Undeveloped Christians are called
babes. Christian teachers sometimes rebuked these
babes and manifested sorrow and disappointment because they had not made development in the Christian
life (1 Cor. 3:1 ff; Heb. 5:12 ff.). Peter exhorts Christians to grow in grace (2 Peter 3:18).

---

[7] See, for instance, the argument by H. F. Tillett in his *Personal Salvation*.

Jesus set forth the spiritual life in terms of living and growing things. This has sometimes been denied by those who have emphasized the apocalyptic phase of his teaching. But whatever one may say about the relation of the ethical and the apocalyptic elements in his teaching, our Gospels represent him as setting forth the kingdom of God in terms of growing things. He compares the kingdom to seed sown by a farmer (Mark 4:1 ff.); to seed growing of itself (Mark 4:26 ff.); to a small mustard seed growing into a large tree (Mark 4:30 ff.); to leaven permeating a large vessel of dough (Matt. 13:31 ff.). These parables show that he probably thought of the kingdom in its individual phase as well as in its more general aspects, as a growing something. With this the whole New Testament representation of the Christian life is in agreement.

While not many have theoretically denied the need of growth in the Christian life, yet as a practical matter it has been greatly neglected in church life, especially in those denominations that have laid emphasis on the need of conversion as a definite, conscious experience and that have, therefore, placed great stress upon public evangelism and revivals. Some other religious bodies have emphasized teaching and training to the neglect of preaching and evangelism. To get the best results, the two phases of work must go together. Those who have emphasized evangelism have seemed at times to forget that conversion was only the beginning of the Christian life. They have forgotten that the new convert who is today rejoicing in his new experience and walking on the Delectable Mountains may tomorrow be a prisoner in the Castle of Doubt or even floundering in the Slough of Despond. They have forgotten that old habits of sin must often be conquered and that the whole emotional, intellectual, and volitional life of the convert, with all his social relations and activities, needs to be brought into captivity to Christ.

2. *Foes to growth*

There are certain things that stand in the way of growth. We will look at the opposing forces, the forces that must be overcome if any progress is to be made in the Christian life. Sometimes one is deceived by the thought that, when he becomes a Christian, all his struggles are over; but it would be nearer the truth to say that his struggles are just begun. The difference between his present and his past condition is not that he is now put beyond the need of struggle and effort. The difference is rather that now he is given a disposition that will not let him rest in sin and that makes it possible for him to overcome it. But his enemies are not dead and he must fight.

One phase of this opposition to Christian growth can be summed up in the word flesh. By the flesh is meant human nature in its sinful disposition, out from under the dominion of the Spirit. It is unsanctioned human nature. The Christian man finds that he is now two instead of one. There is the "old man" and the "new," the "flesh" and the "spirit," and between these there is ceaseless warfare. The flesh has been crucified, but it must be put to death daily. This must be done until the life on earth is over. The flesh cannot be put to death once for all so that it does not need to be done again. And unless the flesh is kept in subjection, there can be no progress in the Christian life. Progress in the Christian life depends upon the overcoming of those impulses and tendencies in one's life that oppose the will of God.

This fight with the flesh will be all the harder if vicious habits have fastened themselves on the life through years of sinful living. And even where there are not vicious habits fastened on the life, there may be selfish and unchristian methods of thought and activity that must be conquered. These may be seen as unchristian only as one develops in moral discernment and discrimination, and may be overcome only as one grows in character and Christian graces. Moral discernment must be developed as well as strength of will.   In all cases there are inherent weaknesses and evil tendencies that must be conquered.

But opposition to progress in the Christian life comes not only from within but also from without.   The world sums up all those forces operative in human society around us that stand opposed to the will of God.   The general currents of life around us are set against the development of true spirituality.   Jesus did not find a very congenial atmosphere when he was on earth, and he did not encourage his disciples to expect that they would.   On the other hand, he warned them that they would be treated as he had been (Matt. 10:24 ff.).   Not everybody would receive them and their message (Luke 10:16).   Woe unto them when all men should speak well of them (Luke 6:26).   Paul says that the man who lives a godly life life shall suffer persecutions (2 Tim. 3:12).   Peter exhorts his hearers to save themselves from a crooked generation (Acts 2:40).   John regards the world as evil and perishing (1 John 2:15-17).   But the Christian has within him a power that enables him to overcome the world (1 John 4:4; 5:4-5).

This view of the world has often been regarded as too puritanical and pessimistic.   It may be possible to take too puritanical an attitude toward human society and its activities.   Certainly there is nothing in the Bible to encourage the idea that matter is within itself evil and that the natural as such is bad.   It is only the abuse of the material world and the perversion of the forces of nature that constitute the evil.   But the Bible does look on the human race as a fallen race and the world of nature as subject to vanity on account of man's fallen estate; and experience and history strongly suggest that this view of the matter is correct.   To go to heaven on flowery beds of ease, one would have to go from another world than this and one of a different kind.

The Bible also suggests that the forces of evil with which the Christian has to contend are supramundane.

Moral evil seems to be rooted in evil forces that are more than human. Paul warns us that we wrestle not against flesh and blood but against spiritual forces that are too strong for us within ourselves (Eph. 6:12). To win against such foes the Christian needs more than human help.

3. *The means of growth*

By the means of growth we mean those agencies and forces that contribute directly to our advancement in the Christian life. These are sometimes spoken of as means of grace. They include all those means or agencies by which we become familiar with the principles of the gospel of Christ and more fully appropriate that gospel. They are the same as the means by which we are brought into saving contact with the gospel, such as the church, the ministry, the ordinances, the Bible, prayer, personal influence and testimony.

This does not signify that any of these things within themselves have the power to augment the spiritual life. They no more have the power to do that than they have the power at first to regenerate or make alive. It is the power of God alone that can regenerate or develop the regenerate life. This idea is suggested by the expression "means of grace." These things are means by which we are enabled to appropriate the grace of God. Our development in the spiritual life is just as much a matter of grace as our justification or regeneration. We can no more make ourselves grow than we can make ourselves alive at first. They are equally the work of God and equally a work of grace. Paul speaking of his efficiency in the Christian life says: "By the grace of God I am what I am" (1 Cor. 15:10).

4. *The condition of growth*

The conditions of growth are the same as the conditions of entrance upon the Christian life, namely, repentance and faith; or, using faith as inclusive of repentance, we might say it is faith alone. There must be continued and increasing repudiation of sin and opposition to it in our lives and continued and increasing dependence on Christ. Since our development in the Christian life is a work of grace on God's part, it must be a matter of faith on our part by which we appropriate his grace. To put it another way, our growth in the Christian life is the growth of our faith. The increase of faith is the growth of the divine life within us. This is due to the fact that faith is the means or condition of our union with Christ. This does not mean that faith is the only Christian grace, but it means that faith is the means of our fellowship with Christ by which these other graces are developed. Faith is the root principle of the Christian life. It is the germinal grace. Out of it grow all the other graces.

There must be struggle on our part against evil. Faith must not only trust and rest in the Lord; it must also agonize in its contention against sin and evil. There is the rest of faith, but there is also the struggle of faith. The statement is sometimes made to the effect that one cannot any more make himself grow spiritually than he can cause himself to grow physically; that all one can do is to conform to the laws of growth and he will naturally grow without effort on his part. It is true that all Christian development is the work of God and that we grow by conforming to the laws of growth. But there is a difference between physical and spiritual development and the laws governing each. And one of the laws of spiritual development is that there must be struggle against evil in oneself and in the world around him. There must be consecrated service to God and man and striving after holiness. "Blessed are they that hunger and thirst after righteousness; for they shall be filled" (Matt. 5:6). But this hungering and thirsting after righteousness must be more than a passing desire; it must be the deepest passion of the soul; it must be such a passion of the soul as to control and direct the energies and activities of life. God will give to one all the righteousness he wants; but he must want it; must want it so that he would fight for it, even die for it. Righteousness of character is no easily won achievement. The most difficult thing in the world is to be righteous. One must be willing to wade through the fires of hell to attain it.

But someone says: "Is not righteousness the gift of God's grace?" Yes, it is. But God can give only as we receive, only as we attain. The experience of regeneration is no easygoing transaction in which the soul is passively quickened into life. It is the supreme crisis of the soul in which the soul agonizes after God and righteousness and renounces forever sin and Satan. And the progressive sanctification of the life or growth in grace is of the same nature. God makes the soul righteous by creating this passion for righteousness in the soul. He gives, but he gives through our effort. Our achievement is his bestowal. God feeds the birds, but he feeds them through their efforts. God gives the farmer his harvest, but he does so through the farmer's planting and cultivation of the soil and his toil in gathering the harvest. He gives a man an education, but he gives it through years of toil and self-denying study. He gives the musican his skill in winning music from his instrument, but he does so through study and practice. We thank him daily for bread which he gives by the labor of brain and hand. So he gives righteousness of character, but he gives it through struggle and effort. Faith receives what God gives, and God gives what faith achieves.

5. *The perfection theory of growth*

In different forms there has arisen in Christian history the theory that man may attain perfection in this life. Sometimes it is held that this is attained in a great crisis. This crisis has sometimes been spoken of as a second work of grace. This work is spoken of as sanctification over against the first work of grace in regeneration or justification. People are exhorted to seek this experience as definitely as they sought the experience of regeneration. According to this theory, "carnal" Christians or "babes" in Christ are in a moment made into "spiritual" Christians.

There are a number of serious objections to this view. One is that it tends to produce in those holding it a self-satisfied spirit and a pharisaical attitude toward others. They look upon other Christians as "babes" and as "carnal." It is never a good indication for one to claim to be free from sin. The closer one gets to God, the less apt is he to claim to be sinless.

Again, those who hold this view usually lower the standard of righteousness. By being free from sin they often mean free from deliberate and conscious acts of transgression. Or they may mean by Christian perfection a heart of love toward God and a sincere purpose to serve him and do his will. They rarely go so far as to claim that all promptings and tendencies toward evil are taken out of one's nature. So when one comes to discuss perfection, it would be necessary for him, first, to define what he means by perfection. Almost anyone could reach a standard of perfection if you would let him bring the standard of perfection down low enough. Any man could reach the stars if he could bring the stars near enough to the earth. Those who hold this view use such words as "holiness" and "sanctify" with a good deal of glibness and freedom.

This theory is also wrong with reference to its view of Christian growth. Christians do not attain to maturity at one bound. Sin is not completely eradicated from the nature of man at a stroke. One cannot help but feel that those who hold this view do not see as they ought the radical nature of sin and do not realize its stubborn hold upon man.

This theory does not agree with the teaching of the Bible. There are places where men are spoken of as perfect, such as Noah and Job (Gen. 6:9; Job 1:1).

Men were commanded to be perfect (Gen. 17:1; Deut. 18:13.)   The word translated "perfect" here probably means blameless, free from fault, wholehearted, sincere—using all these terms in a relative, not an absolute sense. A perfect man was a full-grown, well-developed, sincere servant of God.   (See in N.T. 1 Cor. 2:6; Eph. 4:13; Phil. 3:15; Heb. 5:14; 6:1. In some of these passages the Greek word is translated "perfect," in others, "full-grown.")   The pure in heart shall see God (Matt. 5:8), and without sanctification no man shall see him (Heb. 12:14); but we are not to conclude that perfect purity of heart or perfect holiness is to be attained at one leap.   John describes the regenerated man as one who does not commit sin, but practices righteousness (1 John 2:29; 3:6-9).   This evidently does not mean that the regenerated man never commits an act of sin; much less does it mean that the nature or disposition to sin is entirely removed in regeneration.   John uses here the present tense of the verb, as elsewhere, to denote a continuous or habitual course of conduct, a fixed or settled tendency of life.   Besides, whatever he means by "sinneth not" and "doeth no sin" he affirms as true of every regenerated man, not of Christians who have been "sanctified" in a second work of grace. If he means by these expressions absolute sinlessness, then he affirms that all Christians are sinless.   That would be affirming too much, even for the modern "santificationist" or the most enthusiastic "holy roller."

Besides, the same author says: "If we say that we have no sin, we deceive ourselves, and the truth is not in us" (1 John 1:8). Here he is evidently speaking of Christians and from a Christian point of view.   It is hardly probable that he would affirm here that no man can claim to be free from sin, and then in the third chapter affirm that all Christians are sinless.

Paul's statement in Philippians 3 is instructive on this point. He does not count that he has obtained or been made perfect (v. 12). He does not count that he has laid hold (v. 13). But he stretches forward with all his might, striving to lay hold of that for which Christ has laid hold of him (v. 12-14). He implies that the "perfect" or full-grown Christian is the one who recognizes his imperfection. The one who claims to be sinless therefore, claims more than Paul could claim. But he does not thereby show himself a man of wisdom, but rather advertises himself as one who is lacking in spiritual discernment.

6. *The goal of development*

The goal or standard toward which we are to strive is nothing less than that of a perfect Christian character. According to the meaning of the law in its spiritual content this would demand that one love God with all the powers of his being and his neighbor as himself (Mark 12:29-31). Christ himself was the embodiment and revelation of what God would have man to be. To be like Christ is, therefore, the goal of the Christian's ambition. Or, as Jesus puts it in Matthew 5:48, we are to strive to be as perfect in character as the Heavenly Father himself is perfect. Here is an ideal that remains as a constant challenge to higher endeavor and attainment in Christian life. No matter what heights of attainment in character one may climb, he finds other heights still towering above him and challenging him to yet greater achievements. To attain these we must do more than sing, "Lord, plant my feet on higher ground"; we must also climb.

Protestant theology has usually held that the complete purification of the soul from sin was accomplished at death when the soul passed into the presence of the Lord and beheld him in beatific vision. While it might be difficult to find Scripture statements that clearly and explicitly teach this, yet it seems to be thoroughly in harmony with Scripture principles and a fair inference from what is taught about the soul's passing into his presence at death. So far as the complete transformation of soul and body is concerned, that seems to be put at the final appearing of Christ when we shall see him as he is (1 John 3:2). There is nothing, however, in this to forbid the idea that we shall go on growing in knowledge and character even throughout the endless ages.

VI. The Church and the Christian Life

Any treatment of the Christian life would be incomplete that did not give some consideration to the question of the church. In his excellent book, *Jesus and His Church*, Dr. R. Newton Flew has conclusively demonstrated that the church is necessary to Christianity as set out in the New Testament.[8] Dr. Flew considers the matter largely from the standpoint of the teaching of Jesus and shows that the church was essential to the mission of Jesus as he himself set it out. The church is also essential to the Christian life as men seek to live that life under the conditions that we find in the world today. The idea of the church is not incidental to the Christian life, but holds an essential place in that life. Our purpose here is not to set out a complete doctrine of the church, but to show something of its fundamental nature and function in the Christian life.

1. *The use of the term in the New Testament*

No exhaustive study of the term as used in the New Testament is here undertaken.[9] In a few places it is used in the Greek sense of an assembly of citizens (Acts 19:32, 39, 41) and in one or two in the Old Testament sense of the national assembly of Israel (Acts 7:38; Heb. 2:12; 12:23, doubtful). We are interested in the use of it in the sense of the Christian ecclesia. In the Christian application, it seems to be used in three senses:

(1) The predominant use of the term is with reference to a local assembly of Christians.

---

[8]See *Jesus and His Church*, by R. Newton Flew, published by the Abingdon Press.

[9]For a good summary, see *A Manual of Ecclesiology*, by H. E. Dana, chap. 2, and *Ecclesiology*, by E. C. Dargan, Part I, chap. 2.

Over and over we find the writers speaking of the church at such a place, or the churches in such a region. It is unnecessary here to give specific references, because the term is used so extensively in this sense and because there is general agreement to the effect that this is the predominant use of the term in the New Testament. Dr. Dana puts 93 of the 114 uses of the term in this class.

(2) The word seems to be used in places in an institutional sense.

This is clearly related to the use just mentioned. Strictly speaking, it is not using the word in a different sense; it is using the term with reference to any church located at any place. This is doubtless the use in Matthew 18:17 where Jesus is represented as saying: "Tell it to the church." After other means of settling a difficulty are exhausted, the last resort was to put the matter before the church. This could not be spoken with reference to any general or universal sense of the term. It is using the word in the sense of a local body, but not with reference to any particular local body. It applies to any such local body wherever found. This may be the sense also in Matthew 16:18.[10] This institutional (or abstract) use in the New Testament is rare, and some do not allow it all.

(3) The term is also used in a general or universal sense.

This use is found mainly, if not exclusively, in Paul's writings, and by him mostly in Ephesians and Colossians.[11] It is used in the sense of Christians generally conceived as an ideal spiritual body. Dr. Dargan says that the word in this sense "denotes the whole body of true believers on earth and in heaven and in all ages."[12] As expressed by Dr. S. D. F. Salmond, it is "the fellow-

[10]*Per contra*, see Broadus, Commentary on Matthew.
[11]Dr. Dana allows this use only by Paul, and all but one in Ephesians and Colossians, the other being 1 Corinthians 12:28.
[12]*Ecclesiology*, by E. C. Dargan, p. 49.

ship of believers regarded as an organic, spiritual unity in a living relation to Christ."[13]

The church in this sense is often spoken of as universal and invisible.   The term universal is appropriate since it includes all believers on earth at one time, (if not all the saints of all times, on earth and in heaven).   It is universal in character, because it includes all believers of all races and places.   It is not confined to any one class or race.   The term invisible, however, is not a happy one.   Paul speaks of the church in this sense as the body of Christ.   The function of the body in relation to man's spirit is to objectify and make visible his inner life.   So the church makes Christ visible to man. One reason for using the term invisible is to distinguish it from the church as a visible organizaton.   But the New Testament knows nothing of any general organization called a church.   The only organized body spoken of as a church in the New Testament is a local body, the church located in a particular place.   The word seems to be used in the sense of a body of Christians assembling at a particular place [(1) and (2) above] and in the sense of an ideal assembly composed of all Christians on earth at any particular time [(3) above].

2. *The nature of the church*

We might next consider briefly something of the nature of the church.   What kind of an institution is the Christian church?   Here we will be using the term mainly with reference to a local assembly of Christians, the only use of the term as applied to an organization.

(1) Christianity is fundamentally ethical, personal, and spiritual rather than legal and institutional.

The question as to the nature and function of the church is not a superficial or surface matter as some seem to think.   It is rooted in the nature of Christianity itself.   And Christianity is personal rather than institutional.   Schleiermacher stated the difference be-

---

[13]*Expositors' Greek Testament,* on Ephesians 1:23.

tween (Roman) Catholicism and Protestantism on this point to be: that in the Catholic view one came to Christ through the church, while in Protestantism one came to the church through Christ.[14] In the Catholic view (Roman, Orthodox, and Anglican) Christ founded an institution and to this institution (and its officials, especially, the bishops and priests) he gave his authority. The church, therefore, is his authoritative representative on earth and men come to him through the mediating activity of the church and her ministry. The church, then, is an authoritative institution acting for Christ and mediating his saving grace and activity to men. On the other hand is the view that the church is an association of individuals who have come to know Christ by an act of faith that is spiritually immediate in its nature. By spiritually immediate we mean that it is not dependent on any official or authoritative activity of priest, minister, or church. For the act of faith that binds the soul in spiritual union with Christ, one is dependent on others only for a knowledge of gospel truth and for such personal and spiritual influences as will help him to receive the truth of the gospel. He is also dependent on the enlightening and enabling power of the divine Spirit working in his heart.

Such agency of the Spirit is not dependent on an "authoritative" ministry or church. It is the immediate dealing of God with the individual soul. As a matter of fact, if a man a thousand miles from any priest, minister, or church should read a New Testament or a gospel message and in his soul turn to Christ, he would be saved as definitely as he would in a church, or in a religious service with ministers preaching sermons or priests administering "sacraments."

Dr. E. Y. Mullins set out very clearly as the chief distinction of the Baptist view of religion the competency of the soul under God in religion.[15] The soul

[14]See *The Christian Faith*, by Schleiermacher (English Translation).
[15]See his *The Axioms of Religion*, chap. 4.

by virtue of its moral and spiritual constitution is
capable of receiving the grace of God and of having
fellowship with God in Christ, and that without the in-
tervention of any ecclesiastical or priestly authority.
Christ in his saving work removed the necessity for any
such mediator. There is one mediator between God and
man, and one is enough. The Catholic conception that
the mediation of the church or the priesthood is necessary in the soul's relation to God implies that the mediation of Christ is incomplete. The book of Hebrews
clearly teaches that Christ is an all-sufficient priest and
his mediation is final in its efficiency. The Catholic
conception rather makes Christ the chief among many
mediators between God and man. It is true that in
Protestantism there is the idea of the priesthood of all
believers. But believers are not mediators in the same
sense that Christ is nor is their priesthood to fill out an
incomplete work on his part. The intercession of believers is purely personal and spiritual. It depends on
spiritual character and fellowship with God, not on official position or ecclesiastical standing. Ecclesiastical
ordination has nothing to do with it. The laying of a
bishop's hands on a man's head has no weight with God.
Such things belong in the realm of ecclesiastical red tape
rather than in the realm of spiritual power.

(2) What we have said about the nature of Christianity determines very largely the nature of the church.

a. For one thing, it determines that the church is a
spiritual body. A man cannot of right be a member of
an organized local church who is not first a member of
the one universal spiritual body of Christ. One becomes a member of that universal spiritual body of
Christ by the new birth, and this new birth is an absolute prerequisite to membership in an organized church.

This is not meant as an effort to settle the relation in
the New Testament between the Church as the universal spiritual body of Christ and the church as a local

body more or less definitely organized.[16]   But we do
mean to say that no person can be a member of the
body of Christ, in either the universal or the local sense,
without being renewed by the Spirit of God. This is the
primary and essential condition. One may be counted
as a member of an organization called a church, but he
cannot be a member of the body of Christ. The body
of Christ is a spiritual body. The bond that binds the
members one to another is not an external bond of
organization; it is a living bond of spiritual fellowship.
It is not a bond of creed, nor one of effort to promote
human welfare or social activity. These are secondary.
It is first of all a bond of spiritual union and fellowship
with the living Christ. All else must grow out of and
express that bond of fellowship with him. A man must
belong to Christ first and to the church as a result of
belonging to him. A Christian's primary relationship is
to Christ; all else follows from that. The church is primarily a fellowship, then, and organization is secondary.
That fellowship is first with Christ, then with other
Christians.   Their fellowship with one another results
from their fellowship with Christ. The organization of
the church is to express and develop its fellowship.

b. Another thing that follows from the nature of
Christianity, as set out already in this discussion, is that
membership in the church is voluntary.

The voluntary principle is fundamental and essential
in Christianity all the way through. Becoming a Christian comes by hearing the gospel and voluntarily accepting it. We might simply say by accepting it, for
accepting the gospel is always voluntary. It can be no
other way. There is no such thing as a "sacramental"
communication of grace. Baptism and the Lord's Supper are not sacraments in the historical sense of the term
sacrament. They convey no grace. They are acts of
obedience and manifest the faith by which we appropriate grace and thus strengthen the consciousness of

---

[16]For a statement on this point, see Dargan's *Ecclesiology*, pp. 44-45.

grace in the believer. But they are acts of obedience on the part of a believer, who has already been drawn into a living union with Christ in the act of believing. They also proclaim the gospel to others so that they may believe. But as external acts, they are to be clearly distinguished from the inner act of faith which is purely a spiritual act or attitude; and, as already stated, a voluntary matter. This act of faith brings one into the circle of the spiritual fellowship of believers. But so far as an organized body is concerned, membership in such a body must be a voluntary act.

Since the voluntary principle is fundamental, there can be no such thing as infant church membership. Nor can there be any such thing as the administration of the ordinances to infants or any others who have not voluntarily submitted to the gospel. Such a performance is not the administration of a Christian ordinance; it is the importation of a foreign element into the Christian order.

Likewise all service in the Christian church must be voluntary. Any service that is not voluntarily performed is not Christian in spirit.

c. The nature of Christianity as set forth above means also that the church is a democracy.

Democracy is a form of government; but it is more than that. It is a spirit; it is an emphasis on personality. It might be more accurate to say that it is an order of things that grows out of a recognition of the worth of personality. We tried to set out in preceding statements that Christianity is fundamentally personal rather than institutional. When Jesus told his disciples that the sabbath was made for man, not man for the sabbath, he was recognizing the worth of human personality. That principle runs all the way through the Christian order of things. Wherever any organization or institution is exalted above human welfare, that organization or institution becomes in that respect anti-

Christian. At the very heart of Christianity is the principle that human persons were so dear in the sight of God that he paid an infinite price for their redemption.

Democracy operates on the voluntary basis. Moreover, the spiritual democracy seen in churches of the New Testament order operates for the development of spiritual persons. Sometimes the objection is made against a democratic organization of the church that it lacks efficiency. But when we face this objection, we need to ask: Efficiency for what? More than likely the objector is thinking of efficiency as represented in a business corporation or governmental bureau. Churches should strive for efficiency, but for efficiency of a different order. The efficiency that a church should strive for is efficiency in developing Christlike character. This kind of efficiency can be attained only on a voluntary basis. Many times church efficiency is thought of in financial terms. Quite frequently some type of organization other than the democratic would extort more money from people than the democratic and voluntary method would. But such a standard for measuring spiritual success is quite superficial. Spiritual efficiency is measured in terms of character, not money; in terms of men, not things. Men are developed on the basis of voluntary activity, not of enslaved labor.

The democratic principle is also involved in the fact that our primary relationship is to Christ, not to men. Every Christian is directly responsible to Christ as Lord and Master. Let no man dare come between the individual believer and his Lord. Every one of us shall give account of himself to the Lord (Rom. 14:9-12), not to pastor, the priest, nor the bishop. Before the Judge of all the earth, men stand on a common level.[17] The same truth is involved in the doctrine of salvation by grace. Nothing brings men down to a common level

---

[17]This has political implications. The American Declaration of Independence asserts that all men have certain unalienable rights immediately after asserting that all men are created equal. Later the framers of The Declaration appeal to God as the Judge of all men.

like the guilt of universal sin and the grace of God that saves from sin. There are no aristocrats in the presence of a holy God who saves sinners as a matter of grace. No form of church life is consistent with the doctrine of salvation by grace except one that is democratic in spirit and principle.

3. *The function of the church*

The nature and function of the church are closely related ideas. What we have said about the nature of the church (as related to the nature of Christianity) will largely determine what we shall hold with reference to the function of the church. Function is determined by nature.

We might get at the question of the function of the church by considering it in relation to Christ as head and Lord.

(1) The church the body of Christ

As already stated, the church is the body of Christ. He is its inner life. Without his abiding presence a company of people might be a religious organization but could not be a Christian church.

The function of the church is to embody the life of Christ and to manifest that life to men. Christ is the light of the world (John 8:12; 9:5), but so are his people the light of the world (Matt. 5:14). They are the salt of the earth (Matt. 5:13). They are the salt of the earth because he abides in them as the Saviour of their lives. He transforms them so that they shine as lights in a darkened world (Eph. 5:7 ff.). Christ is now invisible to the world; but he sends his Spirit to his people and abiding in them he convicts the world of its sin and manifests himself as the Saviour of the world.

He is the head of the body, the church (Eph. 1:22; 4:15; 5:23; Col. 1:18). It is the business of the body to obey the head, to carry out the orders of the head. The church is to be obedient to him as head and Lord.

In order that the church may perform its function in relation to him, it must be filled with the divine Spirit. In 1 Corinthians chapters 12-14, Paul discusses spiritual gifts in relation to the church as the body of Christ. He shows that every gift bestowed on any member should be used for the unification and upbuilding of the body. There are intimations that even spiritual gifts may be used for selfish ends and so as to bring distraction and division in the body. Every gift, the apostle insists, should be used for the upbuilding of the body, not for personal display or aggrandizement.

(2) The church and the Spirit

The church cannot carry out its function of manifesting Christ except as the church is filled with the Spirit of God. The Spirit inhabits every individual member, but the Spirit's work in the body is more than his work in the individual members. His work is also to bring the individual members into a spiritual unity. The Spirit is the co-ordinating, unifying power of the body. More than that, the Spirit is the constitutive factor in the life of the church. The church (any local body of Christ) is more than a society of Christians banded together for practical Christian endeavor. The membership may work together to accomplish practical Christian ends; but the church is more than that. It is a company of Christian people molded into a unity of fellowship in Christ by the same power that made them Christians, the power of God. The Christian's primary relationship is to Christ, not to his fellow Christian.

(3) The primary function of the church

The first business, then, of a church is not evangelism, nor missions, nor benevolence; it is worship.[18] The worship of God in Christ should be at the center of all else that the church does. It is the mainspring of all the activity of the church. But it should not be worship

[18]Cf. Archbishop Temple's statement in *The Church and Its Teaching Today*, pp. 13 ff. and Nels F. S. Ferre in *The Christian Faith*, pp. 212 ff. It is fair to say, however, that my statement was written before seeing theirs.

for the sake of maintaining activity. In that case the worship becomes secondary and activity the primary thing. God should be worshiped for his own sake, not for the sake of what he may do for us. Worship is man's recognition of the worth of God, not for man's sake, but for God's sake. Modern Christianity all along the line has been too prone to subordinate God to man. Our churches have been modeled on the pattern of a business corporation, organized for business efficiency. The voice of God has been lost in the clatter of machinery and the bustle of organization. The modern church has sold its soul for the sake of efficiency. We go to church to hear a "go-getter" in the pulpit rally the forces to put over a program rather than to listen to the voice of God speaking to us about eternal realities. Our theological seminaries train men to be church administrators rather than preachers of the word. The apostles gave themselves to prayer and the ministry of the word; the modern minister gives himself to committee meetings and church suppers.

As a result, the hearers of the apostles cried out: What shall we do to be saved? Our listeners today say to themselves: How many more minutes must I listen before I can get out and start doing something? The church loses its secondary aims in losing the primary one. When worshiping God in the Spirit is put back at the center, other things will fall into their rightful place. When the house of God becomes the house of prayer, it becomes the place where lives are transformed. Paul indicates that when an unbeliever comes into a church dominated by the Spirit, the secrets of his heart will be made manifest (to him) and he will fall down and worship God (1 Cor. 14:25).

When we say that worship is the first business of the church, we must use the word worship in the broadest sense. Worship includes the outgoing of the soul in response to God's revelation of himself to us in Christ. It includes song, prayer, Scripture reading, giving, sermon, the ordinances—every phase of individual and corporate outgo of the soul to God in Christ in response to his grace. It is such a response of the soul as cleanses from sin and brings the soul into a deeper fellowship with God. The life begotten in regeneration is developed in worship. The whole life and organization of a church should spring from worship, center in worship, and end in worship.

Much modern preaching fails just here. Such preaching has for its end some immediate practical need of the church or the community or some section of the population. The preacher may pride himself on the fact that he is practical. He does not get up in the clouds; he stays close to the earth. But oftentimes such preaching is so practical that it is not practical. To produce abiding results the preacher's spiritual life must be grounded in the eternal realities of the gospel and his spiritual vision must go beyond the bread and butter needs of his members. Unless a church is more than a social welfare club, it is not a church. And unless it is more than a missionary or evangelistic society, it will lose its efficiency in missions and evangelism. A church is fundamentally a congregation of people who have been bound to God in an experience of saving grace in Christ, welded into a unity by the Holy Spirit, worshiping God and growing in fellowship with one another in Christ.

(4) Results of worship

Such a congregation will, as a matter of course, engage in practical Christian activity. But it will not be such activity that constitutes them a church. Their first responsibility is to be a church, and a church is primarily a worshiping body. Worship is the first business of such a body and the most characteristic (but not necessarily most obvious) expression of its life. Worship is also the inspiration of all else that the church does as a church. Worship is the perpendicular aspect of the life of the church.

Fellowship with God results in fellowship among men. As men worship God they are brought together in fellowship with one another. Normal church life leads to the development of the spiritual life in all the members. All things should lead to edification. New Testament Christians were exhorted to exercise a loving care over one another for the building up of the individual members and of the whole body. Discipline should be exercised in a constructive manner and if necessary of a punitive nature.

Preaching the gospel to those who have not heard or accepted it is also a normal expression of church life. Worship toward God leads to service toward man, and the primary service toward the world for the church is to bring man into contact with the gospel. A nonmissionary church is not a true church. The true Christian spirit is the spirit of communication.

The spirit of communication will express itself in every realm of life. The Christian spirit is always the spirit of sharing. No true Christian can rest so long as any phase of life in himself or the world in which he lives is out from under the control of the Spirit of God.

THE CONSUMMATION OF SALVATION:
THE COMING OF THE KINGDOM OF GOD

I. Difficulty of Eschatology
  1. Main reason for the difficulty
  2. No systematic treatment of the subject
  3. Sufficient knowledge for religious ends
     (1) Assurance for the future
     (2) Courage for Christian living and activity

II. Meaning and Development of the Kingdom of God
  1. Universal sovereignty of God
  2. Israel as God's kingdom
  3. The kingdom founded by Jesus
  4. This kingdom as a progressive power
     (1) This development as an ideal and as a fact
     (2) The eschatological view
     (3) The social view
     (4) The basic fact
     (5) Retrogression
     (6) Development of good and evil together
  5. The eternal kingdom of God

III. Death and Resurrection
  1. Death
     (1) In the Old Testament
     (2) In the New Testament
     (3) Causes of the change
     (4) The meaning of death for the Christian
  2. The doctrine of the resurrection
     (1) Its meaning
     (2) The time of the resurrection
     (3) Summary
     (4) The resurrection of the wicked

IV. The Consummation of the Age
  1. The expectation of the Jews and the program of Jesus
  2. The revelation of the Messiah and the coming of the kingdom
  3. Various meanings of the coming of Christ
  4. Loss of time perspective
  5. The consummation to be a spiritual kingdom

6. This consummation to be a personal act of Christ
7. The question of the millennium
8. The time of the consummation
   (1) In the teaching of Jesus
   (2) In the expectation of the apostles

V. The Judgment

1. The certainty of judgment
2. The purpose of the judgment
   (1) To reveal character
   (2) To assign destiny
   (3) To consummate history
3. The ground of the judgment

VI. Heaven

1. Where is heaven?
2. Complete deliverance from sin
3. Fellowship with God
4. Freedom from natural evil
5. Ceaseless service to God
6. Endless development

VII. Hell

1. The certainty of future punishment
   (1) Biblical teaching
   (2) The moral order of the world
   (3) Man's moral nature
   (4) The holiness of God
2. The nature and extent of future punishment
   (1) Nature of punishment in conformity with nature of sin
   (2) Extent of punishment in proportion to guilt
3. The duration of punishment

CHAPTER VI

THE CONSUMMATION OF SALVATION: THE COMING OF THE KINGDOM OF GOD

We come now to consider what is usually called eschatology, or the doctrine of last things. We must look at this doctrine in relation to, and in the light of, the doctrine of salvation. Christianity is a religion of redemption. It saves man from sin. The salvation that it gives is a present deliverance from the guilt and bondage of sin and the hope of complete deliverance in the life to come from the presence and from every trace of sin. Eschatology, then, is not only related to the doctrine of salvation, it is also a part of that doctrine. Our salvation is consummated only in the future life. Our relation to God in the future life must be regarded as a continuation and outgrowth of our relation to him in this life. This is the way it is regarded in the New Testament. We have here the first fruits of the Spirit; the full harvest will come by and by.

I. Difficulty of Eschatology

1. *Main reason for the difficulty*

Eschatology is the most difficult phase of Christian doctrine to treat. It is the place where there are, perhaps, the most widely divergent opinions. This is due to the nature of the subject. We are dealing with the future life. When we treat of salvation in its beginning and development in this life, we are dealing with a realm in which we have experience and the testimony of thousands of others to guide us. Scripture teaching can be verified by experience and interpreted in the light of experience. Since we have not had experience of the future life, what is revealed to us about that life must be put in terms of the present. There are no other terms in which it can be put. God must reveal the future, if at all, to

men in terms that they can understand, and that means
in terms of the present life. So the men who received
the revelation must receive it in those terms. In turn,
these men must pass it on to others the same way. This
is a recognized law of pedagogy, that in teaching one
must go from the known to the unknown. This is a great
limitation. We see this exemplified in the Old Testament. The prophets of the Old Testament received the
revelation and stated it in terms of the Old Testament
theocracy with which they were acquainted. They did
this because there were no other thought forms in which
they could put the matter so as to be understood. They
must receive and communicate a revelation, if at all, in
thought forms that were familiar to them. They thought
of the coming kingdom of God as a glorified Judaism, not
as a spiritual kingdom that would supplant Judaism.
To them it was not a universal spiritual religion with
the limitations of Judaism removed; it was rather Judaism extended over the whole earth—it was a new life in
the old forms. When it came, the new life transcended
the old forms and left them forever behind. To them the
messianic reign was to be a great kingdom like that
of David except more glorious. The Temple with its
offerings and priesthood was to be restored (Isa. 2:1 ff.;
Ezek. 40-48 et al.). Jerusalem was to be the center.
To it worshipers from all nations would come (Zech.
14:8, et al.). An expectation of a literal fulfilment of
these prophecies was one thing that kept the Jews of
the days of Jesus from recognizing him as the Messiah.
To insist that these prophecies must yet have a literal
fulfilment is to confuse the form with the substance. If
this program were carried out it would give us Judaism, not Christianity. This will never be. The new
wine must be put in new wine skins; the new religion
must have its own forms, not those of a decadent religion of the Old Testament age. The book of Hebrews
shows that these Old Testament forms and institutions
had their fulfilment in Christ. His work once for all

realized the thing toward which they pointed; therefore it is a fundamentally wrong principle to expect that they shall ever be restored. If that be true, these Old Testament prophecies are not to be fulfilled in form. It is the substance we have; the form we do not need. In fact, there is such an inconsistency between form and substance here that we cannot have both. One excludes the other.

Another illustration of this difficulty of revealing the future is found in the case of Jesus and his disciples. From the Gospel records it appears that Jesus announced repeatedly to his disciples, especially from the time of the great confession at Caesarea-Philippi, that he was to die and rise again; but they do not seem to have laid hold of it with any degree of appreciation or understanding. The idea that Jesus was to die they would not entertain, and the idea of the resurrection, therefore, meant nothing to them. So they could not get the meaning of his statements until they had been fulfilled in the events themselves.

What has been said about the form of Old Testament prophecy needs some qualification. Old Testament religion had in it the personal and spiritual element as well as the national. The national and racial factor determined to a large extent the institutions of Old Testament religion. But deeper than the national and institutional factor was the personal and spiritual. This spiritual element was the permanent element. This is the element that comes to the front in the psalms and the prophets. It is this spiritual religion of the Old Testament order that is perpetuated in the New. On this the New Testament is founded. New Testament religion sloughs off the national and racial factors and forms, and gives a purely personal and spiritual religion. Hence it is a fundamental mistake in interpreting Old Testament predictive prophecy to insist that it must be fulfilled in the form of the Old Testament national theocracy and its institutions. Old Testament prophecy is fulfilled in its spiritual intent, not in its outward form.

2. *No systematic treatment of the subject*

We have here in exaggerated form the same difficulty that we have in other phases of theology, namely, that the New Testament does not give us a systematic or complete treatment of the subject. We have a treatment of some other phases of theology that approaches more nearly a systematic treatment than anything we have on eschatology; for example, Paul's doctrine of justification in Romans. What we do have is a reference at different times to certain events of the future. Sometimes an event may be viewed in a certain line of development or in a certain relation or for a certain purpose. But nowhere do we have all these lines of development unified in a complete view of the future. These events or lines of development are presented in such a way as to bring out their significance for the salvation and future destiny of the individual or their meaning in relation to God's purpose for the race. The purpose of these accounts is not to satisfy our scientific or philosophical instinct, but to develop within us the life of faith. These accounts are intended to bring us to a life of fuller obedience now and trust with reference to the future. They give us the assurance that the God of grace who now delivers us from the guilt and bondage of sin will bring us to a glorious destiny in fellowship with himself; they do not satisfy our curiosity with reference to the details of the future history of the human race or the development of the kingdom of God on earth, nor with reference to many things that concern the future life.

3. *Sufficient knowledge of the future for religious ends*

It is not correct to say that we know nothing of the future life. Agnosticism here is no more satisfactory than it is anywhere else in religion. But it must be recognized that our knowledge is limited. Prophecy is not history written beforehand. We have no such view of the future as that idea of prophecy would imply. We do know enough about God and his dealings with men and we are told enough about coming events to know that the future of the race on earth and the future of the Christian beyond this life are both in the hands of God. We might sum up the purpose of eschatology as we have it in the Bible by saying that it should do two things for the Christian:

(1) It should give the fullest assurance with reference to the future of the race on earth and the Christian's destiny for the future life.

It should assure us that the future belongs to God and to those who work with him for the coming of his kingdom. This does not mean that we can have or need anything like a detailed program of future history. Our assurance here is not based on knowledge, such as we can have of past history, but it is the assurance that grows out of trust in God as he is revealed in Christ and known in our experience. It is the assurance of religious faith, not of scientific knowledge.

(2) Our eschatology should also encourage the Christian to the highest, sanest, most spiritual living and to the most determined and far-reaching endeavor in the spread of the gospel and the development of the kingdom of God on earth.

A man's hope for the future should lead to personal purity of living, to sustained activity in the service of God and fellow man, and to endeavor for the promotion of all forms of human welfare. Any form of eschatological doctrine that leads to laxity of living or cuts the nerve of Christian activity is out of line with the New Testament. The same is true of any doctrine that leads to a pessimistic or defeatist attitude toward the cause of Christ in the world or the cause of truth and righteousness in human life in general.

II. Meaning and Development of the Kingdom of God

We believe that the subject of eschatology can best be understood if treated in relation to the idea of the kingdom of God, especially if we remember that this kingdom is a kingdom of redemption. As already indicated, we must keep in mind that this life is a preparation for the next, and that in some real sense the next life is a continuation of this. God is working out a great purpose for the race, especially for his redeemed children. So far as the future is revealed to us, it is revealed as the development and consummation of the plan that God is working out in human history. Man's eternal destiny is to be the fruition of the moral and spiritual forces that are operative in time. This is clearly the view that is presented in the Bible. We will, therefore, treat the subject of eschatology in relation to the idea of the coming of the kingdom or consummation of God's plan of redemption.

We need first to get before our minds the meaning and development of the idea of the kingdom of God. This term is used in a number of senses in the Bible.

1. *The universal sovereignty of God*

In the first place, it is used with reference to the sovereignty of God over the whole of creation and particularly over mankind. This is expressed in many ways in the Bible. In Psalm 47:2 we have this: "For Jehovah Most High is terrible; he is a great King over all the earth." In verse 7 of the same psalm the thought is repeated, and in verse 8 we find: "God reigneth over the nations; God sitteth upon his holy throne." In Psalm 103:19 are these words: "Jehovah hath established his throne in the heavens; and his kingdom ruleth over all." Again in verse 22 the writer says: "Bless Jehovah, all ye his works, in all places of his dominion." This universal sovereignty or rule of God is necessarily involved in the biblical conception of God. There is only one true God, and he is sovereign over all the universe. He is everywhere present and has all power. He is infinite in wisdom and goodness. He reigns over the universe which he has created. All nations of men and individuals are subject to his moral law and must account to him for their deeds. He sends judgment on Egypt, Babylon, Phoenicia and the other nations, as well as on Israel. There is no point in space or time, no member of the human race, no part of any man's life, that is not subject to his righteous rule.

The kingdom of God means that God is working out a purpose in history. This implies that the world order as we know it, including human life, is not an ideal order. Neither human life, nor the larger order of the world, is a direct expression of the will of God. This world order, including man, is not alien to God, however, in the sense of being self-created, self-sustained, or self-propelled. It is dependent on God, but it cannot be identified with him or his will. It is not alien to God in the sense of being self-sufficient, but it is alienated from him in the sense of being out of harmony with his will. But since the world is God's world, created and sustained by him, he has a purpose concerning it; and the kingdom of God is God's working in the world to bring to pass his purpose in and through it. His kingdom, then, is as universal as his sovereignty over the universe and as particular as his moral will for the individual man. There are as many aspects to the kingdom of God as there are to his sovereignty over the created order of the world.

There are places in the teaching of Jesus where he seems to set out the kingdom as meaning God's moral rule in the lives of men and their consequent accountability to him. Such parables as the tares, the dragnet, the talents, the pounds imply that all men are under the moral government of God, must give account to him, and that in the end he will separate the good from the bad.

Another implication of the biblical concept of the kingdom is this: that, while God is working out a purpose in and through history, the historical order can never be identified with God's will. We referred to the fact that the world order at present cannot be identified with God's will. It never can be identified with his will. It is true that Jesus taught his disciples to pray that God's kingdom should come and his will be done on earth as it is in heaven. But paradoxical as it may seem, Jesus did not seem to expect the final triumph over evil, or the separation of the evil from the good until the final consummation. Here is something parallel to his command to his disciples to be perfect as the Father in heaven is perfect. In either case, he has set an impossible ideal. Neither is an ideal that can be realized in time. The purpose of history can only be realized beyond history. Time exists for the sake of the eternal. History exists for the sake of the superhistorical. The ideal set both for the individual and for the kingdom is such that it can only be realized in that which is beyond time.

2. *The theocratic kingdom of Israel*

Then there is the kingdom of Israel in the Old Testament. God had a purpose for the race which could be best worked out by choosing one man and his descendants as his peculiar people. This he did. He selected Abraham and entered into a covenant with him by virtue of which he and his descendants should possess the land of Canaan and should be a blessing to the whole world (Gen. 12:1-3). This people was formed into a nation, and as an organized nation became God's covenant people on the basis of God's redemptive act in delivering them from the land of Egypt under the leadership of Moses. There was a still further development when the nation became a kingdom under the leadership, but over the protest, of the prophet Samuel. Samuel reminded the people that Jehovah was the true king of Israel and that they should be careful not to allow the human king to stand in the way of their loyalty and service to Jehovah (1 Sam. 8). The spiritual guidance of the nation came mainly from the prophets, God's specially called and Spirit-endued messengers, rather than from the worldly kings or the officially appointed priests.

Israel failed but God succeeded. Israel failed because she thought that God had chosen her for her own sake, when he had chosen her for the sake of the world. God's purpose in choosing any person, group, nation or race never stops with that person or group. He chooses to responsibility as well as to privilege. When any person (or group) thinks he is chosen for privilege only, he misses God's purpose. That is one reason that God's choice is not to be considered a matter of favoritism. It is not a matter of favoritism to be charged with the responsibility of conveying God's will to others; that is, it is not favoritism unless responsibility is to be considered such. And usually when people object to the principle of election, they are thinking of the privilege rather than the responsibility, they want the privilege without the responsibility. It was on this point that Israel failed; she became proud of her privilege and forgot her responsibility. So God had to repudiate her. As a nation she was rejected. As a nation she rejected God's Messiah. He came and offered himself to Israel as God's Messiah and Israel refused him. This theme runs as a solemn undertone through all the music of the good news in our four Gospels. This note is missed by those who deny that Jesus thought of himself as the Messiah, and missing this, one cannot understand the Gospels or the gospel in the Gospels. This is not simply a matter of understanding this particular passage or that; it is rather a matter of missing the theme that gives meaning to the whole.

The paradox of history is that God succeeded through the failure of Israel. Israel refused her Messiah-King who came as the lowly Son of man. She refused him because he came as the lowly Son of man. She wanted

a regal Messiah who would rule from a material throne
with Jerusalem as the center, making Israel his agent
for subduing the nations to himself and to Israel. She
would not have a King who would rule all men as equals
in the sovereign power of redeeming love. But the paradox is that through the rejection of this Messiah by Israel
he became a spiritual King for the whole race, ruling by
the power of redeeming love all who accept him. If he
is to be Israel's Messiah, her sons must now come bowing
as penitents before him. They must come, along with
Gentile sinners, acknowledging him as a Saviour-King
for all men. Thus all racial and national barriers are
broken down and gone forever.

3. *The spiritual kingdom founded by Jesus*

Jehovah promised David that his descendant should
ascend his throne and reign forever (2 Sam. 7:12 ff.).
This promise found its fulfilment in Christ. So did the
kingdom of Israel find its fulfilment in the spiritual kingdom of God founded by Jesus. The Old Testament
theocracy finds its whole significance in relation to the
spiritual kingdom for which it was a providential preparation. When Jesus came to earth, he came as a Saviour-King. The magi from the east worshiped him.
(Matt. 2:11). He was regarded as fulfilling the promise
made to David (Luke 1:32-33; Acts 2:25-36). The
kingdom of God was instituted at his coming. This was
the kingdom prophesied by Daniel (Dan. 2:44). Both
Jesus and John came preaching that the kingdom was
at hand (Matt. 3:2; Mark 1:15). This kingdom was
not a political, earthly kingdom such as the Jews expected the Messiah would institute, but it was the reign
of God in the hearts of men. The Jews expected that
the Messiah would drop down out of the skies with such
great, miraculous displays of power as would overawe his
enemies, break the power of the Roman yoke, and establish a great Jewish kingdom to rule over the earth.
And when Jesus came "meek and riding upon an ass,"
saying that the kingdom of God did not come with out-

ward display such as the world could see and be impressed with, but that it was an inner reality that only the twice-born could see and appreciate (Luke 17:20-21; John 3:3), they rejected such a king and such a kingdom with scorn. Even the most spiritual of the disciples of Jesus did not appreciate the spiritual nature of the kingdom until after the death and resurrection of Jesus and the descent of the Spirit at Pentecost. Even on the occasion of the ascension of Jesus they were still asking if he would at that time restore the kingdom to Israel (Acts 1:6), evidently thinking of a restoration of the Davidic kingdom under the Messiah, but perhaps on a grander scale. Paul says that the kingdom of God is not eating and drinking, but righteousness and peace and joy in the Holy Spirit (Rom. 14:17). It is an inner spiritual experience and a present reality. John says that he is partaker with those to whom he writes in the tribulation and kingdom and patience which are in Jesus (Rev. 1:9). John states this as a present experience of his and theirs. If the tribulation and patience belonged to John and his fellow Christians in this life, so did the kingdom. The kingdom, then, is not put off to some future age for its beginning; it begins here and now. When by the indwelling Spirit men know righteousness, peace and joy, they are in the kingdom of God.

It is sometimes said that there cannot be a kingdom without a king; and since the King is absent, the kingdom is not yet; the kingdom will not be until the King returns. It is true that there cannot be a kingdom without a king; but we do have the King present in the Spirit. He lives in the Christian (John 6:56; Gal. 2:20). He dwells in our hearts by faith (Eph. 3:17). No man is a Christian who does not submit to his spiritual authority. He is now both Lord and Christ (Acts 2:36). The resurrection with the ascension is, according to Peter, the fulfilment of the promise to David that his descendant should sit upon his throne (Acts 2:29-34). The Jews could not reconcile a suffering Messiah with the idea of a reigning Messiah. Some Christian teachers have the same difficulty. Because the Jewish nation did not accept and proclaim Jesus as King, some say the kingdom age was postponed until the second advent. But Paul had truer insight. He understood that the universal spiritual authority of Jesus grew out of his humiliation and death (Phil. 2:9-11). Jesus is King in human hearts and lives because they surrender to his sacrificial love, manifested in the cross. His power is the power of sacrificial love. Jesus did not announce that the kingdom of God is at hand and then have to change his program because of rejection by his own nation. The kingdom of God was initiated at his coming. He ushered in a reign of peace and righteousness when he came to save men from sin. He reconciles men to God and to one another. When the angels sang about peace on earth among men of good will, they were not singing a song altogether inopportune because at least two thousand years too early.

4. *This kingdom as a progressive power in the world*

The kingdom is presented in the New Testament as having a development during the present gospel age. The gospel age and the kingdom age are not to be contrasted as two things. The coming of Christ and his gospel initiated the kingdom; the preaching of the gospel is the means of developing the kingdom. The gospel of the kingdom is the gospel of salvation by the grace of God through faith in Jesus as a crucified and risen Redeemer. There are not two gospels, but one.

(1) This development as an ideal and a fact

In Matthew 13 Jesus gave two parables to illustrate the growth of the kingdom—the parables of the mustard seed and of the leaven (vv. 31-33). Starting from insignificant beginnings it is to become a mighty worldwide power. Some say that the parable of the leaven represents the leavening power of Christianity in the individual life, while the parable of the mustard seed teaches the spread of Christianity in the world at large. Whether this is true or not, it is true that Jesus meant to show that Christianity was to have a growth indefinitely great in the world. Just how great is to be the development, no one can tell. Evidently the kingdom of God is to become a mighty power in the world's life. Some object to taking the parable of the leaven as representing the development of the kingdom. They say that it represents the spread of evil in the "church." One reason given for this is that leaven never elsewhere represents good. Two things should be said in reply. One is that, if leaven did elsewhere represent evil, by no means would this prove that it could not represent the good here. A figurative term does not necessarily have the same meaning every time used. Another thing to remember is that leaven did not in the Old Testament always represent evil. (See Lev. 7:13; 23:17.) There are some passages in the Old Testament that seem to predict a universal reign of peace and righteousness, such as Psalm 46:8-9; Isaiah 2:2-4; 11:6-9; Micah 4:1-4. There are those who deride the idea that wars shall cease before the second advent of Christ. But it must be remembered that many things have come to pass that good people did not believe could come to pass. It is not a safe proposition to hold that what has not been done cannot be done, especially if we take God and his grace into the count.

But it is objected that there are predictions in the New Testament to show that the world will grow worse and worse until Christ comes. This, however, is a mistake. These passages, if examined in the light of the context, we think will usually be found to be speaking of evils arising during the writer's own day, against which he is giving warning. They are not passages that can be taken as indicating an increasing predominance of evil for the gospel age as a whole. Such an interpretation of them is contrary to the genius of the gospel and the teaching of the Scriptures as a whole. Besides, such an interpretation cannot be reconciled with two thousand years of Christian history. Even zealous Christian men may speak deridingly of what Christianity has done for human society. But in spite of that the world, in certain definite aspects, is a much better place in which to live than it was when Jesus was born into it. Woman has been partially liberated, childhood uplifted and, to some extent, protected, human personality valued more highly; and all this because of Jesus and his saving work. Political, industrial, and national ideals are being slowly, but surely, transformed. It is something that nations will now at least apologize for causing a war and try to shift the responsibility in public opinion on others. Great social evils are slowly being outlawed.

(2) The eschatological view

There are those who interpret the kingdom (especially the teaching of Jesus) as wholly eschatological. According to this view the kingdom of God is not man's task but wholly God's gift. This is the view of those who hold to the idea of a postponed kingdom. It is also the attitude of Barth and his followers with their extreme emphasis on a transcendent God. It was also the interpretation put on Jesus and his teachings by such liberals as Schweitzer. The whole view is an overemphasis on the truth taught by Jesus that the kingdom is God's gift to man. The whole New Testament emphasizes the fact that only God's power is efficient in the spiritual realm. Paul may plant and Apollos water, but God must give the increase.

Paul never lost sight of the fact that all man's efforts without God were of no avail. But Paul recognized another thing, namely, that God uses man in producing results. God gives the increase, and God only can give the increase; but God uses Paul's work in planting and the work of Apollos in watering the crop. That is God's method in giving the increase. God works, but he works through us. He uses men and their efforts. He has made himself dependent on us. It is foolish to think that man can produce spiritual results without God's power, but it is just as foolish to think that God is going to bring in the kingdom independently of us and our efforts. Jesus taught his disciples to pray for the coming of the kingdom and make it their chief concern (Matt. 6:10, 33). This shows that he did not consider that the kingdom was something that would come wholly apart from man's concern and efforts.

The same principle holds here that Paul recognizes in Philippians 2:12-13. There he exhorts his readers to work out their salvation—not to earn nor buy it, but to work it out to expression in their lives. And the reason that they are to do this is because God works in them both to will and to do of his good pleasure. God works in them to initiate and to bring to completion what he wills. But they must work to bring it to expression in their lives. And God's work was not completed until these Christians worked out what God worked in them. They were dependent on God, but he was also dependent on them—not in the same way, but just as really.

There are as many phases to God's kingdom as there are to God's activity among men. This is true because the kingdom is God as sovereign acting among men. A God who was "Wholly Other" or wholly transcendent would not be working among men at all. He might be acting above or beyond them but not among men. In that case there would be no kingdom of God in our midst. There might be a kingdom of God in some extra-human realm but not among men.

It is not true, then, as some men tell us, that it is useless to talk about efforts to promote the kingdom or bring in the kingdom. Paul knew that he could not save a sinner. He knew that only God could save any sinner. Nobody ever knew that better than Paul or taught it with greater clarity and emphasis. Yet Paul said that he became all things to all men that by all means he might save some (1 Cor. 9:22). Here we have an exact parallel to the progress of the kingdom. Only God can bring it to pass, but he works through us.

(3) The social view

Over against the extreme eschatological view there has been another that might be designated the social view. This view has had its characteristic development and main emphasis in America. It was (or is) a view that reacted strongly against an extreme other-worldly emphasis in religion. It stressed the ethical teachings of Jesus. It sometimes went so far as to say that to be concerned about one's personal salvation and about the future life is selfish and that one should forget such questions and seek to make the world a better place for those now living and for oncoming generations. We were told that our concern should not be to save a few people out of a bad world, but to seek to transform a bad world into a good one. If we could produce the right social conditions, these conditions would result in good men. This general view was often called the social gospel.

Enough has been said in this book already to make clear that the author does not believe in any narrowly individualistic interpretation or application of the gospel. But in regard to this social view of the kingdom of God, some further words are necessary.

The kingdom of God is not to be identified with any social, economic, or political movement or organization. This is one of the fundamental mistakes of millenarianism. The kingdom of God is not to be identified with anything that can be pointed out as a visible entity. When anybody says, "Lo, here" or "Lo, there." he misses it. Jesus once for all repudiated such a conception of the kingdom. Here we have a direct parallel with the transcendence of God. God is in all things but is not to be identified with them either in their individual reality or in their totality. So the kingdom transcends all human relations, activities, and movements, but should vitally affect and transform them all. In this sense the kingdom is not something to be built by man. The kingdom of God is not something for which any man or set of men can draw the pattern or erect the structure. Here human wisdom and power fail. Our chief concern, and in the broad sense, our only concern, should be to bring human life under the control of God in Christ. This would mean the transformation of the whole of life. And such a state of things would be more than any political, ecclesiastical, or social order. No state or church dares identify itself with the kingdom of God. The kingdom of God affects all human relations, but is not to be identified with any or all such relations.

(4) Unredeemed human nature the basic fact

When we think about the progress of the kingdom, there is one basic fact that must be kept in mind, namely, that in every generation, the basic fact is always unrenewed human nature. The advocates of the "social gospel" have sometimes overlooked this fact. They have discussed social advancement on the assumption that man after all was not very bad, that his main need was enlightenment and good surroundings. Given these we could expect indefinite and unhindered upward advancement on the part of the race. At the beginning of the present century men were drunk with the wine of human achievement. Science was making wonderful progress, inventions were making life easier in a material way. A humanistic philosophy prevailed and greatly influenced theology. Men came to feel that the chief end of man was to glorify man and enjoy himself forever.

This view has been rudely shocked by the events of the past third of a century. Liberal theologians and social reformers are forced to recognize that there does seem to be something in man that is demonic in quality and that it takes more than a formula of evolutionary progress to exorcise the evil spirit. We are coming back to a recognition of the truth enunciated by Jesus: "That which is born of the flesh is flesh." Every generation in climbing the ladder of spiritual progress must begin at the ground level. So far as personal holiness and spiritual character are concerned, a man does not begin where his father left off. And social progress cannot be separated from personal holiness and spiritual character. Moral and social progress are inevitably conditioned and limited by personal character on the part of the constituent members of the social order. In the realm of character at least, acquired characteristics are not transmissible. Goodness of character cannot be inherited; it must be acquired. All talk about Christian culture coming in the blood of the race is sheer foolishness. It is contrary to biblical teaching and the experience of the race.

(5) Retrogression

The fact just discussed helps to explain why it is that over and over periods of retrogression occur as well as periods of progress. All through human history the advancement of the race has been retarded and even turned backward by such periods of retrogression. When we were talking early in this century about a world order in which war would be impossible, the world was suddenly plunged into World War I. Following the war came a period of material prosperity and we began to talk about abolishing poverty from the world (or at least our part of it). Then we were plunged into a worldwide depression that brought hunger and suffering to millions that were accustomed to plenty. This was followed by World War II. And along with the depression and our global war, there is on us (1945) a period of moral declension that is alarming in its extent and intensiveness. There seems no guarantee against such periods of retrogression in human affairs.

All this, however does not justify an attitude of unrelieved pessimism. Such periods of distress have been in the past God's judgment sent on the nations and have often resulted in good. Any man who would undertake to adjudicate the merits and demerits of the case in the present situation except on broad general lines would certainly be foolhardy. Yet one does not need to be able so to adjudicate the merits and demerits of the case in detail to see that God is bringing moral judgment on mankind for its selfishness and folly. Such judgments of God have intermingled with them the element of grace, and in the past have resulted in bringing new eras of spiritual revival and progress. This we can hope will be the result in this case. The lessons of history, with a Christian faith in God, justify us in hoping that there will be moral and spiritual deposits of blessing to come out of this world catastrophe.

(6) Development of good and evil together

Another thing to remember is that there may be the development of the good and the evil over against each other. It is doubtful if the worst forms of evil appear in the midst of "heathen darkness." Evil is not just a negation or absence of the good; it is positive opposition to the good. The grossest forms of evil may appear in the lands without gospel light and influence, but the grossest forms of sin are not necessarily the worst. Jesus denounced most severely, not those guilty of what we call the more fleshly sins, such as sexual immorality and drunkenness, but rather those guilty of the more refined forms, such as pride and self-righteousness. It was those who were opposing his works as the manifestation of the power of God that Jesus warned of the danger of committing an "eternal sin." It was over against the clear manifestation of God's presence and power in Jesus and his work that men were in danger of fixing themselves irremediably in a state of sin. Antichrist appears over against Christ.

Then we must remember that goodness and sin are fundamentally personal qualities. Men do not become good or bad in throngs; they become good or bad by personal self-determination, by moral choice. Goodness is determined by personal choice over against evil. It is choice of the good where there is enticement to evil. The more intense good or evil is in its manifestation, the more intense will be the development of the opposite. Jesus indicates that his coming as the manifestation of

God was the occasion of sin on the part of the people of his day (John 15:22, 24).

The book of Revelation seems to picture the struggle between sin and righteousness as being prolonged and assuming many different forms. Sin appears in myriad forms before it is finally vanquished. When put down in one form, it reappears in another. It is made clear in the parable of the tares (Matt. 13:24 ff.) and in other places that sin will not be entirely overcome until Christ comes again at the end of the age when there will be a final separation of the good and the bad. Nevertheless our aim as Christians should be to make every man on earth a Christian if possible and to bring every Christian into complete subjection to Christ. Our aim should be to bring the whole social order of the world under the sway of the principles of the gospel and the Spirit of Christ. If it be objected that this is an ideal that is impossible of attainment in this age, it might be well to remember that, although the ideal is impossible of attainment, yet Christ has commanded us to be perfect as the Father in heaven is perfect (Matt. 5:48). The Great Commission sets before us as high an ideal with reference to Christianizing the social order in which we live as does this command of Jesus with reference to individual Christian character. The command to pray that God's kingdom shall come and his will be done on earth as it is in heaven places before us the same high ideal and on us the same great obligation.

5. *The eternal kingdom of God*

It is made clear in the New Testament that the final stage of the kingdom is the eternal kingdom to be ushered in at the second coming of Christ. A good deal of confusion of thought appears at this point. Some insist that the kingdom is yet to come, that it is to be initiated at the second coming of Christ. But the New Testament makes it clear that the second coming does not initiate but consummates the kingdom of God on earth, and ushers in the eternal kingdom. The following passages make it clear that the word is used in this latter sense: Matthew 13:43; 25:35; 26:29; 1 Corinthians 15:24; 2 Timothy 4:1, 18. This phase of the matter will be discussed further in connection with the consummation of the age.

The topics that follow may be considered as steps in the establishment of the eternal kingdom or aspects of that kingdom when established. Death, the second coming of Christ, the resurrection, and the judgment are steps in the establishment of the eternal kingdom, while heaven and hell are aspects of the order of things when God's authority and power shall have been established over all things.

III. Death and Resurrection

1. *Death*

(1) In the Old Testament

We have already considered the fact that death is viewed in the Bible in relation to sin. We do not here need to treat that phase of the matter any further. But there is the fact that in the Old Testament death and the future life were generally given a rather gloomy aspect. The religion of the Hebrews was a religion mainly for this life. It is rather difficult for us to put ourselves in their place and realize that this is true, but nevertheless it is, as the Old Testament clearly shows. The promises were mainly for this life, and more largely than in the New Testament were connected with temporal good. Death at times was spoken of as the cessation of conscious communion with God and active service to him (Psalm 6:5; 30:9; 88:10-12; 115:17; Eccl. 9:10; Isa. 38:18). The continuance of life on earth was the mark of God's favor (Isa. 38:18-20). At times the writer seems to look beyond death to life with God, but even then the matter is not dwelt upon. It is simply asserted (Psalm 16:8-11; 73:24 ff., et al.). Only once or twice is resurrection clearly and definitely asserted (Isa. 26:19; Dan. 12:2). The passage in Daniel 12:1-3 is the only undisputed one. The one in Isaiah is almost as clear. The figurative use of the expression by Ezekiel shows that the idea was not unfamiliar (Ezek. 37:12 ff.). The teaching of Peter (Acts 2:25 ff.), of Paul (Acts 13:33), and of Jesus (Mark 12:24 ff.), shows that they regarded the Old Testament as teaching the doctrine. The translation of Enoch and Elijah shows that the Old Testament writers did not regard death as the end of existence. We might sum up by saying that the Old Testament as a whole clearly does not regard death as the cessation of existence, but it does not give us much light on life beyond the grave.

(2) In the New Testament

The remarkable thing is that in the New Testament all this is changed. The outlook upon death is completely transformed. This does not mean that death within itself has come to be regarded as a good; it rather means that the evil of death has been overcome and death is looked upon as the entrance for God's child upon a more glorious and a fuller life. Jesus calls death a sleep (Mark 5:39). For this his enemies laughed him to scorn. He speaks of the death of Lazarus as a sleep (John 11:11). This his disciples could not understand. He speaks of Abraham, Isaac, and Jacob as living, not dead (Mark 12:26-27). In the story of the rich man and Lazarus, Jesus shows that he does not regard death as the cessation of conscious existence, but for the righteous as the entrance upon a state of rest and peace (Luke 16:19 ff.). Stephen is said to have fallen on sleep (Acts 7:60). Paul names death as one of the things that cannot separate us from the love of God (Rom. 8:38), and again he includes it as among the Christian's possessions (1 Cor. 3:21-22). This last expression shows that Paul regards death as becoming, by God's grace, an asset rather than a liability, a blessing rather than a curse. In his own case he says that it would be far better to depart and be with the Lord; this is his desire for himself (Phil. 1:23). Later on when he thinks his time is about up, he quietly says that the time of his departure is at hand, henceforth there is laid up for him a crown of righteousness (2 Tim. 4:6, 8).

(3) Causes of the change

What are the causes that have wrought this changed view of death?

Leaving aside the theological development of the inter-biblical period, we find in the New Testament itself an explanation. There are three primary reasons. One is the resurrection of Jesus; a second is the communion with God that came to men through faith in the crucified and risen Redeemer; and a third is the teaching of Jesus. The disciples had seen their hopes concerning Jesus as the Messiah dashed to pieces by his cruel death upon the cross at the hands of sinful men. But their hopes were revived by his resurrection from the dead, and their conception of his Messiahship and the nature of his kingdom transformed. The resurrection also wrought a transformation in their view of death. They had before them a living demonstration of the fact that death had been conquered. They interpreted the death and resurrection of Jesus to mean that he had dealt with the two great problems of human life. He died for our sins according to the Scriptures (1 Cor. 15:3). In his death he met the problem of sin and solved it. He struggled with it as man's greatest enemy and conquered it. In conquering sin he conquered death, for sin and death are inseparable. The other side of the matter is that by faith in Christ men came into fellowship with the living God and thereby had conscious victory over sin and death in their own lives. They were conscious that the fellowship they had with God was one that death could not terminate. The power of sin and death had been broken in their lives by the incoming of a new power, the power of the Spirit of life in Christ Jesus (Rom. 8:2). Christ came and took the nature of man that through death he might deliver all those who through fear of death were all their lifetime subject to bondage (Heb. 2:14-16).

Then, as just indicated, our Gospels represent Jesus as speaking of death in a manner that nobody else ever had. He speaks with a quiet assurance. There is a note of confidence and certainty. He spoke of death as a sleep (Mark 5:35; John 11:11). By this he did not mean a state of unconsciousness; but doubtless he meant a state of rest as compared with the trouble and turmoil of this life. John's Gospel also represents Jesus as saying: "If a man keep my word, he shall never see death" (8:51). Again, he said to Martha: "He that liveth and believeth on me shall never die" (John 11:26). That indeed was a new way to talk about death.

(4) The meaning of death for the Christian

Instead, then, of death being something to be dreaded, it is the hour of deliverance for the Christian, the hour of entrance into a more glorious life. Death is not the termination of life, it is the entrance upon a larger life. The main element in this larger life is that it is to be a life of continued fellowship with the Lord. That was the thing to which Paul looked forward with eager longing (2 Cor. 5:1 ff.; Phil. 1:23). Death is the means, then, by which we are translated into the "upper and better kingdom."

This confident assurance concerning death and life beyond death is not to be found except where men have found communion with the living God through faith in Christ. We do not mean to say that men outside Christian circles have not died heroically. They have. But it is one thing to meet death with stoic heroism, and another thing to meet it, like Paul, saying: "To die is gain; it is far better to depart and be with the Lord." (Cf. Phil 1:21-23.) Such assurance does not come from philosophical reasoning. The philosophers have been able to give us good reasons for believing in life beyond death. This belief has been very general among men as far back as the history of men's thoughts can be traced. No doubt such belief has exercised great influence over men in their lives. But man needs something more vital than a belief in immortality that can be summed up in a "perhaps." That something can be found only in a faith that joins one to the living Christ in such a way as to give a realization of a death-transcending life here and now. Such an experience New Testament Christians had; and millions since then have had a similar experience. It cannot be logically demonstrated. It can be experimentally realized. This, and this alone, will meet the needs of men.

In broad terms, here is the difference between the Greek belief in immortality and the Hebrew doctrine of resurrection. The Greek reasoned that the soul would probably live on after the death of the body. The Hebrew thought rather in terms of the resurrection of the whole person. The Christian belief is rooted in the Hebrew tradition rather than in the Greek. The Christian belief is not that the soul will live on apart from the body, but that through resurrection the whole person overcomes death and rises above it.

2. *The doctrine of the resurrection*

In line with what has just been said, we do not get the Christian view of death apart from the doctrine of resurrection. It is not the idea that the soul will live on after the death of the body that gives hope in view of the fact of death; it is rather the doctrine of resurrection. And this doctrine is that through the power of God the person will be delivered from the embrace of death into a glorious life beyond the grave. This is in line with what was said about the resurrection of Jesus in relation to the Christian view of death. We find our hope in the living Christ.

Belief in God and in life beyond death for man will likely stand or fall together. Men believe in life beyond death because they believe in God. As Christians we believe in God as the One who raised Jesus Christ from the dead. To believe thus in God means to trans-

form a general belief in life beyond death into a living
hope. (Cf. 1 Peter 1:3.)

(1) The meaning of resurrection

We are considering resurrection here with reference to
its meaning for us as Christians. What is the significance of resurrection as we find it in the New Testament?
What is meant, for instance, when in the sixth chapter
of John, it is said four times that God will raise his people "in the last day" (vv. 39-40, 44, 54)? This hope
runs like a thread through the whole New Testament.

There are three instances recorded in the Gospels in
which Jesus raised people from the dead. Although
nothing directly is said to that effect, the impression
gathered from the accounts is that these were raised
back to their former condition, lived out their natural
lives and died a natural death. What is meant by the
resurrection "in the last day" is something different from
this and vastly more meaningful. These were the resuscitations of dead bodies, not resurrection in the true
meaning of that term. Their significance lies in the fact
that they manifest Jesus as the Lord of life and death.
They throw light on his statement to Martha when he
said: "I am the resurrection and the life" (John 11:25).

There are places where the reappearance of people on
the earth is thought of as a possibility or a reality, and
such a reappearance is spoken of as a rising from the
dead. In the parable of Dives and Lazarus, Abraham
says to Dives that, if his brothers will not hear Moses
and the prophets, neither will they repent if one rise
from the dead (Luke 16:31). Moses and Elijah appeared on the Mount of Transfiguration with Jesus
(Luke 9:30-31). Nothing is said about the form in
which they appeared except that Luke says that they
appeared "in glory." The impression gained from the
account is that they appeared as complete persons, not
merely as disembodied spirits.

One of the most instructive passages in the New Testament on the question of the resurrection is the one in

which Jesus answered the question of the Sadducees on
that question. These Sadducees did not believe in any
resurrection. So they brought to Jesus the question
about the woman who was the wife of seven brothers in
succession, all dying and leaving no children. They
wanted to know whose wife she would be in the resurrection. (See Mark 12:18-27 and parallels in Matt.
and Luke.) Jesus answered them by referring to the
passage in Exodus 3:6 in which God is spoken of as the
God of Abraham, of Isaac, and of Jacob. He reminds
them that God is not the God of the dead but of the
living. His argument seems to imply that to live as
Abraham, Isaac, and Jacob were living at the time this
was spoken of them was the same thing as a resurrection.
In fact, it is expressly said that he cited this passage
(Ex. 3:6) to show that the dead are raised. To continue to live after death in fellowship with God is the
same thing as resurrection. The Sadducees erred, said
Jesus, in denying the resurrection, not knowing the
Scriptures nor the power of God. The Scriptures, in assuming that Abraham, Isaac, and Jacob lived in fellowship with God beyond death, proved the resurrection.
The natural explanation of this passage is that Jesus
means that for Abraham, Isaac, and Jacob to live after
death is the same thing as resurrection from the dead.
Any other interpretation of the passage is somewhat
forced.

There are places where the idea of the resurrection is
applied specifically to the raising of the body. A few
passages will be sufficient to show this in the New Testament. In John 5:25 Jesus is quoted as saying: "The
hour cometh, and now is, when the dead shall hear the
voice of the Son of God; and they that hear shall live."
Here is something that takes place in the present and
evidently refers to a present, spiritual resurrection. Those
who live in sin are dead in trespasses and in sins. God
quickens them by his Spirit into new life. He makes
them to live (Eph. 2:1 ff.). This is what Paul calls a

new creation (2 Cor. 4:17). Jesus in John's Gospel calls it a new birth (3:5, 7). But in John 5:28-29 Jesus says: "The hour cometh, in which all that are in the tombs shall hear his voice, and shall come forth." In verse 29 it is made clear that this includes the good and the bad. This resurrection is universal and is "from the tomb."

In 1 Corinthians 15, Paul has an extended discussion of the resurrection. He seems to place it at the second coming of Christ, it is limited to the righteous (so far as Paul's discussion goes), and is stated in terms of a bodily resurrection. Paul has an elaborate discussion in which he answered the question: "With what kind of a body do they come"? (v. 35) He sets out in considerable detail the kind of body that is sown and the kind that is raised. Then in 2 Corinthians 5, Paul gives us his conception of the house from heaven with which the Christian is clothed at or after death. He shrinks from a disembodied state, but is confident that, when the earthly house of this tabernacle is dissolved, we shall not be left unclothed or naked spirits, but that we shall be clothed with the new house or body from heaven.

One thing that comes out clearly from these passages, and others that could be cited, is that resurrection means victory over death. God may and does raise people from the dead spiritually now. The spiritually dead are given life in this world. Jesus brought people back to natural life while he was here in the flesh. These were probably only resuscitations, raising back to natural life those who had experienced death in the body. Yet they were resurrections of a kind. Those who continue to live beyond death or who appear on earth after having died are thought of as being raised from the dead or as experiencing resurrection. So the general idea of resurrection is that of deliverance from death or victory over death. It is always the work of God, as only God can conquer death.

The idea may have a specifically spiritual application in places; that is, it may be the raising of man from the dead in the spiritual sense here and now. Or it may be applied to the body in places. Those who are made children of God are made to long for the redemption of the body. We have assurance that this ultimate deliverance is coming through the Spirit who dwells in us as the first fruits of our salvation (Rom. 8:23). In its full meaning, then, resurrection is the deliverance of the whole person from the dominion of death. It signifies the complete salvation from sin and death of the whole person. Sin and death are two aspects of one dark and dreadful reality. Salvation and life belong together. Fulness of salvation means the complete deliverance of the whole person from the dominion of death as well as from sin. In our discussion here we are concerned with resurrection as the final and complete deliverance of the Christian from death. It is the deliverance which the Lord promised those who believe in him—the deliverance that would come in "the last day" (John 6:39-40, etc.).

(2) The time of the resurrection

One of the most difficult questions concerning the resurrection as the final deliverance of the Christian from death is the question as to time. When does this final deliverance from death come to the Christian? Does it come at death, at the second coming of Christ, or when? This is a difficult question from an exegetical point of view, as well as otherwise.

As to the time of the resurrection, there are in general three positions, with modifications of each.

One position might be designated as the premillennial. Those who hold that the second coming of Christ is for the purpose of establishing a reign of a thousand years on the earth usually hold also that the first resurrection spoken of in Revelation 20, is the resurrection of the righteous and that there will be a resurrection of the wicked at the end of the millennium. Moreover, those who hold that people will be born, live their natural lives and die during the millennium hold that there will be a third resurrection at the end of the millennium. This will be the resurrection of the righteous who die during the millennial reign of Christ.

The evidence for this view is the evidence for the whole premillennial scheme and need not be reconsidered here. So far as we can see, the choice must lie between the two views yet to be presented as to the time of the resurrection.

The view that has been generally accepted in Protestant theology has been the view that there would be one general resurrection of all the dead at the second coming of Christ, including both the righteous and the wicked, and that this resurrection would consist in the raising of the bodies of the dead and the reunion of these bodies with the spirits of the persons to whom they belonged. The apostles' creed even speaks of the "resurrection of the flesh."

The third view as to the time of the resurrection is the one that holds that every individual comes into possession of his resurrection body at death. This view holds that the resurrection is universal in the sense that it includes all men, but that it is not simultaneous. In that sense it is as individual as regeneration and death.

This question of time as related to the resurrection may be impossible of final solution. We shall give some consideration to it in the following summary. But the important thing for us is not the time of the resurrection; it is rather the fact and the nature of it.

(3) Summary of the doctrine

In summarizing this matter, we note the following points:

a. This discussion takes account only of those views that hold in some sense to a bodily resurrection.

We are not taking account here of those views that assume either that there is no such thing as a bodily resurrection or assume an agnostic attitude in regard to the matter. One of the values of the biblical doctrine of the resurrection is the assurance that salvation includes the whole man; it does not include only the soul or spiritual nature of man. Biblical religion did not regard the body, as some types of Greek philosophy did, as evil and as an impediment to the soul. This tendency came into Christian thought after New Testament days and was a strong factor in the development of the monastic type of piety. Such a view regarded the death of the body as the hour of deliverance for the soul. The body was regarded as the prison house of the soul and the death of the body as the time of the soul's release.

On the other hand, Hebrew thought looked on the body as an essential factor in the life of the person. Full salvation included the body as well as the soul. In 2 Corinthians 5, Paul shrinks from the thought of being a disembodied spirit after death and gives expression to the hope that we shall be clothed with another house not made with hands, eternal in the heavens. What Paul has to say about our being sealed in the Spirit and about the first fruits of the Spirit looks toward the redemption of the body (Eph. 4:30; 2 Cor. 1:21-22; Rom. 8:23). The earnest of the Spirit is the Spirit himself dwelling within us as God's pledge of our final and complete redemption. We groan within ourselves, Paul says, waiting for our adoption, namely, the redemption of our bodies. In this sense, we are saved in hope. We earnestly look forward to the deliverance of our complete personality, including body as well as soul.

b. The resurrection of the body does not depend on the idea that the new body shall be composed of the same particles of matter as the body that is buried in the ground.

The continuous identity of the body in this life does not depend on its having throughout life the same particles of matter. We know that the particles composing the body are constantly changing. A man's body at any particular time probably has in it no particle of matter that it had a few years ago and very few that it had a few months or weeks ago. The matter composing the body constantly changes, yet it remains the same body. Evidently the principle of continuity lies in something higher than matter. That is true even in the animal. In man the principle of identity probably lies in the soul or spiritual nature of man. The body is more than matter. It is a living organism. The thing we call life (*psyche* in Greek) is more than matter. It is doubtless the organizing principle that gives unity, continuity, and identity to the body. It is entirely possible that there is something in the "life" that inhabits the body that determines the peculiar qualities of the body and determines its continuous identity. Moreover, it is in God that we live and move and have our being (Acts 17:28), and he can fashion another body for the soul when and as it pleases him.

Paul's analogy of the grain of wheat is suggestive. The grain of wheat falls into the earth and dies. It springs up in a new life. The new stalk may have in it no particle of matter that was in the old grain, yet it is continuous with it. That connection is a life connection, not a material one. So it is with the old body and the new. The new body grows out of the old rather than being connected with it in a material way. The essence of the bond of connection between the old body and the new lies in life not in matter.

It is instructive to note that, according to John's Gospel (12:24), Jesus uses of the whole person the analogy of the grain of wheat as dying and thus bearing fruit, applying it to himself as well as to his followers.

c. There are grave difficulties in what we have recognized as the standard view of Protestant theology as to the time of the resurrection.

One difficulty grows out of the fact that it involves belief in an intermediate state between death and the second coming of Christ in which the soul exists in a disembodied state. It would seem that it was from such a disembodied state that Paul was shrinking in 2 Corinthians 5:1 ff. Some have held that during this disembodied state the soul is unconscious and that it will return to consciousness only after being reunited with the body which is to be raised at the second coming. But this view is materialistic in its fundamental assumption, namely, that there can be no conscious life apart from a material organism such as our present bodies are. It avoids the difficulty of believing in a long state of conscious or semiconscious life for the soul in the intermediate state; but it does so at the cost of holding a view that amounts to saying that the soul is annihilated at death and recreated at the resurrection. Such a price is too high to pay.

We have already seen that in the Christian view death is entrance into fuller life than we knew here. But it is difficult to believe this with reference to a disembodied state. I think it will be found also that those who hold this "soul-sleeping" view regard the resurrection as giving us bodies very much like the bodies of flesh and blood which we have in this life.

One thing against this view that the soul exists in a disembodied state between death and the second coming is that it offers little consolation with reference to our Christian friends who die.[1] It is not much consolation to tell the bereaved that somewhere in the indefinite future their loved one will be raised from the dead. Whatever else one may hold in regard to the matter, the New Testament does not teach an intermediate state in which either the righteous or the wicked are unconscious or semiconscious waiting for a resurrection to come in some indefinite future. The righteous dead enter upon

---

[1] See the remarks of Dr. T. P. Stafford on this point in *A Study of Christian Doctrines*, pp. 591 ff.

a fuller and more complete life immediately after death. The parable of the rich man and Lazarus definitely implies that both the righteous and the wicked go to a life of full consciousness at death and that they enjoy (or suffer) the fruits of the life lived here (Luke 16:19-31). When Martha met Jesus after the death of Lazarus, she said that her brother would rise again in the last day. But as if to call her attention to something more immediate and cheerful than that, Jesus said: "I am the resurrection, and the life: he that believeth on me, though he were dead, yet shall he live: and whosoever liveth and believeth in me shall never die" (John 11:25-26). For the Christian there is no death; he simply passes out into a larger life. That was Paul's hope. He says that for the Christian to die is gain. It means to depart and be with the Lord (Phil. 1:21-23). Death does not break the Christian's fellowship with the Lord. Jesus says again that the one who keeps his word shall never see death (John 8:51).

What Jesus said to the Sadducees (Mark 12:18 ff.) and what Paul says in 2 Corinthians 5:1 ff., would rather indicate that they thought this life after death was an embodied life now. On the other hand, are the passages, such as 1 Corinthians 15, that seem definitely to locate the resurrection at the time of the second coming of Christ.

One attitude that we might assume in regard to the matter is that, for all practical purposes, death brings us to eternity. That is true for the individual, while the second coming of Christ brings the end of the age and the eternal order for the race. Whether we get our resurrection bodies at death or at the consummation of the age, the doctrine of the resurrection gives us the assurance that salvation is for the whole man. It brings man's whole personality to complete development in fellowship with God in Christ. We are doubtless limited in our understanding by our lack of knowledge as to what eternity will mean when we get to it.

Paul definitely indicates that the living will be transformed at the second coming of Christ. He seems also to hold that the resurrection for the dead in Christ will take place at his appearing. But we have also seen that the reappearance of the dead on the earth is spoken of as their rising from the dead. Could it be that they receive their resurrection bodies at death and "rise from the dead" when they come back with the Lord in these bodies?

After all, our knowledge as to what time means to those who have gone within the veil is very limited. What does time mean to those who have entered the eternal order? Of one thing we are sure: their existence is not an unconscious or a semiconscious one; nor is it a depersonalized one. God's people one by one enter the eternal world by death. In all essential respects we judge that this means finality for them. Christ's second coming means finality for the whole historical order as well as for the individual.

d. The new body has higher powers than the old

This is evident in the case of the body of Jesus. He seemed to come through closed doors at will (John 20: 26). At the time of the ascension his body moved through space. Possibly our resurrection bodies will largely transcend the limitations of space, as those limitations belong to matter as we now know it. Paul calls the resurrection body a spiritual body. As pointed out already, this does not mean a body composed of spirit, but one perfectly adapted to the ends and uses of our glorified spirits. Paul says that flesh and blood shall not inherit the kingdom of God (1 Cor. 15:50). Some interpret this to mean that the resurrection body will not be composed of matter but spirit. This would not agree with the statement of Jesus that his resurrection body was flesh and bone. The context shows that Paul's statement rather means flesh and blood as we now know them, subject to corruption and decay. Corruption, decay, and death will be done away with, and our resurrection bodies will be immortal, incorruptible, and glorious. As to the definite respects in which its powers will transcend those of the present body, we are not told.

From what we are being told these days about the nature of matter, one can get glimpses of wonderful possibilities of bodies composed of refined forms of matter, especially after this matter is transformed and glorified. When one beholds the beauties and grandeur of nature or is enraptured with the wonders of music, he will be slow to speak of "dead matter." Possibly dead matter is not so dead after all. Our present bodies are capable of inexpressible joys. Rather our poor sinful selves inhabiting and working through an organism of flesh and blood can experience thrills of holy joy and high hours of conscious blessedness in fellowship with God and kindred spirits. What will it be when soul and body have been delivered into the liberty of the glory of God?

But it is a mistake to limit the idea of the resurrection to the body. The body has significance only in relation to the life of the person. The language of Jesus and Paul, dealt with above in regard to death and resurrection, has significance for the whole personality. Man's whole being will be renewed and brought to a state of complete conformity with the ideal set before us in the glorified Christ.

e. The resurrection life of the Christian grows out of his union with Christ.

We have seen that this resurrection life applies, not simply to the body, but to the whole person. As in the case of Jesus, resurrection for the Christian means the elevation of his whole person to a higher plane of being. Paul's doctrine of the indwelling Spirit here comes to mind. This Spirit dwelling in man is God's seal, the first fruits of the coming harvest, thus being God's assurance of the final and complete deliverance of the whole person from the dominion of sin and death (Eph. 4:30; 2 Cor. 1:21-22; Rom. 8:23). The doctrine of union with Christ as set forth by Paul and John is a guarantee of both the fact and the nature of the resurrection life of the Christian. It is our assurance that our resurrection life is to be the development of the best that we experience here in fellowship with God in Christ.

Christ is the first fruits of them that are asleep, not necessarily in the sense of being the first in point of time to rise from the dead, but in the sense that his resurrection is the ground and pattern of ours. Because he lives, we shall live also (John 14:19).

This truth comes out in another way. It is our original union with Christ by faith that is the germ of all that grows out of it. John's Gospel and First Epistle especially emphasize the fact that the believer has eternal life the moment he believes in Christ. This eternal life is everlasting, but it is more than everlasting; it is eternal in its quality. It is death-transcending in nature. It is timeless and imperishable. Its nature guarantees final and complete victory over death for the man united to Christ by faith. In his resurrection Christ abolished death and brought life and incorruption to light (2 Tim. 1:10). Our participation by faith in his incorruptible life is the guarantee of our triumph over death.

What we have said means that assurance of life beyond death is a matter of religious faith, not of scientific demonstration. All talk of "scientific" demonstration of life beyond death is futile. Our assurance is of a different type. This does not mean that it is only a matter of fancy or fantasy; but it does mean that our assurance grows out of our trust in God as made known in Christ. Such trust is the foundation of our religious life. It is a foundation that stands sure.

(4) The resurrection body of the wicked

As to the nature of the resurrection body of the wicked, we are left almost entirely in the dark. About all that we learn is the fact that the wicked are raised and that they rise to a resurrection of shame and condemnation. Possibly in some ways their bodies will conform to their depraved and deformed spirits, but we are not told; and where nothing is revealed and we have no suggestions in experience as to which way to go, we had better practice a reverent silence.

IV. The Consummation of the Age

What we are here considering is usually discussed under the expression, the second coming of Christ. It is doubtful, however, if there is any one term or phrase that adequately describes the hope that is meant to be described by it. Perhaps the expression used here will come as near as any other. In approaching this question, several facts need to be kept in mind. Some of these facts lie on the surface in the New Testament. Some of them do not; they are more in the nature of implications than direct statements. We will try to summarize the matter under the following points:

1. *The disappointment of the Jews and even of the disciples with Jesus and his program*

All that we know about the Jews of that day indicates that they expected a Messiah of a radically different kind than the one that Jesus proved to be. They had long expected one who should come as their deliverer. They expected him to come as a great national leader and hero, deliver the Jews from their oppressors, set up a kingdom and rule over his people and with them rule the world. This expectation of theirs is so generally accepted in its main outline that it is not necessary to dwell on the question here.

When Jesus entered upon his mission, he definitely set aside that messianic ideal and that kind of a program for the kingdom. We believe that Jesus recognized from his entrance on his public ministry that he was God's Messiah and that his task was to set up the kingdom of God among men. After his baptism, in which he devoted himself to this task, he worked out in the wilderness experience the question as to what kind of a Messiah he was to be and the general lines of his work in establishing the kingdom. He definitely refused to be the kind of Messiah that the Jews expected and set his face to establish a spiritual kingdom, by spiritual methods at any cost to himself.

Two things resulted. One was that he was rejected by the Jewish nation. To them he offered himself as their Messiah. But when he refused their ideal of messiahship, they refused him. They would not have him unless he would be the kind of Messiah they wanted, and this he would not do. The result was that they rejected and crucified him. The other result was that his disciples never understood him or his program until after his death and resurrection. They came definitely to accept him as the promised Messiah, but could not grasp the idea of his being a suffering Messiah. When this was suggested to them, they sometimes indignantly rejected it (Mark 8:31 ff.) and sometimes seemed perplexed and confused by it (Mark 10:32 ff.). Under the very shadow of the cross, they kept planning their ambitious futures and looking for a great worldly kingdom (Mark 10:35 ff.). They even seemed to be hanging on to such a hope after the resurrection and just before the ascension (Acts 1:6).

2. *The revelation of the Messiah and the coming of the kingdom*

Another thing that we need to keep in mind here is that the revelation of the Messiah is the coming of the kingdom. Sometimes it is insisted that the kingdom has not yet been instituted in the world on the ground that we cannot have a kingdom without a king; and since the King was rejected and has gone away, the kingdom has been postponed until his return; at his return the kingdom will be set up.

We can readily agree to the idea that we cannot have a kingdom without a king. But we cannot agree to the proposition that, when the Jews rejected Jesus as their king, he therefore postponed his kingdom to a future age. We must remember that their conception of the

kingdom was wholly different from his. He did not post-
pone setting up the kind of kingdom they were looking
for; he set it aside once and for all. He did not set up
that kind of a kingdom during his earthly life, and he
never will. He did initiate a spiritual kingdom which
was to be promoted by spiritual methods. But he did
not complete that kingdom. It was not set up full-
grown. It was initiated as a small affair; it was to grow
and someday be consummated. The manifestation of the
Son of man as the incarnation of the love and saving
grace of God was the initiation of the kingdom; the progressive coming of the Son of man during this age is the
development of the kingdom; the final manifestation of
the Son of man will be the consummation of the kingdom.

Take a statement found in all three of the Synoptics
as illustrating the point that the coming of the kingdom
and the coming of the Son of man were the same thing.
Luke quotes Jesus as saying in one place that there were
some standing there who should not taste of death until
they should see the kingdom of God (Luke 9:27). Mark
says that they should not taste of death until they should
see the kingdom of God come with power (Mark 9:1),
while Matthew says until they should see the Son of
man coming in his kingdom (Matt. 16:28). Some New
Testament critics might take this as a case of confusion
and inconsistency among the writers of the Gospels. Why
could it not just as well be taken as a case where the
Gospel authors state the same idea in different forms?
It is evident that all three accounts refer to the same
occasion. All three Gospels place the saying in the same
setting between Peter's confession at Caesarea-Philippi
and the transfiguration. And the different forms of
statement bear witness to the fact that the followers of
Jesus thought of the coming of the Son of man and the
coming of the kingdom as the same thing and that this
identity goes back to Jesus himself.

3. *Various meanings of the coming of Christ*

It is evident from what has been said that the coming of Christ might be spoken of in a variety of senses or applications. And that is exactly what we find. If one thinks that a future coming of Christ spoken of in the Gospels or in the New Testament necessarily refers to his final manifestation at the consummation of the age, this is wrong and will surely lead to confusion. He was to come in a variety of senses. John's Gospel represents the coming of the Spirit as a coming of Christ. In promising to his disciples the coming of the Spirit, he says: "I will not leave you comfortless [orphans]: I will come to you" (John 14:18). This is in line with the Johannine method of thought that the Spirit comes to represent Christ, to make him real, that the Spirit's presence is the presence of Christ. The Spirit's work is not so much to take the place of an absent Christ as it is to make real to us a present Christ. The coming of the Spirit is the coming of Christ.

The resurrection was a coming of Christ. According to Peter on the day of Pentecost, the resurrection of Jesus was his exaltation as the Son of David. It was the fulfilment of the promise made to David that his Son should occupy his throne forever (Acts 2:29 ff.). The Son of man in the resurrection was coming in his kingdom.

This might throw light on the statement of Jesus made before the Sanhedrin when he was on trial before that body. When asked by the high priest (on oath, according to Matthew) if he was the Christ, the Son of God, he answered in the affirmative and added: "Ye shall see the Son of man sitting on the right hand of power, and coming in the clouds of heaven" (Mark 14:62). This coming does not seem to refer to the final advent, because Matthew says that they shall see this from *now on.* The King James Version gives this as "hereafter" and the American Standard as "henceforth." The Greek means that it takes place immediately. Luke says, "from now the Son of man shall be sitting at the right hand of the power of God" (Luke 22:69). The expression in Mark and Matthew about coming in the clouds of heaven is omitted by Luke. But it probably expresses in different language what is meant by the Son of man sitting at the right hand of power. And the whole passage refers to the exaltation of Jesus to his throne in his spiritual kingdom. In the resurrection and exaltation he was to come into the position that belonged to him as the Messiah and Son of God. In the Bible clouds often symbolize the divine presence and power.[2] Jesus is hurling into the teeth of his enemies, who are about to put him to death, the fact that God will crown him with authority and power as the messianic Son of God. As the Messiah of God, crucified and risen from the dead, he will be invested with authority and power over the universe. The language is apocalyptic in form; but it is saying what is said in many places in the New Testament, that he was to be enthroned at God's right hand and made King in God's kingdom. That took place in the resurrection and ascension.

Another manner in which Christ should come was in the judgments of history. This is made evident in what he says about the coming judgment on his own nation and people. In such passages as the twenty-fourth chapter of Matthew and the parallel passages in Mark and Luke, Jesus foretells this calamity that will come on the Jewish people. But he evidently goes beyond that coming judgment on the Jews and looks on to the final advent and the consummation of the age. Many attempts have been made to distinguish in these passages just where he passes from the fall of Jerusalem to the final consummation. It is the present writer's conviction that no such effort will succeed. Jesus seems to look on to the end through this judgment on his own people and the two are inextricably blended. But it does seem to be true that the coming of judgment on the nation, to-

²See the article on clouds in Hastings' *Dictionary of the Bible*.

gether with countless other such judgments since, was a coming of the Son of man in his kingdom.

4. *Loss of time perspective*

The last example discussed is a good illustration of another phenomenon which we have in the sayings of Jesus and the writers of the New Testament about the future. This phenomenon is that, as they look into the future, the temporal perspective is largely lost. They see certain realities looming large on the horizon, but nowhere undertake to relate these in a definite temporal series for us. What seems to take place is that they see the coming kingdom, in its varied aspects; they see the King coming into his kingdom; but the varied phases of the kingdom and in particular its temporal development are not distinguished for us.

Something like that took place in the Old Testament as the prophets looked forward to the coming of the Messiah and his kingdom. The prophets grasped something of the glory of the coming messianic reign, but they give us no detailed description of it. Here is the fundamental error in the saying that prophecy is history written beforehand. This saying assumes that future events are not only described before they come to pass, but that they are so described that they can be related in a temporal, if not in a causal, sequence. All the efforts that have ever been made to relate coming events in such a sequence on the basis of prophecy have failed, and they always will fail, because this is not the purpose of prophecy. The prophets of the Old Testament had visions of a glorious kingdom that was coming. With these visions they encouraged their own hearts and those of their fellow worshipers. They were encouraged to hope and wait and work until God's plans should mature. These prophecies were specific enough that, when they came to pass, the spiritually minded could recognize the fulfilment of God's purpose as revealed in the prophecies. But they were not specific enough that anybody could make a program of events beforehand.

Something like that took place in the New Testament. Jesus came. He offered himself as Messiah to his people. They did not receive him, because he was not the kind of Messiah they looked for and desired. His disciples were left stunned and disappointed. But in substance Jesus said to them: "Wait. Do not be in too big a hurry. Better things are coming. The Son of man will reign. His kingdom will come." His disciples got visions of the coming reign. It seems that sometimes they saw it in its beginning, sometimes in its consummation. But they did not seem to see, at least they do not give us, any definite program of its coming or of its consummation.

The New Testament writers were aware of the fact that the messianic reign had begun; but they also knew that it was not yet here in the fulness of its power. To this they looked forward. Both thoughts came from Jesus. Jesus regarded his kingdom as having begun, but as destined to grow in power. He also taught that it was coming to a consummation.

But neither in his teaching nor in the New Testament as a whole is there a definitely outlined program. The coming kingdom looms large. As in the case of the Old Testament prophets in setting out the Day of the Lord, the coming kingdom (or whatever form it is put in) in the New Testament is represented as "impending."[3] It loomed large on the horizon. It was the next thing in God's program. It might be too hasty to decide from this that the consummation of the age was necessarily at hand.

5. *The development and consummation of a spiritual kingdom*

Whatever may be said about the development and consummation of the kingdom, it must be kept in mind that it is to be the development and consummation of the kingdom founded by Jesus. It is not to be something

---

[3]See *The Prophets and the Promise* by Willis J. Beecher, p. 311.

unrelated to, or out of line with, what he did in founding that kingdom. Jesus ran counter to Jewish expectation when he founded a spiritual rather than a political kingdom. He reversed the Jewish program. To hold that he will someday return and set up a political kingdom is to hold that he will then reverse his own program and adopt that of the Jews. Such a procedure would be an absurdity.

This has a definite bearing on a much debated question. Was the teaching of Jesus fundamentally ethical and spiritual or was it apocalyptic? What kind of a kingdom did he expect? Did he expect the kingdom to come with a catastrophic upheaval or by ethical and spiritual means and processes? Here again we do not believe that it is merely a question of explaining this or that particular saying of Jesus, but rather one of interpreting his whole life and mission. We believe that his life and mission are set out in our Gospels on the assumption that he planned to found a spiritual order and that in line with God's purpose for his life he did found such an order. Moreover, the paradox of the situation was that in founding that order he used the opposition of his own people and their rejection of him and their effort to destroy him. Here lies the meaning of the cross and resurrection. He founded a spiritual kingdom in spite of the opposition of his people. Yea more than that, he founded his kingdom by means of their rejection of him. By means of the cross he turned defeat into victory. The cross was followed by resurrection and enthronement in the spiritual realm.

Whatever else the consummation is to be it is to be the consummation of the kingdom founded by Jesus, not the displacement of the kingdom founded by him with another of a different order. We believe therefore that they are wrong who hold that Jesus expected a kingdom founded by catastrophic methods. He rejected such methods in the wilderness temptations. He rejected such methods, because he refused the ideal of the kingdom presupposed in such methods. A kingdom founded by such methods would not have been the spiritual kingdom founded by Jesus. It would have been more on the order of the one he refused to accept as his ideal.

This will probably help to explain the fact that, in both the Synoptics and in John, Jesus constantly refused the demand of the Jewish leaders to work a miracle to prove his messianic claim. The kind of miracle that they demanded would have been one to overwhelm the moral and spiritual sensibilities of men and bring them into submission by a display of spectacular power. Jesus was giving them signs, but they were signs that did not signify much except to those with spiritual eyes. They wanted signs that would overwhelm the intelligence of men and compel submission to a kingdom of political power.

Jesus' conception of the kingdom was apocalyptic in two respects. In the first place, it was apocalyptic in that it was to be brought in by the power of God. The kingdom was to be God's gift to man. Only God's power could bring it in. The parable of the seed growing of itself teaches that the power of growth lies in the seed, not in the man that sowed the seed (Mark 4:26-29). The man who sowed the seed went home and went to bed. Yet the seed grew. It had the power of growth within itself. This is not to be taken to mean, however, that God brings in the kingdom by catastrophic methods wholly apart from our prayers and efforts. If that were true, the teaching of Jesus that we are to pray for the coming of the kingdom (Matt. 6:10) and make God's kingdom our chief care (Matt. 6:33) would have no meaning.

Then perhaps the teaching of Jesus concerning the kingdom was apocalyptic in the sense that God uses great upheavals in history to work out his will for men. This is true in the destruction of Jerusalem. That was God's judgment on the Jewish nation. It was a coming of the Son of man. Such events have been used since

and will doubtless be used until the end of the age as
God's judgment on men and to set forward his redemptive program in the world. How much this factor
will enter into the final consummation it may be impossible for us to say. But the language of Jesus in
Matthew 24, and in other places would suggest that it
may be a large factor in the consummation.

Cataclysmic events are God's judgments on men. They
are the coming of the Son of man. The final manifestation of the Son of man could easily be in connection with
some universal upheaval of nature or history. The coming of the kingdom is the coming of the eternal into time.
The consummation of the kingdom will be the end of
time in an act of God that brings to final judgment all
things temporal and human.

6. *The consummation of the kingdom a personal act
of Christ*

The resurrection and ascension of Christ meant that
the historical Christ became the superhistorical Christ.
The Christ who had lived in space and time now rose
above the limitations of space and time. He sat down at
the right hand of God (Acts 2:33, ASV margin; Heb.
1:3; 10:12, etc.). This means that he was enthroned
under God over the universe. The ideal that God had
for man in the beginning (Gen. 1:26 ff.), and expressed
in Psalm 8, is being realized in Christ (Heb. 2:5 ff.).
But his enemies have not yet all been conquered. He
sits at God's right hand awaiting the day when all his
enemies shall be put beneath his feet (Heb. 10:13 ff.).
God's purpose for mankind will then have been realized.
The temporal kingdom will be consummated and the
eternal kingdom ushered in.

The exalted Christ is revealed in the New Testament
as the Lord of history. He acts on history from above.
Luke seems to imply in Acts 1:1 that the book of Acts
is meant to tell us what this risen Christ continues to do
and teach. What he did while living in the flesh was only

the beginning of his activity among men. That program is to be carried forward. One big mistake that Christians make in thinking about Christ is to think that his work for us was completed on the cross, or at least in the resurrection and ascension. Sometimes we think that he now acts in intercession in a faraway realm that we call heaven. But the book of Acts tells us that on the day of Pentecost he poured out his Spirit on his people, that he entered into their hearts and took possession of their lives. And even then we are tempted to think that this is the end of his activity in the Spirit. But the New Testament says it was just the beginning. He is to continue to pour fresh accessions of spiritual power into human history. He acts on history in perpendicular fashion. He acts from above. He pours himself into the lives of men as Spirit. But he never becomes identified with the men to whom he gives himself. He transcends them. He is Lord over them. He is the Lord of the world of men. He is the Ruler of the kings of the earth (Rev. 1:5). The book of Acts tells us how he works by his Spirit through his people for the coming of his kingdom. The book of Revelation has the same theme, but looks on to the consummation. In the midst of world darkness and strife, the author of this book stops again and again to look forward to that consummation and to praise God for the time when the kingdom (sovereignty or rule) of this world shall become the kingdom of our God and of his Christ[4] (Rev. 11:15).

This consummation toward which history moves is to be the personal act of Jesus Christ. The Christ who founded the kingdom of God and who now works in and through human history for the development of that kingdom is to bring it to its consummation. The expression, the consummation of the age, is used five times in the Gospel of Matthew (13:39-40, 49; 24:3; 28:20). The

---

[4]It is interesting to note how scholarly men still follow the faulty text of the King James Version and quote this text as if it meant that the national governments of the world would one day pass into the hands of Christ —a thing utterly at variance with the text.

New Testament as a whole looks forward to that consummation. The book of Revelation, after describing in various ways what appears to be an almost interminable struggle with the satanic forces of evil, pictures this consummated state in the last two chapters as the New Jerusalem come down out of heaven from God to the earth. The point we are now concerned with is that this consummation is to be the act of Christ in which he manifests himself to bring about this consummation.

This personal act of Christ is usually spoken of as his second coming. This expression, however, is not used in the New Testament and may even be misleading. We have already pointed out that there are other comings of Christ besides this final coming. So the expression, second coming, might make the impression, and some people seem to think of it that way, that he left the world after his resurrection and has no touch with it until he shall come in his final manifestation. This is very unfortunate. Any view of Christianity that looks on Christians today as orphans serving only an absent Lord is out of line with the New Testament. He said he would not leave us thus (John 14:18). He came back in the Spirit. He is a present Saviour. He works now in and through his people. He is to be with us until the consummation of the age (Matt. 28:20). He is to bring his kingdom to that consummation.

There are two terms used in the New Testament that may throw some light on this matter. One is the term *parousia*. It is used in several places with reference to Christ's final manifestation (Matt. 24:3; 1 Cor. 15:23; 1 Thess. 2:19; 3:13; 4:15, etc.). It is sometimes translated coming, but it means primarily his presence. It suggests that this act of Christ in consummating his kingdom is more of the nature of a manifestation of a Christ already here than the coming of a Christ who is absent. This is even more definitely suggested by the other term which means manifestation (*epiphaneia*). He is to manifest himself in glory and power, as he was manifested before in humility and death. (See 2 Thess. 2:8; 1 Tim. 6:14; 2 Tim. 4:1, 8; Titus 2:13; 1 John 3:2.)

7. *The question of the millennium*

Certain theological systems are determined at this point by their attitude toward the "millennium." This idea of a millennium comes from Revelation 20, where the author speaks of the risen saints as living and reigning with Christ a thousand years. This passage has been the center of much controversy, and no interpretation of it has been found that has won anything like general acceptation. Those who take it to mean an actual period of time, either a literal thousand years or a period indefinitely long, have disagreed as to when this time should be, whether it would come before or after the second coming of Christ. Those who have held that Christ would come before the millennium have been called premillennialists, while those who held that the millennium would precede the second coming have been called postmillennialists. There have been all kinds of variations in the ranks of both premillennialists and postmillennialists. The premillennialists have agreed pretty well on these points: that Christ would come before the millennium and raise the righteous dead; that his coming was for the purpose of ushering in the millennium; that Christ would establish a visible kingdom on earth and reign for a thousand years; and that following the millennium there would be a resurgence of wickedness on the earth which Christ would suppress, this to be followed by the resurrection and judgment of the wicked. Many premillennialists have held that the millennium would be the great age of salvation for the world.

Postmillennialists have not been so well agreed even as premillennialists. There have been wide variations among them as to what the millennium would be, how long it would last, and so on. They have pretty well agreed on the point that Christ's coming would not only follow the millennium, but also that it was for the purpose of raising the dead, both the righteous and the wicked, and judging the world, assigning all men to their eternal destinies.

In these two systems it will be seen that the idea of the millennium plays a leading role. There is today, however, an increasing number of theologians who believe that the whole idea of a millennium is out of place in theology. This is not on the ground that they deny the authority of the New Testament for belief, but on the ground that the whole idea of a millennium is so obscure that it should not be made determinative in relation to theology as a whole. In only one passage is the millennium mentioned. That passage is a highly figurative book in the New Testament. All millennial schemes, so far as they have been tested out in history, have been proved false. They have usually been connected with a method of interpreting prophecy that regarded prophecy (in particular the Apocalypse) as meant to enable one to forecast in a more or less definite manner the course of history. Here is where all schemes have failed so far as tested by the course of events.

There is a growing number of conservative interpreters who prefer to call themselves amillennial; that is, they believe that the whole millennial idea should be left out of theology. The author confesses that he is more and more convinced that this is the correct attitude. He agrees, however, with postmillennialism on the point that the second coming of Christ means the end of history, the consummation of the kingdom of God in relation to time and history, and the ushering in of the eternal kingdom of God.

8. *The time of the consummation*

In the teaching of many, great emphasis is laid on the idea of the imminence of the coming of Christ; that is, the idea that his coming may take place at any time. It is said that the New Testament teaches the imminence of his coming and that the value of the doctrine of the second coming depends on it. It is said that the value of the doctrine as an incentive to holy living and Christian activity is lost unless the coming of Christ may be expected at any time. This is perhaps the most difficult phase of this question. Let us look at it to see if we can come to a satisfactory conclusion.

(1) In the first place, what did Jesus teach his disciples concerning the time of his return?

We have seen that in his teaching there does not seem to be any possibility of separating his statements about the final advent and his statements about the fall of Jerusalem and perhaps some other events.

Jesus did teach his disciples that certain things would take place during that generation (Matt. 24:32-34, and parallels). But he must have been referring to the fall of Jerusalem, the transfiguration, Pentecost, and possibly other such events. He solemnly affirms in some of these passages that heaven and earth shall pass away, but his words shall not pass away (Matt. 24:34). This solemn statement of Jesus would not be true if he had predicted his final return in that generation, since it did not take place. Besides, in this same connection Jesus said that only the Father knew the time of his return (Matt. 24:36). What Jesus seems to say, then, is that there are some things that he is telling them about that will come to pass during that generation; but lest they should think that he means his return to earth he puts in a warning word to the effect that he himself does not know the time of his return, and he says that no one knows but the Father. So, if any man claims to know, he contradicts Jesus on that point. And Jesus indicates that his coming will be sudden and unexpected (Matt. 24:37 ff.). Moreover, there are indications in the teaching of Jesus that he did not expect to return immediately. In the parable of the ten virgins he said: "While the bridegroom tarried, they all slumbered and slept," (Matt. 25:5). He said in the parable of the talents: "After a long time the lord of those servants cometh" (Matt. 25:19). One thing, then, we can count as settled; that is, that Jesus did not teach that he would return soon, nor did any of his teaching necessarily imply that he expected to return soon.

(2) Did the apostles expect Jesus to return during their lifetime?

Many of their statements make that impression. This seems to be generally agreed upon by New Testament students; yet many New Testament interpreters have placed an undue emphasis on this idea. Probably all that we are justified in saying in that direction is that the New Testament Christians regarded it as possible that Jesus would come back during their lifetime. Such seems to be implied in Paul's statement in 1 Corinthians 15:51: "We all shall not sleep, but we shall all be changed." We must remember, however, that there is a difference between affirming that Jesus would come during their lifetime and assuming the attitude that his coming was a possibility. The first would need to be based on definite knowledge as to the time of his return; the latter is based on a conscious ignorance as to the time of his coming.

There is another distinction that needs to be noted. When New Testament writers are speaking of the coming of Christ without reference to intervening events, they speak of it as an event that looms large and often seems to be near. This is doubtless due to the fact that the second coming is the great event of the future for Christians and for the kingdom of God. It is like looking at a great mountain peak that rises above the surrounding plain through a clear, rarefied atmosphere. It rises so high above the surrounding and intervening objects that it appears to be near. When one begins to move over the intervening territory and view the peak in relation to intervening objects, it is seen to be much farther away than it seemed at first sight. Something like this seems to be true with reference to the second coming of Christ. When the New Testament writers are looking at that event with reference to its meaning to themselves, it seems to their hearts, eager and longing for a restoration of face-to-face fellowship with him, to be near. But when they look at his coming with reference to intervening events, they affirm that it is not immediately at hand. When Paul was reported as teaching that the Lord was immediately at hand, he denied it and said that the Lord would not immediately appear. The man of sin must first be revealed (2 Thess. 2:1 ff.). When the report went out that Jesus had said to Peter that the Beloved Disciple should not die, but remain until Jesus returned, that disciple corrected the report (John 21:18 ff.). Some think that he added the twenty-first chapter of his Gospel after coming to a close in chapter 20, for the purpose of making that correction. Some say that the apostles expected Jesus to return during their lifetime. If Peter did, he must have disregarded what Jesus told him, for Jesus told him by what manner of death he should glorify God (John 21:18-19). Paul, in his old age at least, expected to die (Phil. 1:21-24; 2 Tim. 4:6 ff.).

It hardly represents the situation correctly, then, to say that the New Testament writers spoke of the second coming as imminent in the strict sense of the word; that is, as liable to occur at any time. Paul expressly repudiated the idea, as shown in the preceding paragraph; while Peter and John knew that Peter was to die. It does seem true that, under what one might call an impressionist view, the second coming seemed near, due to the tremendous significance of the event. Doubtless other things that contributed to this view, along with the importance of the event, was their desire to see Jesus again in objective vision and the fact that the time of his return was concealed from them. After considerable delay, when Jesus did not return and people began to become skeptical about the matter, Peter falls back on the principle that a day is with the Lord as a thousand years (2 Peter 3:1 ff.). That is, he says that God does not hurry as man does. He takes his time. Christ will return, for God is not slack concerning his promise. His delay does not mean his failure. It means rather that God is delaying because he wants to give men more time to repent. Christ will return and that when men are not looking for him.

One might say, then, that in the New Testament, when the writers saw the second coming through their eager desire to see Jesus again and in relation to the meaning of his coming to themselves, it seemed near. But when seen in relation to intervening events and the salvation of sinners, it seemed to recede. This is not a false impression, for the only opportunity that any man has to prepare for the Lord's coming is now. The time is brief. One must prepare before death comes. It is now or never. Consequently so far as individual preparation and readiness are concerned the second coming is near; so far as the history of the world and the coming of the kingdom of God are concerned, it may be millenniums away.

Some people insist, however, that unless we can say that Christ may come any minute, we lose the value of the doctrine as a motive to holy living. As a matter of fact, Jesus never urges the nearness of his coming as such a motive. He does urge the uncertainty of the time as such a motive (Matt. 24:44). The certainty of his coming, together with the uncertainty and brevity of time to prepare for it, does constitute a valid appeal to holy living, and this can be urged on any view as to the time of his coming. The man who says that it is the imminence of the final advent that makes it an incentive to holy living will preach on the judgment, urge its certainty and the uncertainty and brevity of time for preparation as a motive to repentance and holy living, when, according to his own view, the final judgment must be at least a thousand years in the future. In the New Testament the second coming and the judgment are put on a par in this respect (James 5:8-9). On the other hand, Christian history shows conclusively that a strong emphasis on the idea of the imminence of the Lord's coming, not only may promote fanaticism, but will almost certainly promote a form of Christian activity that emphasizes evangelism of a type that is not any too thorough and overlooks other forms of Christian activity that are just as essential to carrying out the full commission of Jesus and necessary to the building of a Christian civilization.

V. The Judgment

1. *The certainty of judgment*

The principle of judgment in God's dealings with man runs all the way through the Bible and through human experience and history. The fact of judgment is involved in man's moral freedom and in his responsibility to God. Judgment is not wholly deferred to the future. No man can do either good or evil without reaping immediately a reward of good or evil in accordance with his deed. Perhaps it could not be otherwise under a reign of moral law. And yet we can see that it would probably interfere with man's freedom, at least to some extent, if every deed were immediately followed by its full reward, especially if such a result were open and manifest. Man would follow the right course then, not so much because he loved the right and hated the wrong as because he feared to do the wrong. Such an arrangement would hardly be one of moral freedom and discipline, but rather one of coercion. Much of our moral discipline and spiritual development we now get out of loyalty to right in face of the fact that right often seems to go unrewarded and sin unpunished. Such rewards as do follow the doing of right or wrong are often of such a nature as not to be evident to the world. Many times they consist in the approval or the disapproval of our own consciences. The full reward of our deeds does not follow immediately upon the commission of a deed right or wrong, nor is such reward as does follow immediately fully evident to the world. Such an arrangement as we have in this life seems to be necessary in a world designed as a place of moral discipline and probation.

The Scriptures are full of examples showing how God bestows his blessing upon the individual or nation that does right or his curse upon the one that does evil. This is especially evident in such periods of judgment as the flood, the destruction of Sodom and Gomorrah, the deliverance of Israel from Egypt with judgments upon Egypt, and the Babylonian captivity of the Jews. In the history of the Jews we have another outstanding example in the destruction of Jerusalem in A.D. 70. We have the prophecy of this in the New Testament, but not the record of its fulfilment. Jesus foretold this coming destruction upon the Jewish nation as a judgment for their rejection of him as the Messiah and God's Son.

As in the case of the resurrection, there is difficulty as to when future judgment takes place. In the Old Testament the emphasis is upon judgment in this life; in the New Testament final judgment is postponed until the next life. Final judgment seems to come at the final advent of Christ. This is shown in Matthew 25. It may be that final judgment is postponed until the end of human history in order that our deeds of good and evil may have time to work themselves out in human history to their final consequences. All our deeds will then have had plenty of time to manifest themselves in their moral quality in their effects upon the lives of others. Every man will then be judged, not as an isolated individual, but as a member of the race. The race in its unity and totality, as well as the individual units of the race, will be judged. God will be vindicated in his work of creating the race and in his providential direction and redemption of it. The judgment comes at the end of the history of the race on earth and as the consummation of that history.

Yet there are places where judgment for the individual seems to come at death. Hebrews 9:26 simply indicates that judgment comes after death. As to whether it comes immediately after death or long after, the statement is not decisive. The parable of the rich man and Lazarus seems to indicate that both of these came to their final state immediately upon death. The state of each seems to be fixed, and each is reaping the consequences of the life he lived on earth. It is possible that, in places at least, the writers of the New Testament spoke of what they saw to be true of the life beyond death without reference to the element of time. Temporal distinctions may be largely lost beyond death. It is also possible that the "hour and article of death" constitutes in some respects the judgment of the soul, while in some other phases judgment comes at the end of the temporal world order. At any rate, the fact and principles of judgment may be clear to us whether the time and process are altogether clear or not.

There is no contradiction, then, between the idea of partial judgment in God's dealings with individuals, with nations and the race during the course of history, and the idea of a final judgment at the end of human history. The latter comes as the completion and vindication of the former. Each implies the other and neither would be complete without the other.

2. *The purpose of the judgment*

The purpose of the judgment is not to institute an investigation to determine whether or not the individual will be saved or lost. The God of infinite wisdom and knowledge needs no such court of investigation. Known unto him are all man's ways, man's character, man's destiny, without any such court of inquiry. Nor is it necessary in order that the individual himself shall know what his destiny is. This is known to everyone at death, if not sooner. Death itself is doubtless a great crisis of judgment in which character is manifested and crystallized, when one comes into the immediate presence of God. But in spite of this, it seems that there is still necessity for a final judgment at the end of human history.

What, then, is the purpose of the judgment? We might sum it up as follows:

(1) To bring out into the light every man's character as revealed in his words and deeds in relation to his fellow man, and in the effects of his deeds upon the lives of others.

Perhaps this is the reason that final judgment does not come until the end of human history at the second coming of Christ. The purpose of the judgment is not to weigh over against each other a man's good and bad deeds and determine his destiny according as the good or bad preponderates. But his words and deeds are brought into the judgment as indicating his character. Character determines destiny, and character is indicated and determined by deeds.

(2) To assign one a destiny in accordance with his character

As just stated, this does not mean that one must wait until the judgment to know whether he is saved or lost. Nor does it mean that one does not enter upon the enjoyment of the fruits of a good life or the suffering of the evil consequences of a bad life immediately upon death. The teaching of the New Testament is to the contrary. But it does mean that the final and complete possession of such rewards for good or evil does not come until the end of time and the consummation of the historical order. In some respects, man does not come to his final destiny this side of the second coming of Christ and the judgment. Everyone comes to his final destiny along with every other member of the race.

(3) It is, then, to bring the affairs of human history to completion and to vindicate God's dealings with the race as well as his dealings with the individual.

If it were only to assign the individual, strictly speaking as an individual, his destiny in accordance with character, then the judgment might possibly not be a necessity. But God created man as a race, not as isolated individuals; the race as a race fell in the sin of the first man; God provided redemption for the race in the last Adam; he preserves and governs the race in him; and he will judge the race at his final manifestation. It is especially stressed in the New Testament that the judgment is to be universal (Matt. 25:32; Rom. 14:10; Rev. 20:13). All men will be there, and the affairs of the race in its history in time on the earth will be consummated. God's ways with man will be vindicated.

3. *The ground of the judgment*

The ground of the judgment is the fact that man is responsible to God as the Creator of the world and of man's being. Man is responsible to God, because God creates and preserves him in existence and gives him all that he has in life. He lives in God's world. God is the ground and support of our being. "In him we live, and move, and have our being" (Acts 17:28). As free, man can choose or reject God and his service. To him, therefore, we are accountable for our lives.

The New Testament nowhere regards salvation by grace as delivering man from responsibility and accountability to God. This is why Paul repudiates the idea that justification by faith abrogates or nullifies the law. He says rather that it establishes law (Rom. 3:31). Salvation by grace does away with the law as a method of salvation, but it does not do away with man's responsibility to moral law and his accountability to God. The opposite view is the antinomian view of salvation by grace and would undermine the moral order. It has been urged from New Testament days as an objection to salvation by grace (see Rom. 6:1 ff.), but it is based on a misunderstanding of what salvation by grace means. Man is not saved by being delivered from obligation to keep the righteous requirements of the moral law; he is saved by being freely forgiven on the basis of Christ's atoning blood and so reinforced by the power of God's renewing grace that he can meet the requirements of the law (Rom. 8:1-4).

The gift of God's grace to sinful man does not deliver man from responsibility to God; it increases his responsibility. Since God has dealt with man in grace, certainly God's gracious dealings with man will be taken into account in the judgment. This may give a suggestion of what Paul means when he says that God will judge the secrets of men according to his gospel (Rom. 2:16). The judgment will be the vindication of God's past dealings with the race and with the individual members of the race. And since all God's dealings with man have been in and through Christ, Christ will be the judge of mankind. In Christ the race was created, preserved, and redeemed; in Christ the race will be judged (Matt. 25:31 ff.; Acts 17:31; Rom. 2:16).

VI. Heaven

By heaven we mean the eternal blessedness of the saved. Sometimes theology has set forth a definite doctrine of an intermediate state between death and the resurrection or the second coming of Christ. Whatever may be true about an intermediate state, one thing is clear, as we have already stated: namely, that there is not for the Christian (nor for the unsaved) an intermediate state in the sense of an unconscious or semiconscious state after death. The condition of the Christian after death, in the New Testament, is regarded as being one of conscious blessedness immediately following death. Paul looks forward to being with the Lord immediately after his departure from this life and thinks of it as being "very far better" than his life of service to the Lord here (Phil. 1:21 ff.).

It is entirely possible, however, that the Christian does not come to the full and final enjoyment of the blessings of redemption until the re-creation of a new humanity in Jesus Christ is completed. Our salvation is a part of a plan that a redeeming God has in mind for a new race now being created in the image of Jesus Christ. The individual Christian comes to his final destiny as a member of this new redeemed race of which Christ is the head. Apart from those who come after and those who have preceded us, we shall not be made perfect. We have a foretaste of the blessedness of redemption in this life; we enter upon a fuller possession of that blessedness at death; we come into full possession of it after judgment. What is said here, however, about the eternal blessedness of the redeemed will apply very largely to their condition between death and the consummation of the age.

1. *Where is heaven?*

Heaven is not primarily a place but a state of character and relationship to God. It is freedom from sin and fullness of fellowship with God. A man with sin in his heart could not be happy anywhere in God's universe. He would convert any paradise into a hell. Character is more than environment. A perfect environment will not make perfect character. Some modern soapbox orators seem to think that a full dinner pail is all that is needed to turn sinners into saints and the world into a paradise. But experience rather indicates that, without the regenerating grace of God, the easier conditions are for the sinner the more perverse he will likely become.

On the other hand, salvation would not be complete without a change of environment as well as a change in character. We have seen that there are indications in the New Testament that there will be a renovation of the physical universe along with the deliverance of the children of God from the bondage of sin and corruption (Rom. 8:19 ff; 2 Peter 3:13). There will be new heavens and a new earth for a new humanity to inhabit. This will be true whether Peter's statement refers to the renovation of the physical universe or is a figure for the regeneration of the moral universe. The fact that we are to inhabit bodies will probably call for a "local habitation and a name." Heaven will doubtless be a location as well as a state of character. Will it be on this earth? Nobody knows, and there is no use to speculate about the matter. Our glorified bodies may have the power to move through space at the behest of our glorified wills. We do feel safe in holding that, while the primary thing about heaven is a state of character, it will also include a perfect environment.

2. *Our eternal state will be complete deliverance from sin*

Or, to state the matter affirmatively, it will be holiness of character. To be like Christ will be heaven. We know that when he shall appear we shall be like him (1 John 3:2). To make us like Christ in character is the thing that God has had in mind for us from eternity. He predestinated us to be conformed to the image of his Son (Rom. 8:29). Nothing grieves the heart of the Christian so in this life as his own sins and moral lapses. He longs with unutterable longing for complete deliverance. This comes to him in the next life. To be free from sin will be one of the chief elements in the Christian's blessedness in the coming age. Not only will sin be taken out of us, but also out of the whole social order of which we shall be a part. The dogs, the sorcerers, the fornicators, the murderers, the idolaters, and every one that loveth and maketh a lie—all these shall be left outside the Holy City (Rev. 22:15).

3. *Our eternal state will be a life of unhindered fellowship with God in Christ*

The Christian's fellowship with God is his chief joy in this life. It is this that brings joy and hope and conquering power. It is for a fuller fellowship with the Lord that the Christian longs in the next life. Paul says that it would be very far better to depart in death and be with the Lord (Phil. 1:23). This is the explanation of the eager looking toward the second coming that we find in the New Testament. While Jesus was on earth, his disciples had fellowship with him in the flesh. During the present age we have fellowship with him in the Spirit.

When he returns to receive his people, we shall have with him a fellowship that combines the values of the inner and the outer, the spiritual and the physical. In this life our fellowship with God is hindered by our sins and spiritual blindness. When we see the Lord face to face and are completely transformed into his image, then our fellowship with him will be full and complete. This carries with it the idea that heaven is the complete realization of the life of fellowship that man has with God here and now.

Fellowship with God carries with it fellowship with his people. Those we have known on earth we will probably know there, as well as the host of the redeemed. Earthly relations, however, will be swallowed up in a higher relationship. That is true to some extent here. It will be more completely true there. The fundamental relation there will be our relation to God. If family relationships are remembered, they will be subordinated to the higher. There will be no marrying and giving in marriage (Mark 12:25). There will be social relations in heaven, but they will be subordinate to the religious. God will be first, our fellows second.

4. *The eternal order will be one of freedom from natural evil, such as sorrow, sickness, and death*

There are abundant indications in the New Testament that all forms of natural evil will be transcended in the glorified life of the Christian during the coming age. God will wipe away all tears from the eyes of his people (Isa. 25:8; Rev. 7:17; 21:4), and sorrow and sighing shall flee away (Isa. 51:11). The complete conquering of sin carries with it complete transcendence of all other forms of evil. When man is entirely right with God and in complete harmony with his will, then all is bound to come right for man. "There shall be no curse any more: and the throne of God and of the Lamb shall be therein" (Rev. 22:3). And the reason there shall be no curse is because the throne of God and of the Lamb is there.

God's authority and rule will have abolished all evil and everything that is accursed. This is relatively true for this life, but comes to full realization in the life to come.

This complete transcendence of evil is beautifully pictured in Revelation 21 and 22 under the figure of the New Jerusalem come down out of heaven to men. In the book of Revelation we do not get out of the atmosphere of turmoil and strife until we get past the judgment in chapter 20 and come to the New Jerusalem in chapter 21. But when we get to chapter 21, we seem to have come into an altogether new atmosphere, one of eternal calm and joy. The strife and disappointments of this earth life are past. We come into a perfected social life in which love to God and one's fellows reigns. God is supreme. All his enemies and ours are vanquished. Life abundant is the portion of God's people, and eternal peace is theirs.

5. *There will be ceaseless service to God. His servants shall serve him in the eternal order (Rev. 22:3)*

Heaven is no place for inactivity; it is no lazy man's paradise. It is a place of abundant life, and life means activity. In the very nature of the case, created beings would serve the God who created them. What forms our service will take we are not told. It is enough that we are assured that we shall serve God. Doubtless praise and adoration will forever be given to the God who has redeemed us (Rev. 12:10). But doubtless also we will do something more than sing and praise. Even singing might grow monotonous if it were not mixed with other forms of activity.

6. *Also, heaven will be, doubtless, a place or state of endless development*

It will be asked at once: Is not heaven a state of perfection, and does not perfection exclude the idea of growth? Heaven is a state of perfection. It is freedom from sin and its total curse. But a perfect state for man is not a state in which there is no growth. This is shown in the case of Jesus. He was sinless, but he grew. A state of perfection for a created being is rather a state in which everything that hinders growth is removed. The great hindrance to growth in this life is sin. When sin is taken out of us and we are placed in an environment in which sin as an obstruction to growth is removed, we will then be in a condition to begin to grow as we should.

In 1 Corinthians 13:9-12 Paul indicates that there will be a great change in the method and character of our knowledge. Here he is perhaps referring to the eternal order. Doubtless our knowledge then will be more direct and intuitive than now. We shall then see face to face and know fully as we are known. But we cannot interpret this to mean omniscience. Only God is omniscient. For a being who is not omniscient there is always room for growth. And when we come into face-to-face communion with God, there will doubtless be such a renovation and readjustment of our rational powers as to make it possible for us to grow in knowledge as we do not now dream possible.

Again, Paul indicates that faith, hope, and love are the abiding virtues of the Christian life (1 Cor. 13:13). Knowledge passes away in that it is swallowed up in fuller knowledge, as the knowledge of the child is swallowed up in that of the man (1 Cor. 13:8-11). Faith, hope, and love do not pass away. They abide forever. But hope looks to the future. It looks for something not yet realized. This indicates that even in heaven there will always be before us possibilities toward which we are moving that we have not yet attained. And Paul's statement indicates that faith and hope are just as eternal as love. This would seem almost to necessitate the idea that the future life for the Christian will be a life of eternal growth. Boundless possibilities of development in knowledge, power, and holiness are our inheritance in Christ Jesus, and endless ages are ours in which to attain our possibilities.

VII. Hell

1. *The certainty of future punishment*

As pointed out in connection with the judgment, the idea of judgment runs through the whole Bible. The ideas of divine judgment and of punishment for sin are inseparable. What was said, therefore, about the certainty of judgment will apply to punishment for sin.

Men are punished in this life for their sins. This is made clear in the examples and teachings of the Bible. It is also verified in experience. But men do not get the full punishment for their sins in this life. The full punishment for sin, therefore, must come in the next life. We maintain that men will be punished in the future life for the following reasons:

(1) It is distinctly taught in the Bible

Punishment for sin is emphasized in the Old Testament, but it is mainly punishment in this life. In the New Testament punishment for sin in the future life is clearly taught. Nobody teaches this more clearly and emphatically than does Jesus. He solemnly and repeatedly warns men against the dangers of a hell of fire in which God will destroy both soul and body (Matt. 5:22, 29; 10:28; 18:9). The teaching of Jesus is set forth with special clearness in connection with what he says on the judgment (Matt. 25:41-46). The book of Revelation speaks of the lake of fire into which the wicked will be cast after the judgment and identifies it with the second death (Rev. 20:10, 14-15; 21:8).

(2) The very existence of a moral order requires that sinners shall be punished

The reason there is a hell is because there is sin in the world. In a moral world there must be a difference between the righteous and the wicked. If the righteous and the wicked were treated alike, there would be no moral order it; would be nonmoral. The very existence of sin, then, demands the punishment of sin. The man who lives in sin can never be made happy. Sin and

punishment cannot be separated. Christ saves men first
from sin, then from punishment. He cannot save from
punishment except as he saves from sin. The same word
in the Old Testament may be translated iniquity or punishment. (See Gen. 4:13.) This shows that in Hebrew
thought punishment could not be separated from sin.
Sin carries its own punishment. Many men think that
if they can just stay out of the fire after they die they
will be all right. What they need is to see that they
must get the fire of sin out of their souls. Man cannot
be made happy while he remains in sin. The moral
order of the world makes it impossible. Looked at from
this viewpoint, man makes his own hell. He reaps what
he sows. His violence comes down upon his own pate.
His feet are ensnared in the gin that he sets for others.
He digs a ditch and falls into it himself. (See Psalms
7:15-16; 9:15-16; 57:6, etc.)

(3) The sinner's moral nature is a guarantee that sin
will be punished

Because man is what he is, he will suffer for sin. He
cannot escape from himself. The lashings of conscience
and memory, the vain regrets and remorse that follow in
the wake of a misspent life will make a hot enough hell
for any man.—"Myself am hell." So many a man finds
out. He thinks, at first, that if he can escape the law
and public reproach, he will be safe. But he soon comes
to find out that he may escape from the law, but cannot
escape from himself, and he cannot have peace anywhere
until he comes to be at peace in his own mind and heart.

(4) Sin must be punished because it is opposed to the
holy nature of God

Sin violates the moral order of the world; but that
order is a revelation of the holy nature of God. This
is God's world. The very nature of sin is such that it
would dethrone God. God must punish sin or abdicate
his throne. As stated already, man brings down destruction upon himself. But it does not follow from this that

God does not punish the sinner. God made and sustains the moral order under which the sinner suffers. That moral order is so made that man cannot sin without suffering, and the reason it is that way is because God wills that it should be. It may be truly said, then, either that the sinner destroys himself, or that God destroys him.

2. *The nature and extent of future punishment*

(1) Such expressions as those spoken of—"the hell of fire," "the lake of fire," and "the second death"—indicate the awfulness of the fate of the impenitent.

There are those who insist that the fire spoken of must be literal fire. Some insist on this with great emphasis and seem to think that to interpret the language as figurative means to do away with the reality of future punishment. But one could maintain this position only on the assumption that a figure of speech does not represent a reality. Jesus speaks of the place of punishment as a place of outer darkness (Matt. 8:12; 22:13; 25:30). It could not be a place of both literal fire and literal darkness. But there is no more reason for taking one expression as literal than there is for taking the other as literal. Besides, literal fire would destroy a body cast into it. Some would say that it is a literal fire, but not the kind of fire that we are accustomed to. But to say that it is not the kind of fire we are used to is equivalent to saying that it is not literal fire. Moreover, to inflict purely physical pain on the sinner would not be to adapt his punishment to the nature of his sin. The sinner's punishment in this life is adapted to the nature of his sin, and there is no good reason why the same should not be true in the next world. Since we reap the final reward of our deeds in the next life, it would seem that the conformity of punishment to sin in its nature would probably be closer even than in this. Physical suffering would not be an adequate punishment for spiritual sins. It is entirely possible, then, that the nature of the punishment in the next life will depend on the nature of the sin for which it is a punishment, and that there will be as much variety in the kinds of punishment inflicted as there is variety in the kinds of sinners punished.

(2) It is made clear in the New Testament that punishment will be in proportion to the greatness of one's guilt.

Jesus recognized this when he says that it will be more tolerable in the day of judgment for Tyre and Sidon than it will be for the cities that have rejected him and his message (Matt. 11:22). Paul also manifests a belief in this principle. He says: "As many as have sinned without the law shall also perish without the law: and as many as have sinned under the law shall be judged by the law" (Rom. 2:12). He says also that those who do not have the law are a law unto themselves in that they show the work of the law written in their hearts, their consciences bearing witness therewith (Rom. 2:14-15). This principle clearly commends itself to man's sense of justice. There is nothing in either reason or the Scriptures to justify the idea that all the impenitent will be punished to the same extent in the next life.

3. *The endlessness of future punishment*

It seems to be made clear in the Bible that the future punishment of the wicked is endless. In the parable of the rich man and Lazarus, in answer to the rich man's request that Lazarus dip his finger in water and cool the rich man's tongue, Jesus represents Abraham as saying: "And besides all this, between us and you there is a great gulf fixed, that they that would pass from hence to you may not be able, and that none may cross over from thence to us" (Luke 16:26). Here Jesus seems to be expressly teaching that, if a man dies unrepentant, there is no hope of mercy in the next life. His condition is unchangeable. There is no crossing from one place to the other. Another passage that seems to be decisive on this point is on the judgment in Matthew 25. Jesus says: "These go away into eternal punishment: but the righteous into eternal life" (v. 46). Here the Lord uses the same word to describe the endurance of the punishment of the wicked that he uses to describe the endurance of the blessedness of the righteous. If the word as applied to the blessedness of the righteous means never ending, why should it not mean the same thing as applied in the same context to the punishment of the wicked?

In general, there are two views that deny the endlessness of future punishment. One is the view of restorationism or universalism. This holds in different forms to the idea that man will suffer in the future life for his sins, but that this suffering will be remedial in its nature, and that through his sufferings he will be purified from sin and finally delivered from it. There is no evidence in the Scriptures, however, that suffering in the future life will be remedial in its nature, but positive teaching to the contrary. Suffering is remedial in this life, but not wholly so. There is no teaching in the New Testament that the next life will be redemptive in its purpose. All that we have on the subject is in the contrary direction.

Then it is held by some that sin and its punishment are destructive in the sense that the soul and its powers are blotted out of existence. It is pointed out that sin here tends to dissipate and destroy. This destructive tendency of sin is the punishment for sin, and the second death is the complete annihilation of man's existence. But this would lead to the conclusion that the greater sinner one became the sooner would his conscious existence come to an end and, therefore, the less his suffering. Besides, sin does not always tend to destroy one's conscious powers in this life. And when it does so, it may be due to the fact that man's soul inhabits an organism of "flesh and blood." This may not be true of the soul during the intermediate state nor after the resurrection of the body.

So the only hopes of deliverance from sin and its awful consequences held out in the gospel of Christ are for this life, and the evidence indicates that no man will be saved after he departs this world. This does not mean, as sometimes held, that evangelical theology teaches that the great mass of mankind is damned to an eternal hell, since only a small portion of the race has professedly accepted Christ. It means that it is made clear in the New Testament that the man who consciously and definitely accepts Christ as Saviour and Lord is assured of eternal blessedness with him in the next world; and that the man who consciously and wilfully rejects God's mercy manifested in Christ and dies in impenitence is solemnly warned that he will be eternally punished for his sins. The great mass of mankind lying in between these two classes we can safely leave in the hands of God, being assured that he will do what is right with reference to every son of man and that he knows to which of these two classes every man belongs.

How much moral light and spiritual knowledge one must have before he can so commit sin as to seal his destiny for evil, we cannot determine. Nor is it our business to do so. To decide this question is God's prerogative. It is ours to give to every man that we possibly can the full light of the gospel, so that he may have conscious salvation through faith in Christ, or be left without excuse because of the rejected grace of God.

GENERAL INDEX

INDEX TO SCRIPTURE REFERENCES